"Malphurs and Penfold have de-n process without factoring out the necessary dependence on the Holy Spirit. They have provided principles and processes to follow. They have supplied evaluative tools for both the church and the pastor. And, most importantly, they have centered it all in Scripture and prayer. This will be a resource every pastor leading in a revitalizing effort will want to have."

—**Phil Stevenson**, assistant district superintendent, Pacific-Southwest of the Wesleyan Church

"What leadership is to healthy and growing churches, vision is to effective leadership. Penfold and Malphurs have rightly targeted and identified the need for weary pastors and waning church leaders to team up around a renewed vision that will direct and align their energies and resources toward a revitalized church. What they present may well be the remedy for the declining direction of the church in America."

—**Rich Frazer**, president, Spiritual Overseers Service International

"Integrating statistical analysis, biblical theology, and pastoral wisdom, Aubrey Malphurs and Gordon Penfold have compiled a marvelous work that will help leaders think through how to lead their teams to re-envision their leadership structures for the glory of Christ."

—**Kevin Peck**, lead pastor of The Austin Stone Community Church

"Church planting is on the rise, but what about all the existing plateaued, dead, or dying churches in America that are in desperate need of revitalization? Is there hope for them? Very few pastors are turnaround leaders, yet the majority of churches in America are in desperate need of renewal. Most pastors don't know how to lead a church out of a downward spiral. Here's a book that will help pastors do just that—turn around a church."

—**Jim Tomberlin**, founder and senior strategist, MultiSite Solutions; author of many books, including *125 Tips for MultiSite Churches*

"In this invigorating, timely, and prophetic work, Malphurs and Penfold paint a necessary future picture for the American church. Not content to only describe and lament the decline of the American church, the authors provide marching orders for pastors, congregations, judicatories, and denominations. Substance is added to the picture as the authors provide processes useful to the pastor who desires to bring about the re-envisioning of a local congregation."

—**Matthew Bohling**, pastor for preaching and vision, Living Hope Presbyterian Church (PCA)

"*Re:Vision* acknowledges the state of the church, declining denominations, and what it takes to reverse those trends. Through quantitative and qualitative research, Malphurs and Penfold unpack the significance of pastoral vision and how it directly influences the heart, health, and future of the church. This book will help leaders regain the momentum they need to revitalize the work God has called them to do."

—**Tami Heim**, president and CEO of Christian Leadership Alliance

"This book should be required reading for every pastor and staff member in our churches. Aubrey and Gordon have produced a phenomenal user's manual for kingdom and church growth. They have covered all the bases plus brought into the mix of material behavioral requirements that are needed for pastors. Every reader should be challenged to make personal changes that will allow God to use them in an extraordinary way as well."

—**Ken Bratz,** owner, Ken Bratz Consulting

"This practical leadership book adds tremendous value to church leaders. The research, real life stories, and reflection sections will help move you from ideas to implementation. *Re:Vision* is not only a great read, it's a great training tool."

—**Mac Lake**, visionary architect, The LAUNCH Group

"This is a book pastors will return to again and again. Every pastor should read it and read it again when it is time to dream new dreams and lead toward the next season of ministry. This is a great book for a mentor and protégé to enjoy together."

—David Bowman, executive director, Tarrant Baptist Association

"Malphurs and Penfold offer us their marvelous wisdom, creativity, practical analysis, and motivating vision—envisioning—with regard to pastoral leadership in the church. In this present situation in North America, there is much confusion over what could and should be done to lead churches toward health and growth. One thing we do know is that without vision—without envisioning—congregations slowly decline and die. This book is a treasure trove of down-to-earth, immediately usable advice for all of us called to lead the church today."

—**Charles Van Engen**, professor of Biblical Theology of Mission, School of Intercultural Studies, Fuller Theological Seminary

Re:VISION

Re:VISION

THE KEY TO TRANSFORMING YOUR CHURCH

AUBREY MALPHURS
AND GORDON E. PENFOLD

BakerBooks
a division of Baker Publishing Group
Grand Rapids, Michigan

Published by Baker Books
a division of Baker Publishing Group
P.O. Box 6287, Grand Rapids, MI 49516-6287
www.bakerbooks.com

Printed in the United States of America

Library of Congress Cataloging-in-Publication Data

Malphurs, Aubrey.
Re:vision : the key to transforming your church / Aubrey Malphurs and Gordon E. Penfold.
pages cm
Includes bibliographical references.
ISBN 978-0-8010-1682-0 (pbk.)
1. Church renewal—United States. 2. Pastoral theology—United States. 3. Christian leadership—United States.
BV600.3.M34 2014
253—dc23 2014018021

14 15 16 17 18 19 20 7 6 5 4 3 2 1

We dedicate this book to those pastors and their families who commit themselves, often at tremendous personal cost, to transforming established churches from the throes of death to new life and vitality. You have hung in there in spite of people's resistance to change and innovation. Sometimes the saints can make church work difficult. Regardless, out of a deep love for Jesus Christ and his body, you struggle against all odds to direct the churches you serve back to the Great Commission and the Great Commandment. We thank God for your dedication and sacrifice not only to the church, but to those who are not yet Christ-followers. May your number grow exponentially and may the Lord use you to create such a stirring that North America will never again be the same. You are our heroes. We need more leaders like you.

Contents

Appendixes

Acknowledgments

Thanks to all those pastors who contributed in some way to our exploration. Your willing participation made this book possible. Your love for Christ's church and your desire to aid in her growth is commendable. Thanks for making yourselves vulnerable as you shared your ministry life with us.

Special thanks to Brad Bridges, who helped us gather some of the material to make this book possible. Due to your push at the end of the discovery phase, we were able to reach pastors whose ministries touch each state and each Canadian province. Thanks for your investment.

To Ken Bratz of Ken Bratz Consulting: Your gift of the DISC profiles made this project doable. Thanks for your wonderful generosity that enabled us to reach such a large and diverse group of pastors. The extensive nature of this exploration would have been most difficult, if not impossible, without your generous contribution.

From Gordon:

Thanks to Sandy Ferguson, who tirelessly entered information into our massive database. Your commitment to accuracy and detail made life much simpler for all of us!

First Baptist Church of Holyoke, Colorado, made a commitment seven years ago to support me in this ministry. This project would not have succeeded without your faithful support and belief in this work. Thank you for your wonderful partnership in this venture and the ministry of Fresh Start.

Bob Humphrey, you initiated ministry to plateaued and declining churches decades ago. Your wisdom and insight into the body of Christ give constant courage and hope to me in the midst of the struggle to re:vision churches. Thanks for believing in me to carry on the work you began.

Gary McIntosh, you coached and mentored me through the D.Min. program and Talbot Seminary. Your insight into the church and your willingness to lead me through Discovery 1 are not forgotten. Thank you for your investment in me. You have been a true mentor.

Aubrey Malphurs: Thank you for your patience as you helped this rookie writer take steps in completing this volume. We began the journey as colleagues and have grown to be friends. I have been enriched greatly by that friendship. Without you this book would still be only a distant dream.

Thanks to all who have supported Fresh Start with prayer and financial support. Without your help this project would not have succeeded.

To my wonderful wife, Beth, who patiently stands by my side. We have walked together on this faith journey often surprised and delighted by the many twists and turns along the way. Your resolute support and encouragement spur me on toward the finish line. Thank you for your investment in me. Above all others, I dedicate this book to you.

Introduction

During the 1970s and '80s, churches and denominations were on the cusp of decline but did not see it coming. Consequently they weren't interested in church envisioning (church planting) and church re-envisioning (church revitalization).

Early in the twenty-first century, however, 70–80 percent of churches and denominations have plateaued or are in serious decline. If 70–80 percent of our churches are plateaued or declining, what might this signal about the state of those who are pastoring these churches? The answer is that many are disillusioned, are questioning their "call to pastoral ministry," are questioning whether they have a leadership gift, and wonder if they should even be in the ministry. Others have jumped every two to three years from church to church, looking for the perfect place where they can make a difference, and in the process they, not necessarily the church, may be the problem. Somewhere along the way the vision has been lost.

As a result, many denominations, networks, conferences, and churches have become most interested in church planting or church envisioning, knowing it is key to their very survival. However, in their pursuit of visionary church planters who can plant spiritually healthy churches, they've overlooked the need for and importance of the re-envisioning or the revitalization of our established churches. Re-envisioning or revitalization are so essential to our future because most successful church plants are nurtured by a strong, vital, supporting established church. The demise of established churches means there are fewer strong churches to nurture church plants, making planted churches less viable. We must place as much emphasis on re-envisioning our churches as we do planting new ones if we are to have any hope for the future of the church in America.

Most important, the key to re-envisioning churches that are able to plant healthy, robust churches is visionary leadership, especially on the part of the senior pastor. The problem is that church re-envisioning is a fairly new solution and most know very little about it. We believe that everything rises or falls on visionary leadership. Thus the focus of this work is on *who* more than *how*, though it will include a chapter on how.

The major reason so many churches are plateaued or in decline is that they've either lost their vision or adopted the wrong vision. When churches experience lots of turnover in their pastors and personnel, vision is one of the first things to be lost. And in America today the tenure of pastors is often short. Ron Sellers, president of Ellison Research in Phoenix, Arizona, writes:

> The average SBC minister has been a senior pastor at 3.6 churches in his career, and 37 percent of all SBC pastors have led four or more churches. Only Methodists exceed this—but Methodists usually are assigned positions by their denomination, and the average assignment lasts only about four years before the pastor is moved to another church by the denomination.[1]

Todd Breiner writes, "The average tenure for a youth pastor is 1 year to 18 months."[2] Finally, Thom Rainer writes, "In our national surveys of pastors, we found the average pastoral tenure to be 3.6 years. But in different studies of effective leaders, those pastors had an average tenure ranging from 11.2 to 21.6 years."[3] Then they and their churches need to be re-envisioned, and it takes visionary leaders to re-envision Christ's church. Note that in this book, we will use such terms as *re-envision*, *re:vision*, *revitalize*, and *turnaround* as synonyms and not separate concepts.

This book is based on our exploration of envisioning and non-envisioning pastors and their churches. Our work is observation based. We're not sitting in some ivory tower guessing at the characteristics of re-envisioning pastors or basing our work on hearsay or on one or two unique examples. We've conducted quantitative research (using the Pastoral Leadership Survey), which we've given to more than one hundred pastors. We've followed this up with qualitative research, interviewing each pastor one-on-one.

I (Aubrey) must confess that initially I was concerned about using a research approach. Would it turn some pastors off? Would it confuse others who aren't familiar with the terminology? We realize that the average leader isn't as interested in the research itself and how it was done but in the results. Therefore we've tried to be careful not to overwhelm our readers with research terminology, statistical studies, and other concepts and have put some of our findings in the appendixes and endnotes.

Using a research approach has turned out to be a delightful process of exploration resulting in exciting discoveries. The differences in God's leaders and the ways he has wired them to lead his church are most exciting and can really make a difference. We've discovered much about how he's wired us for ministry as well.

We have several suggestions for how you can get the most out of this book.

- If you're a senior pastor or the point person of a parachurch ministry, you should work through the material on your own as it asks some hard questions that you might not be ready to answer in a group.
- Before working your way through this material with your key leaders, such as the staff and the board, consider the vulnerability of these people and their willingness to speak out honestly and lovingly on the material. Then it would be your call as to whether you work through the material together.
- If you are attempting to lead a church through revitalization, you should work through the material with your leaders after you've read through it at least once. Again, be prepared for resistance on the part of some of your people.
- If you're a leader in a denomination, midlevel judicatory (for the purposes of this book defined as a subgroup of churches in a denomination or association of churches, often called districts, associations, or presbyteries), network, or conference, this material can be extremely important to you, as outlined in chapter 14. Early in the twenty-first century, such organizations, like their churches, are struggling for viability. Younger pastors in particular are asking why they should be loyal to or a part of these groups. However, we will proclaim that for such ministries this material can mean a new day! You may use it to counsel pastors under your leadership or help churches to find the right person for their ministries.
- If you're a seminary professor, you might find it most instructive to assign the re-envisioning process presented in this book as a vocational project for your students. It will help them understand themselves better and determine if they're really wired to lead a plateaued or declining church or possibly some other ministry. And this could save them from much unnecessary pain and disappointment in the future.

All of the chapters include questions at the end for personal reflection, discussion, and application for you and/or your team. You would be wise to work your way through them.

PART 1

Preparation for Discovery

Before we launch into the "how to" or process portion of this book found in chapters 6–8, we must first prepare ourselves for that process; otherwise we will likely fail in our attempts to re-envision Christ's church. We see this in the world of sports. Teams do not launch their season without some type of preparation for it. Baseball has what they refer to as spring training. Football sponsors summer minicamps. Months before the season begins, the players report to camp where they prepare for their season by learning the plays, conditioning their bodies, and addressing any injuries. Those who lead churches would be wise to learn this lesson from the sporting world. Preparation precedes process and practice. So we begin with preparation in chapters 1–5.

1

The State of Pastoral Leadership in America

It was the typical "First Church," founded within a few weeks of the establishment of a railroad town on the old Santa Fe Trail. This was truly a Wild West town. A few concerned parents gathered to launch what was considered to be the first church west of Dodge City, Kansas. The original church building doubled as the community's only school and community center. In 1874 the first bell to be rung in Southeastern Colorado pealed from the steeple of the brand-new building. Joy filled the hearts of those committed to serving the Lord Jesus Christ in this newly developing frontier.

The church grew, matured, and declined. In 1979 the graying congregation knew that times were desperate. Their pastor of thirteen years was on cruise control. Effective in his first three years of ministry, their shepherd was gliding toward retirement, and the church followed suit. He was comfortable and secure, but the church was in steep decline, moving precipitously toward death. Eventually the pastor was released.

In 1980 the church called as their next pastor a recent graduate from Fuller Seminary, a young man deeply schooled in the principles of church growth but with little experience in church life. He came to the church full of ideals, ideas, and passion. Slowly the church began to alter its course. However, in his youthful exuberance the pastor alienated about half of the congregation while endearing himself to the other half. This young man bore the marks of a turnaround pastor but his rough edges had rubbed too many influential people the wrong way. When he left after two and a half years, this church that was already on the downside of its life cycle was one step closer to its own funeral.

In 1983 the church called another pastor. This one was a little older with a few years' experience. While helping to unload the U-Haul at the parsonage, the church treasurer casually said to the new pastor, "I suppose you know this church is ready to split right down the middle." The new pastor was stunned. No one from the pulpit committee or the church had bothered to mention that rather important fact!

The good news was that the young Fuller graduate had primed the church for change. This congregation, whose average age easily exceeded 65, was ready to do whatever was necessary to continue a long tradition of effective ministry. The church turned around and 14 years later had grown from 86 to 110 in spite of 64 funerals for church members. The average age of the church membership dropped to about 35. All of this occurred in the midst of a shrinking population base.

Down the street one block to the north stands another church facility, the largest in the county. The building boasts a seating capacity of 440 in a community that at one time had a population of 5,000. This church could and did accommodate almost 8 percent of the city's population. It had a storied history. In the 1930s when the congregation hosted Billy Sunday for a two-week crusade, the church was packed with standing-room-only crowds. Several hundred people came to Christ in that two-week period. Every evangelical church in the community was impacted.

In the late 1980s this church also called a young man, a recent seminary graduate. He was energetic and had lots of ministry ideas. Outwardly he was very much like the current pastor of Old First Church. However, his ministry did not go well. The church closed its doors in the mid-1990s. The pastor's idealism and dreams for ministry were dashed on the rocks of discouragement and disillusionment. He left the ministry.

Now the building's only inhabitants are pigeons and bats. The structure with its massive stained-glass domed cupola sits as a dark, empty hulk, a bleak reminder of the death of a vision.

Many factors contributed to the death of one church and the renewal of the other. Both had dreams of effective, fruitful ministry. Both were looking for the "right" pastor. Both were seeking renewal. Certainly the makeup of the congregations contributed to the demise of one church and the renewal of the other. However, pastoral leadership was a major factor, perhaps the key factor, in the differing outcomes.

The authors have observed over the years that there are two essential elements for church renewal. The primary need is the right pastor. The second factor is a willing congregation. When these two dynamics come together, vibrant, renewed ministry is the outcome.

So how are we doing? What is the state of the American church and the state of pastoral leadership in the church?

The State of the American Church

THE STATE OF THE AMERICAN CHURCH
Majority of Churches Plateaued or in Decline
Percentage of Church Attenders Declining
Young People Leaving Church
Growth of Cults and Non-Christian Groups
Church-Planting Needs versus Church-Planting Ability

In this chapter we will explore the state of the American church and the state of pastoral leadership in the American church. These two subjects are inextricably linked.

Majority of Churches Plateaued or in Decline

In the mid-1960s church leaders began to notice a disturbing trend, something hitherto unnoticed in America: many major denominations had ceased growing. In 1988 Win Arn, church growth pioneer, shocked the American church world with the following statement. "Today, of the approximately 350,000 churches in America, four out of five are either plateaued or declining. . . . Many churches begin a plateau or slow decline about their fifteenth to eighteenth year. 80–85 [percent] are on the down-side of this cycle."[1] After the shock wore off, Christian leaders began to examine more closely the state of the church. Arn's statement proved to be disturbingly accurate!

Troubling signs do appear at every juncture. Church researcher David T. Olson, whose database includes information from 200,000 churches, declares, "In summary, the future looks grim for the American church. The conditions that produce growth are simply not present. If present trends continue, the church will fall farther behind population growth."[2] He explains that if the church continues on its present course, the percentage of the population attending a Christian church each weekend will decline from 20.4 percent in 1990 to 14.7 percent in 2020.[3]

Church researcher Thom Rainer describes the state of the church in North America based on his years of consulting with many different churches and denominations, saying, "Eight out of ten of the approximately 400,000 churches in the United States are declining or have plateaued."[4] He includes the following in a footnote: "Of the churches for which we have data, 84 percent are declining or experiencing a growth rate below the population growth rate for their communities. The latter is defined as a plateaued church."[5]

The church of Jesus Christ in North America is in a free fall with no bottom in sight. Consider the comments of the leaders of two large judicatories in the Rocky Mountain Region that I (Gordon) received while collecting information for Discovery 1 (research for my doctor of ministry thesis project at Talbot Seminary). One stated, "I am reluctant to direct you to pastors who have led churches into decline, not wanting to subject them to further humiliation." This district superintendent supplied the name of only one turnaround pastor. Another judicatory leader wrote, "We do not have any pastors in our district who meet your requirements for turnaround." This means that this judicatory had no churches growing at what we determined for our study was a minimum rate of 2.5 percent per year!

While speaking at the Great Commission Research Network in 2011, Gary McIntosh declared, "I have been working with a judicatory in the Midwest. In their district 97 percent of the churches are in decline. Not plateaued, but in decline."[6]

Here's another example of the challenges we face. I (Gordon) completed a study of a midlevel judicatory in 2008. Between 2001 and 2008 the judicatory lost 15 percent of its affiliate churches. This same group lost 23 percent of its average worship attendance in the remaining churches between 1997 and 2007.

These examples from four different judicatories reflect the realities that denominations, districts, and churches face in present-day America. The need for revitalization is great. Struggling churches, disillusioned pastors, and disenchanted believers litter the church landscape. Many of the survivors have no vision for the future! They are simply hanging on by their fingernails hoping for a better day.

Recently church renewal specialist Matthew Bohling of the Presbyterian Church in America made this statement to me: "We can no longer simply ignore struggling churches. We must give attention to these churches before they die or we all lose!" With proper care, plateaued and declining churches can become healthy. Healthy churches are normally the incubators of church plants. Vibrant, healthy churches produce vibrant, healthy offspring.

By the way, we are not advocating that every church should be rescued. The stark reality is that some churches need to die. They have outlived any further usefulness. They need to die with dignity and invest their resources in healthy church plants and church renewal efforts.

Percentage of Church Attenders Declining

Once again, researcher David Olson paints a realistic portrait of the state of the American church. He shows that the percentage of the population attending church on any given weekend in America in 2007 was 17 percent. This figure includes Catholic, evangelical, mainline, and orthodox churches.[7]

The Census Bureau tells us that the population in the United States continues to climb. It went from 248,709,873 in 1990 to 308,745,538 in 2010, a 24 percent gain, which yields an average annual growth rate (AAGR) of 1.1 percent. At the same time Olson informs us that the number of worshipers remained virtually unchanged: 51.8 million in 1990 and 51.7 million in 2006.[8] Large churches have grown larger, smaller churches have grown smaller, and many churches ceased to exist. The net effect is no measurable growth in church attendance. These figures scream, "Stagnant!" Had church attendance simply kept pace with population growth, the number of those attending would have grown at 1.1 percent per year for 16 years, resulting in church attendance of 61,708,000 people, an increase of nearly 10,000,000 people!

Young People Leaving Church

Many churches lose their young people between their teenage years and age thirty. David Kinnaman comments:

> The ages of eighteen to twenty-nine are the black hole of church attendance; this age segment is "missing in action" from most congregations. . . . Overall there is a 43 percent drop-off between the teen and early adult years in terms of church engagement. These numbers represent about eight million twentysomethings who were active churchgoers as teenagers but who will no longer be particularly engaged in church by their thirtieth birthday.[9]

This is a huge problem considering that young people in this age group will soon need to take the mantle of leadership from their parents' generation. Our discovery process clearly reflects this reality as only a small number of our pastors were under age forty.

Growth of Cults and Non-Christian Groups

In contrast to the stagnant condition of the church, cults and non-Christian groups continue to grow. In the United States, the Mormons have grown from 2,487,000 to 3,158,000 from 1990 to 2008.[10] The Jehovah's Witnesses have increased from 1,381,000 to 1,914,000 in the same time frame.[11] Between 1990 and 2008 the number of adherents to Islam expanded from 527,000 to 1,349,000.[12] Those who follow Buddhism have enlarged their camp from 404,000 to 1,189,000 during the same period.[13] The fastest growing religious group has been the Wiccans, who have increased dramatically from 8,000 in 1990 to 342,000 in 2008.[14]

The table below shows the growth rates for various cults and non-Christian groups and compares them to the growth rate in the church.

Total Growth, Percentage of Growth, and Average Annual Growth Rate (AAGR) for Cults and Non-Christian Groups Compared with the Church in the United States

Group	Total Growth	Years	Percentage of Growth	Average Annual Growth Rate (AAGR)
Mormons	2,487,000–3,158,000	1990–2008 (18 years)	27%	1.3%
Jehovah's Witnesses	1,381,000–1,914,000	1990–2008 (18 years)	39%	1.8%
Muslims	527,000–1,349,000	1990–2008 (18 years)	156%	5.4%
Buddhists	404,000–1,189,000	1990–2008 (18 years)	194%	6.2%
Wiccans	8,000–342,000	1990–2008 (18 years)	4,175%	23.2%
U.S. Population (U.S. Census Bureau)	248,709,873–308,745,538	1990–2010 (20 years)	24.1%	1.1%
U.S. Church Attendance	51,800,000–51,700,000	1990–2006 (16 years)	−0.2 %	−0.01%

Before looking at these statistics one might think that people in America simply aren't interested in spiritual things. Obviously this isn't the case. They are interested in spiritual matters, but they're not looking to the church for the answers as did earlier generations.

Church-Planting Needs versus Church-Planting Ability

Not only does the picture look grim for existing churches, but the overall outlook is not much better when one considers the impact of church plantings compared to that of church closings. We are simply not able to plant enough churches to replace those that close. Olson notes that, based on current trends, church closures will nearly equal the number of church plants between 2005 and 2020. He asserts:

> Approximately 55,000 churches [sic] will close between 2005 and 2020, while 60,000 new churches will open, producing a net gain of 4,500 churches. However, to keep pace with population growth, a net gain of 48,000 churches will be needed. In those 15 years the American church will fall short of this mark by almost 43,500 congregations.[15]

The table below gives a graphic view of this reality.

Estimated change in the number of churches in America, 2005–2020[16]

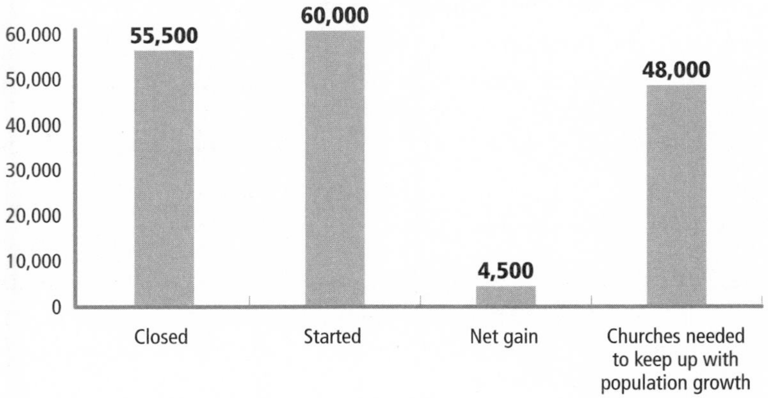

Church planting and church closure can be likened to a truck at the loading dock. Forklifts on one side of the truck load the freight—that's church planting. On the other side of the truck there are forklifts that unload it—that's the effect of church closures. The truck never gets loaded! Church planting alone will not solve the problem of the decline of the church in the United States.

Reflect on the following sobering reality. An aggressive evangelical church-planting denomination recently celebrated the successful planting of forty-five new churches out of fifty attempts (a 90 percent success rate), when one of the pastors reminded them that they were also closing one church every eleven days! The denomination closed thirty-three churches that same year. The result was a net gain of twelve churches, a positive gain for that denomination. However, most denominations do not enjoy a 90 percent success rate with church planting but they may experience the same rate of closure. We must let these figures sink into our thinking. Coming back to the truck metaphor, we unload the truck at nearly the same rate we load it.

The church in America faces great challenges. Most churches are plateaued or declining in worship attendance. The percentage of people attending church is shrinking, and young people eighteen to twenty-nine are abandoning the faith. The problem is not a lack of concern for spiritual things but a turning from the things of God to cults and non-Christian groups or simply dropping out of church altogether.

The State of Church Leadership

The state of the church reflects the state of church leadership in America. If 80–85 percent of churches are struggling, what does that say about those who are pastoring these churches? We believe there is a direct correlation between the state of the church and the state of pastoral leadership in those churches.

A Key to Success or Failure

A number of years ago I (Gordon) heard this statement: "Everything rises and falls with leadership." At first, I battled with the concept. Could it be true? I think it troubled me because it painted a bull's-eye squarely on me as a pastor. Is there any justification for such a statement?

Leadership is a key to success or failure of a given enterprise. On the football field, the success or failure of the offense normally rides on the shoulders of the quarterback. In a school, good administration will draw the best out of the teachers, and good teachers will draw the best out of their students. A business leader such as Steve Jobs produces a work environment conducive to massive creativity that leads to exceptional success. In the local church, pastoral leadership is also a key, if not the key, to vibrant church life.

Unfortunately, pastoral leadership appears to be absent or seriously restricted in many churches. Perhaps the dearth of leadership in the church points to a deeper problem—poor pastoral preparation. A secondary cause may be the high expectations placed on pastors by the church membership. Pastors stay so busy chasing the church's tail that they have no time to dream and lead. Pastors are considered the hired guns to do the work of the ministry—something far removed from Christ's design (see Eph. 4:11–12).

Let's see if this leadership maxim, Everything rises and falls with leadership, is discoverable in the Scripture. Indeed, we see this truth reflected in many places: in Old Testament kings and leaders; statements from the prophets; Jesus's words to the scribes, Pharisees, and Sadducees; New Testament statements concerning pastoral leadership; and finally, Jesus's communication to the seven churches of the Revelation.

Leadership in Ancient Israel

When trouble reared its head in Israel, the Lord frequently held the leader accountable for his actions as well as the actions of the nation. This can be seen in Moses' striking the rock (Num. 20:7–13), King Saul's disobedience concerning the Amalekites (1 Samuel 15), Ahaz and Judah's rebellion against the Lord's rule (Isaiah 7), and Elijah and his classic conflict with King Ahab (1 Kings 17:1). Had the people sinned in these situations? Of course they had. But the Lord made the leader answerable for the nation. In the following telling account, Manasseh's sins caused judgment to fall on all Jerusalem and Judah (2 Kings 21:10–13, emphasis the authors').

> The Lord said through his servants the prophets: "*Manasseh king of Judah has committed these detestable sins.* He has done more evil than the Amorites who preceded him and has led Judah into sin with his idols. Therefore this is what the Lord, the God of Israel, says: *I am going to bring such disaster on Jerusalem and Judah* that the ears of everyone who hears of it will tingle. I will stretch out over Jerusalem the measuring line used against Samaria and the plumb line used against the house of Ahab. I will wipe out Jerusalem as one wipes a dish, wiping it and turning it upside down."

Manasseh was called to account for the sins of the nation. Why? It's very simple. He led and the people followed. Both the king and the people were accountable to God, but Manasseh, as king, bore the greater responsibility because of his leadership. This theme repeats itself many times in the Old Testament.

Jesus's Words to the Scribes, Pharisees, and Sadducees

In the New Testament our Lord Jesus Christ often spoke tenderly to those who humbly sought him, but his words to the leaders of the day were harsh. He called them to account for the anemic spiritual condition in Judea and Galilee. "Woe to you, scribes and Pharisees, hypocrites," is echoed through Matthew 23:13–36. He held these contemptible leaders responsible for "all the righteous blood shed on earth, from the blood of righteous Abel to the blood of Zechariah" (v. 35 NASB). On another occasion he called the Pharisees blind leaders of the blind (see Matt. 15:14). Those in leadership carry a heavy weight of responsibility.

New Testament Statements Concerning Leadership

The apostle Paul stated, "Follow my example, as I follow the example of Christ" (1 Cor. 11:1). Hebrews 13:7 states plainly, "Remember your leaders, who spoke the word of God to you. Consider the outcome of their way of life and imitate their faith." Both of these passages speak to the tremendous impact of a leader's influence.

Hebrews 13:17 (NASB) reverberates with leadership responsibility. "Obey your leaders and submit to them, for they keep watch over your souls as those who will give an account. Let them do this with joy and not with grief, for this would be unprofitable for you." This statement ought to weigh heavily on every Christian leader and every church member. Leaders will give an account for their leadership. Members are to make their leadership task a joy!

Jesus's Communication to the Seven Churches of Revelation

This brings us to what we believe to be the strongest statement about pastoral responsibility found in the New Testament. As a young pastor I (Gordon) was preaching a series on the seven churches of Revelation. As I read the texts of Revelation 2–3 in Greek for the first time, I stopped in my tracks. I noticed that the pronouns (you) were second person singular. As I read and reread these texts, they shook me to the core. I understood that the "angels" of Revelation 2:1, 8, 12, 18; 3:1, 7, 14, the messengers, were the pastors of the churches.[17] It is highly significant that the messengers were the ones being evaluated by the Lord. All of the pronouns in the opening lines addressed to the messenger of each church are masculine singular. When the Lord rebukes, he rebukes the messenger. Thus the Lord Jesus Christ spoke to the earthly shepherds, the pastors, whose character had become the character of the church. For example, when the Lord Jesus said, "Yet I hold this against you [singular]: You have forsaken the love you had at first" (Rev. 2:4), he was addressing the earthly shepherd, the pastor of Ephesus, whose character had become the character of the church. Each church had become the lengthened shadow of its pastor. I understood this to mean the Lord Jesus himself would hold me accountable for the churches that I would pastor for the time that I led them. Understanding the gravity and responsibilities of serving as the pastor, I nearly resigned from ministry.

Ultimately Christ extends the application of the text to all churches and all believers when he says, "Whoever has ears, let them hear what the Spirit says to the churches" (2:7, and others). But don't miss the initial point: Christ addresses the pastors first!

When pastors have been leading a church for five years or longer, the church assumes the character of their pastor. As goes the leadership, so goes the church! So the maxim, Everything rises and falls on leadership, is discovered and confirmed repeatedly on the pages of the Word of God and practically in the lives of pastors and the churches they serve.

How Are Church Leaders Doing?

A great number of churches are characterized by an inward, self-serving focus, territorialism, bullies, power brokers, passivity, disillusionment, lack of a clearly defined purpose and vision, all accompanied by division and conflict. The result of such attitudes and actions is a mass of churches that are plateaued or declining in membership, attendance, and vitality. Many have become havens for the disgruntled and fortresses against the Great Commission. These "country clubs" have become the antithesis of everything the gospel represents.

Where are the pastors in all of this? Many pastors feel they have their backs against the wall. They want to make changes but either they are afraid to roil the waters or they don't know how to lead. Church bullies intimidate them. Church boards are uncooperative and controlling. Consequently, pastors struggle and the churches they pastor struggle. The resulting gridlock causes attenders to leave in frustration.

Other pastors are simply on cruise control. They draw their pay and don't rock the boat. Many are content to leave Jesus outside knocking at the door (Rev. 3:20). Many also lack the skill and backbone to develop a vision of a preferred future and pursue it to a fitting conclusion. Others simply walk down the path of ministry blissfully ignorant of the impending cliff before them.

The Problem

Lack of Strong, Visionary Leadership

The problem is that there's a lack in the church of strong, visionary leadership, not necessarily a lack of leaders (there's a difference!). Churches aren't really developing visionary leaders. How many churches have in place a process for developing leaders at every level of the church? The answer is few. How many churches in the search for a new pastor or staff person ask about the candidates' ability to develop leaders, because the church believes it is an important role of their ministry? Following are some insightful questions that every pulpit committee should ask of a potential pastor or staff person, though the answers may not be encouraging.

1. Do you know how to develop leaders?
2. How many leaders have you developed over the years?
3. Who are you currently developing as a leader?
4. Who has developed you as a leader?
5. Who is developing you now as a leader?
6. Is it okay to include your development of leaders on your annual evaluation?

J. L. Penfold, Gordon's brother, clearly articulated the leadership crisis in the American church. One of his district superintendents in Florida lamented, "Only about 25 percent of our pastors can get the job done. We simply hope the churches can endure through three pastors before we can finally send another good one." The problem is not a lack of pastors. It is the lack of capable, visionary pastors. A large segment of pastors occupy the pastoral position but don't lead their congregations into fruitful ministry.

Lack of Seminary and Bible College Training

Seminaries aren't *fully* developing visionary leaders. If you check the catalogs of most major seminaries, you'll find little if anything in the curriculum on leadership and leadership development. There is much on church history, the original languages (Hebrew and Greek), Bible knowledge, preaching, Christian education, and so on, and these are important to the curriculum. It's what's missing that concerns us. Seminaries tend to attract leaders but are doing little to train them specifically in the area of leadership. At best, most seminaries train scholar-chaplains, not scholar-leaders. The church is crying out for visionary leaders.

In 2010, I (Gordon) traveled to the Russian Far East to train pastors and denominational leaders in the principles and practices of visionary leadership. During the last two weeks, a team traveled nearly sixteen hundred miles visiting and assessing four local churches. One of the churches was pastored by a middle-aged man with a remarkable story. After perestroika, he rode his bicycle seventy kilometers in the winter (-30 degrees Celsius) one way to hear the Word of God. He did this week after week. After he came to Christ, he and his wife sold their possessions and moved their family to Donetsk Christian University where he graduated with a three-year degree in theology. He and his family of five then returned to Primorye, the Russian Far East, to minister.

His nineteen-year-old congregation was languishing in deep conflict. The primary cause of the conflict was lack of leadership on the part of the pastor. The church people wanted to move forward; they desired to be led, not to lead. (In Russian culture no one moves without the okay from the leader.) My friend could not point the church in a direction and pull the leadership trigger. The church people longed for him to point them in a direction, any direction, and they would follow! The pastor is a great guy, a wonderful father, but he has no leadership skills and little vision. The result is a fractured, struggling church.

This problem is not unique to Russia. It is prevalent in North America.

The Challenge

On the one hand, re-envisioning pastors (REPs) are swimming upstream against the prevailing current. They are fighting, scratching, clawing to move the church toward fruitfulness and joy. Often their efforts exact a terrible cost from them and their families. Nevertheless, they move forward, impelled and compelled by their love for the Savior and his commission to return churches to their glorious Head and to productive ministry.

On the other hand, non–re-envisioning pastors are often paralyzed by fear, afraid to upset the power brokers, church bullies, the status quo, and the sacred cows of ministry. At the very core of their being, their divine design prevents them from leading their churches out of the doldrums to vitality and new life. Bob Humphrey, founder of Fresh Start Ministries, notes, "Others have positioned themselves as 'hirelings' rather than shepherd-leaders of God's flock. Some seem incapable of articulating a vision for the church. They have not been trained to see the dream, say the dream and seize the dream. . . . Others see themselves as bricklayers rather than architects."[18]

In *Courageous Leadership* Bill Hybels describes the wondrous beauty of a vibrant local church.

> There is nothing like the local church when it's working right. Its beauty is indescribable. Its power is breathtaking. Its potential is unlimited. It comforts the grieving and heals the broken in the context of community. It builds bridges to seekers and offers truth to the confused. It provides resources for those in need and opens its arms to the forgotten, the downtrodden, the disillusioned. It breaks the chains of addictions, frees the oppressed and offers belonging to the marginalized of this world. Whatever the capacity for human suffering, the church has a greater capacity for healing and wholeness.
>
> So to this day, the potential of the local church is almost more than I can grasp. No other organization on earth is like the church. Nothing even comes close.[19]

He further describes the role of visionary leadership in the life of the church.

> *The local church is the hope of the world and its future rests primarily in the hands of its leaders.* For the first time, I realized that from a human perspective the outcome of the redemptive drama being played out on planet Earth will be determined by how well church leaders lead. Many churches are filled with sincere, talented, godly people who would love to leverage their spiritual gifts in order to impact the world for Christ. The question is this: Will the men and women who have been entrusted with leadership gifts take their gifts seriously, develop them fully, and deploy them courageously, so that the willing and gifted believers in their churches can work together to make a difference in the world?[20]

If Hybels is correct in saying that "the outcome of the redemptive drama . . . will be determined by how well church leaders lead," and if 80–85 percent of the churches are failing for lack of visionary leadership, then the church in America may have little hope left.

The hour is late, the challenge is great. Let's rise to the challenge and allow the Lord once again to awaken the church in America. President Kennedy once asked, "If not us, who? If not now, when?" Will you join our Lord in this great adventure of church renewal? If you will, then we all win!

Questions for Reflection, Discussion, and Application

1. Is your church in the 15–20 percent of churches that are growing in worship attendance? If it is stagnant, do you understand the reasons why?
2. Is your district, association, or fellowship of churches growing or declining? Have you done anything to try to reverse the trends? If so, what? Has it been successful?
3. Do you think the statement, Everything rises and falls on leadership, is fair? Why or why not?
4. Are you the "hireling" of the church or are you the "servant of the Lord"? Stated another way, whom do you serve first: the congregation or Jesus Christ?
5. Are you a chaplain or are you the leader in your congregation? Which role should take precedence?
6. Does the loss of young people in our churches trouble you? Are you retaining your eighteen- to thirty-year-olds? Why or why not?

2

Re-Envisioning Pastoral Leadership

The solution to the state of the church problem is a renewed vision for both church planting and church revitalization among our pastoral and denominational leaders. Again the state of the church is symptomatic of a deeper problem—*leadership*. We need leaders in general who can re-envision churches in particular.

A Renewed Vision for Church Revitalization

It's imperative that we launch a nationwide movement to develop pastors not only as church planters but as visionary church revitalizers. We believe that church planting is critical and certainly worth pursuing and we hope this message is clear. Without church planting we wouldn't be here today. If anything, we must turn up the heat on our church-planting efforts in North America and abroad. However, along with this increased emphasis, we must do better at training pastors as visionary leaders, not as chaplains, caretakers, or scholars, but people who can re-envision their churches.

What we've discovered is that, while some are wired to re-envision established churches, others, perhaps the majority, aren't. (We will say more about this in chapters 6 and 7.) They simply don't have the skills or divine wiring to re-envision churches. So they experience conflict, frustration, and anguish.

Eventually they burn out and in time drop out. Thus the focus of this research is on developing visionary leaders who'll lead in re-envisioning our churches.

We have noted an increased nationwide interest on the part of denominations and judicatories in renewing established churches. When Gordon and I bring this topic up, these people are all ears. We have also been invited into a number of groups—especially denominations—to address this issue. We believe that this very well could be the prompting of the Holy Spirit that he will use to turn our churches if not our nation around so they get back on their spiritual feet.

What we envision and are praying for is a nationwide movement prompted by the Holy Spirit that sees churches making U-turns and moving in a new direction, one that honors and glorifies the Savior. When asked about my (Aubrey's) vision for church planting, my response, much to people's surprise, is that I'm not interested in planting a church! I'm interested in planting church-planting churches. It's not enough that we plant a single church. It's imperative that our goal be to plant a church that, in turn, plants a number of churches. That's a movement. Such movements are how cities can be won. For example, if I were to plant a church in Dallas, Texas, where I live, my goal would be that this church would start church-planting churches all over Dallas. If you were to ask for my vision for church re-envisioning, it would be much the same. Let's begin to re-envision existing churches with the goal that each, in turn, re-envisions other churches that re-envision other churches and on and on. Combine envisioning (church planting) with re-envisioning (church renewal) and watch a movement spring up that will powerfully impact our cities and suburbs for the Savior. And this must not be an either-or mentality but a both-and mentality.

Mini-Bio: How a Re-Envisioning Pastor Thinks

Les Magee served as a missionary in both Portugal and Brazil. At age 50 he accepted the call to become the pastor of Washington Heights Church in Ogden, Utah. The church, in the heart of Mormon country, averaged 140 in worship.

Soon after Les arrived, the church showed the film, "Temple of the God-Makers." The church members spread fliers all over the community inviting people to come. The community people stayed away in droves!

Afterward Les thought, "If I were in a Catholic country, the last thing I would do is to show a Catholic-bashing film in the church." At that point he determined that he needed to think like a missionary. In his words, "I had to change the culture of the church. The church drew up the drawbridge rather than reach out. Our church had a fortress mentality. It was really based on fear in two ways: they were fearful of being overwhelmed by the Mormons and also they didn't know how to share their faith with the Mormons. As a result the Mormons were the enemy rather than people God loved and for whom Christ died. The church's attitude was against Mormons. We had to change that mindset." The church realized they could no longer be a fortress against Mormons but a mission to the Mormons. The church adopted a new vision: "Building bridges, not walls."

Many said, "This is Utah, you can't do that here." But Les had a deep conviction of what God could do and he would not be satisfied with less.

The Lord's favor fell on the congregation. In 20 years the church grew from 140 to 1,200. After 20 years of ministry, Les passed the torch to Roy Gruber, and the church continues to thrive. In great measure this is because Les introduced a new vision to a "fortress" church. The results: spectacular!

Questions for Reflection, Discussion, and Application

1. Do you agree with the authors that the solution to the state of the church problem is a renewed vision for both church planting and church revitalization among our pastoral leaders and denominational representatives? Why or why not? Do they make their case? Why or why not?
2. Do you see a connection between vision and church leadership? Have we truly lost our vision for our ministries? Is it possible we've not had a vision or we didn't have the right vision to begin with?
3. The authors speak of a nationwide movement to re-envision America's churches as well as plant them. Do you agree? Why or why not? Is this merely a pipe dream or do you believe it could happen? Do you believe it must happen?
4. Have you noted a growing interest on the part of denominations and judicatories in church renewal? If so, how has it manifested itself?

3

The Biblical Basis for Re-Envisioning Ministry

In the context of this book, the question naturally arises: What does the Bible say about turnaround or re-envisioning pastoral ministry? Quite frankly, the Scripture says little about pastors renewing churches. However, God weaves the concept of transformation, renewal, and revitalization throughout the fabric of the Word of God. In essence, the whole of the work of God with humanity revolves around the work of transformation and renewal. Two key passages, 2 Corinthians 5:17 and Romans 12:1–2, speak of transformation, first, of the unredeemed and, second, of the believer. In addition, new birth or regeneration stands at the heart of God's ministry with the children of Adam in this present age (John 3:3)! This chapter will examine three areas of biblical revitalization.

First, we will unpack the influence of key leaders of the Bible to demonstrate the biblical basis for re-envisioning ministry. The key to remember is this: vision drove each of these leaders to accomplish the work of God.

Second, we will explore the relationship between the Lord Jesus and the seven churches of Revelation 2–3 to understand the connection between pastors at the end of the first century and re-envisioning pastoral leadership today.

Third, the concept of mentoring played a vital role in producing transformational, visionary leaders found in the Bible. Thus we will lay a rudimentary foundation for the mentoring process. However, the subject of mentoring will be more fully expanded in chapter 12.

Re-Envisioning Leaders in the Bible

Throughout history the Lord has used multitudes of individuals to lead the transformation of his people. They are diverse characters, each uniquely designed and used by God for his purposes. This section will look at seven of these leaders: Moses, Hezekiah, Josiah, Elijah, Nehemiah, apostle Paul, and the Savior.

RE-ENVISIONING LEADERS IN THE BIBLE
Moses
Hezekiah
Josiah
Elijah
Nehemiah
Apostle Paul
Our Lord Jesus Christ

Moses

Moses is one of the most significant transformational leaders found on the pages of biblical history. His vision was to take a nation of Hebrews and move them from the slavery of Egypt to the freedom of the Promised Land. One might argue that little is said about the early life of Moses that would indicate a driving passion to deliver the slave-nation of Israel to freedom, yet Acts 7:25 reveals that Moses knew God would use him to deliver Israel from bondage. Unfortunately, the Israelites didn't understand Moses' role as deliverer. Hebrews 11:24–28 is particularly instructive in understanding the passion and vision that drove Moses.

> By faith Moses, when he had grown up, refused to be known as the son of Pharaoh's daughter. He chose to be mistreated along with the people of God rather than to enjoy the fleeting pleasures of sin. He regarded disgrace for the sake of Christ as of greater value than the treasures of Egypt, because he was looking ahead to his reward. By faith he left Egypt, not fearing the king's anger; he persevered because he saw him who is invisible. By faith he kept the Passover and the application of blood, so that the destroyer of the firstborn would not touch the firstborn of Israel.

Initially, at age forty, Moses failed. Then, at age eighty, he succeeded in leading the children of Israel out of captivity (Exod. 3:10).

Moses' initial failure is instructive. Here are some points to ponder for those involved in re-envisioning ministry.

- Immaturity marked Moses at age forty. Today that would be like being in our mid-twenties. Often lack of maturity leads to initial failure. At age forty Moses felt he could conquer the world in his own strength. His immaturity coupled with his volatility resulted in the death of an Egyptian.

- His attempts were premature. His timing predated God's plan. Moses' initial effort to deliver Israel came 40 years ahead of God's timetable. God promised Abram that the children of Israel would suffer hardship in the land of Egypt for 400 years. The total length of the sojourn came to 430 years (Exod. 12:40–41; Gal. 3:17). Moses was just a bit ahead of God.
- Moses based his actions on his human strength and position, rather than recognizing his human weakness and God's divine power (compare Exodus 2:11–12 with 2 Corinthians 10:3–5).
- Moses' failure prepared him for success.
- At age eighty, after tending sheep for forty years, Moses knew he could do nothing on his own. His maturity led him to usefulness in the hand of the almighty God. Moses gives testimony that we're never too old to be used after proper preparation!

Initial failure can lead to the development of transformational, visionary leaders. This truth not only fit Moses, but the same pattern describes many pastors today. An initial failure does not relegate an individual to a life of failure. Wise leaders use their failures to build toward future successes. In an interview with Gordon, Robert Humphrey, founder of Fresh Start Ministries (the ministry Gordon now directs), stated, "If a guy bombs at the first church, he may become a good church planter or a good turnaround pastor."[1] A ministry failure is not necessarily the end of the road for a Christian leader. However, the leader must be teachable and learn from his past or be doomed to repeat it!

Premature action can be as debilitating as failure to act at all. On more than one occasion I (Gordon) have missed God's direction completely. When I become unsettled or angry, I am often "just a bit early" or completely out of sync with God's will and/or timing. Placing God in our leadership box inevitably produces frustration because God chooses to do his work his way (see Isa. 55:8–11). Our vision does not bind him, but his vision better captivate us!

In Deuteronomy 8:7–9 Moses reveals his passionate vision. See the description in chapter 10 of Moses' vision and his communicating his vision to the nation. This is a powerful description of the vision-casting process. Don't miss it!

Though he did not see the fulfillment of his vision for Israel in his lifetime, Moses made it possible for Joshua to complete the transformation of Israel from a nation of slaves to a nation living under the theocratic leadership of the Lord in the Promised Land.

Hezekiah

The importance of Hezekiah's life and impact is seen in the fact that the account of his reign over Judah is recorded in three major sections of the Old Testament (2 Kings 18–20; 2 Chronicles 29–31; Isaiah 36–39). Hezekiah's reign followed the destructive reign of his father, Ahaz, one of Judah's most wicked kings. The summary statement regarding Ahaz in 2 Kings 16:2–4 provides ample evidence of his spiritual corruption.

> Ahaz was twenty years old when he became king, and he reigned in Jerusalem sixteen years. Unlike David his father, he did not do what was right in the eyes of the LORD his God. He followed the ways of the kings of Israel and *even sacrificed his son in the fire*, engaging in the detestable practices of the nations the LORD had driven out before the Israelites. He offered sacrifices and burned incense at the high places, on the hilltops and under every spreading tree (emphasis the authors').

Hezekiah's vision drove him to restore the proper worship of YHWH during his reign. We read of his passion in 2 Chronicles 29:3–11:

> In the first month of the first year of his reign, he opened the doors of the temple of the LORD and repaired them. He brought in the priests and the Levites, assembled them in the square on the east side and said: "Listen to me, Levites! Consecrate yourselves now and consecrate the temple of the LORD, the God of your fathers. Remove all defilement from the sanctuary. Our parents were unfaithful; they did evil in the eyes of the LORD our God and forsook him. They turned their faces away from the LORD's dwelling place and turned their backs on him. They also shut the doors of the portico and put out the lamps. They did not burn incense or present any burnt offerings at the sanctuary to the God of Israel. Therefore, the anger of the LORD has fallen on Judah and Jerusalem; he has made them an object of dread and horror and scorn, as you can see with your own eyes. This is why our fathers have fallen by the sword and why our sons and daughters and our wives are in captivity. Now I intend to make a covenant with the LORD, the God of Israel, so that his fierce anger will turn away from us. My sons, do not be negligent now, for the LORD has chosen you to stand before him and serve him, to minister before him and to burn incense."

We cannot appreciate his passion until we fully understand the newly crowned, twenty-five-year-old king's background. It is easy for us to miss the negative impact of Ahaz on Hezekiah when he "sacrificed his son in the fire." Hezekiah survived the carnage of his father, King Ahaz. Lorin Woolfe, businessman and Christian writer, captures the significance.

> Hezekiah, one of the sons spared this sacrifice, realized that strong symbolic measures were necessary to put the people of Israel back "on purpose." The first thing he did was to open the doors of the temple and repair them. This was not just the repairing of pieces of wood; it was a rededication of purpose. He then exhorted his subjects: "Listen to me, Levites! Consecrate yourselves now and consecrate the temple of the Lord. . . . Remove all defilement from the sanctuary" (2 Chron. 29:1–11). Many of the sacred items had become impure or unclean, and Hezekiah wanted to restore the temple to its former level of cleanliness.[2]

The past marked and marred Hezekiah. His re-envisioning reforms were some of the most sweeping and complete recorded in the Old Testament. His vision consisted of two parts. The scars of his past drove him powerfully and emotionally (1) to separate the nation from the reprehensible deeds of his father and (2) to return Israel to spiritual fruitfulness through restored worship and consecration to the Lord God of Israel. His vision captured him and the hearts of his countrymen.

Hezekiah's problems were not unique to his time and place in history. Re-envisioning pastors face the same types of issues. Like Hezekiah, they must return their people to godliness.

Often pastors must deal with a shadowy past when they arrive at a new church. The pulpit committee may paint a rosy picture of life in the manse. However, when the pastor arrives, he discovers lots of skeletons in the closet: a forced resignation, unrepentant sinful attitudes, unresolved issues with a church bully, unfettered gossip, just to name a few. True worship cannot exist because of the continuing sinful behaviors of the church.

For example, a friend of Gordon's became the pastor of a declining church of about three hundred members. The church leadership team completed a re-envisioning process prior to his arrival. The church appeared primed to move from decline to growth, health, and vitality. But the pastor hit a stone wall. No matter what he tried, nothing changed. Then sin issues began to surface one after another. It turns out that fourteen of the twenty individuals who served on the envisioning team had significant immorality issues. Sexual sin infiltrated and permeated the church to its very core. The revisioning process, of necessity, made a huge U-turn. Only after dealing with the sin issues could the congregation return to genuine worship.

How can we overcome such obstacles? A vision of a preferred future must drive us forward.

Josiah

During Hezekiah's extended fifteen years of life, Manasseh, his son, joined the family. After the death of Hezekiah, Manasseh began his rule at age twelve (2 Kings 21:1). He basically reversed all the reforms his father had instituted (vv. 2–9) and sinned even more than his grandfather Ahaz. During his fifty-five-year reign the nation lost the Scriptures! After Manasseh's death, his son, Amon, ascended the throne. He reigned for just two years before being assassinated. Josiah, Amon's son, assumed the throne at age eight. These conditions set the table for another period of great reform, greater even than the reforms of Hezekiah (23:25).

During the renovation of the temple under Josiah's direction, Hilkiah, the priest, discovered the book of the Law. It had been lost! The worship of the Lord had been so neglected that Israel "lost" the Law!

The events that followed are most remarkable (22:8–23:28).

- In an act of contrition, King Josiah tore his clothes when he heard the Word of God that spoke of the judgments pronounced against Judah.
- He immediately inquired of the Lord.
- Because of Josiah's brokenness, the Lord promised to postpone the inevitable judgment.
- The king instituted massive reforms in Judah. He cleansed the temple, removed idols and idolatrous priests, destroyed the high places, burned the bones of the false prophets from Bethel according to the Scriptures (1 Kings 13:2), and defiled the valley of the Son of Hinnom (effectively ending child sacrifice).
- Josiah reinstituted Passover and observed it in a manner not seen since the days of the judges, a period of more than four hundred years.

Josiah's tenderness toward God caused him to turn "to the Lord . . . with all his heart and with all his soul and with all his might, according to all the Law of Moses" (2 Kings 23:25 NASB). His vision consisted of two parts: (1) postpone the inevitable judgment of Judah by cleansing the land of sin and (2) restore the proper worship of YHWH—a worthy vision graciously fulfilled.

Many churches are at the precipice, ready to close unless drastic measures are taken. How should re-envisioning pastors respond when ungodliness and worldly attitudes surface in the church? Like Josiah, we should repent and seek the Lord on our behalf and on behalf of the church. We must seek spiritual cleansing and restoration. In many cases church discipline must be carried out. Failure to do so may result in the Lord removing the "lampstand" (Rev.

2:5)—the closure of the church. However, when churches respond appropriately, the Lord may grant them an extension of life. These attitudes and actions are at the heart of revisioning leadership.

Elijah

Elijah, an ordinary man and prophet to the Northern Kingdom of Israel, preceded chronologically both Hezekiah and Josiah. The Word of God records that there were no "good kings" in Israel. Each king followed in the sins of Jeroboam, the son of Nebat, who erected two golden calves as objects of worship (1 Kings 12:25–33). As the leaders led, the people followed. King Ahab, with whom Elijah dealt, superseded all the previous kings from the Northern Kingdom with his wicked ambitions.

The prophet's vision for transformation is plainly seen when he confronted the prophets of Baal on Mount Carmel. His vision was to destroy Baal worship and restore the nation to the worship of YHWH, the God of Israel.

> Elijah went before the people and said, "How long will you waver between two opinions? If the LORD is God, follow him; but if Baal is God, follow him." But the people said nothing. . . . At the time of sacrifice, the prophet Elijah stepped forward and prayed: "LORD, the God of Abraham, Isaac and Israel, let it be known today that you are God in Israel and that I am your servant and have done all these things at your command. Answer me, LORD, answer me, so these people will know that you, LORD, are God, and that you are turning their hearts back again." Then the fire of the LORD fell and burned up the sacrifice, the wood, the stones and the soil, and also licked up the water in the trench. When all the people saw this, they fell prostrate and cried, "The LORD—he is God! The LORD—he is God!" Then Elijah commanded them, "Seize the prophets of Baal. Don't let anyone get away!" They seized them, and Elijah had them brought down to the Kishon Valley and slaughtered there.
>
> 1 Kings 18:21, 36–40

The passionate, visionary Elijah literally brought the people to their knees in worship as they experienced the power of the Lord firsthand. His vision originated in the very presence of the Lord (17:1) and found its voice through mighty, kingdom altering prayer (James 5:17–18). Not bad for an ordinary guy.

Christian leaders who desire to help re-envision a church ministry must, like Elijah, stand first in the very presence of God. We must not spend our study time simply building sermons. The Lord must grip our hearts with a vision of what can be, a vision of a preferred future. Our time with the Lord must move us to prayer, and prayer, in turn, moves the hand of God. As someone once stated, "Prayer is the only bit of God's omnipotence he shares with us." Become an ordinary person whom God uses in extraordinary ways.

Nehemiah

Nehemiah was a remarkable character whom God used in many ways. His vision developed in two phases. The first and most recognizable launched his great adventure in rebuilding the walls and gates of Jerusalem. The second arose out of necessity in response to the decadence of the Israelites. Not only did he find the city in disrepair, but the people were equally in spiritual disarray. In partnership with Ezra, Nehemiah helped lead a movement of spiritual restoration of repatriated Israel.

Phase 1

While serving in the privileged position as the king's cupbearer, Nehemiah received a troubling report concerning Jerusalem: "Those who survived the exile and are back in the province are in great trouble and disgrace. The wall of Jerusalem is broken down, and its gates have been burned with fire" (Neh. 1:3).

Nehemiah responded with a dangerous, well-planned, and wise strategy. The danger lurked in a recent decree that King Artaxerxes had issued concerning Jerusalem. The Jews under Ezra had tried to rebuild the walls, but their efforts were halted by a decree from Artaxerxes himself (Ezra 4:7–23). In essence, Nehemiah needed to persuade the king to reverse his earlier decree.

The efforts of Nehemiah were precise and courageous. According to Ezra 4:21, only King Artaxerxes could give the command to resume the work. Nehemiah, living in the palace, would have undoubtedly been well aware of the decree since it involved his people and his city. For four months Nehemiah prayed, planned, and prepared for the right moment, the precise instant, when he would present his petition to the king. He demonstrated great wisdom in his request to Artaxerxes in that he never once mentioned Jerusalem, only Judah and the city of his ancestry. God granted favor, and the king granted his request. Nehemiah set out with everything in place to complete the mission—the rebuilding of the walls and gates of ancient Jerusalem.

Nehemiah's vision moved him to action. Two passages give us a hint as to this passion and drive. In Nehemiah 1:4 the text tells us that the report concerning the trouble and disgrace that had fallen on Jerusalem crushed

Nehemiah. This reproach and distress fueled his passion to see a restored Jerusalem. In Nehemiah 2:17 he speaks to the inhabitants of Jerusalem, "You see the trouble we are in: Jerusalem lies in ruins, and its gates have been burned with fire. Come, let us rebuild the wall of Jerusalem, and we will no longer be in disgrace." Nehemiah's original vision was to rebuild the city to remove the reproach from his people.

The results of his mission were stunning. In spite of terrific opposition from both the enemies of Israel and the Jews themselves, Nehemiah led the Jews in rebuilding the walls, gates, and dignity of Israel in fifty-two days! This was an extraordinary feat directed by a vision-driven leader.

Phase 2

Often leaders must "retool" their vision once the initial phase is complete. It takes a driven visionary to accomplish such a task. Nehemiah proved himself such a leader.

Phase 2 of his vision was not evident initially. However, the need for a second step became apparent through the following two incidents. On his return to Jerusalem from Susa, Nehemiah discovered that Tobiah, his enemy, had actually moved into the temple! Nehemiah promptly threw him out along with all his goods, cleansed the temple, and helped restore proper worship. Then, in dramatic fashion, he also enforced the law against intermarriage with the women of Ashdod, Ammon, and Moab, marriages forbidden by the Law. This he accomplished rather forcibly:

> I rebuked them and called curses down on them. I beat some of the men and pulled out their hair. I made them take an oath in God's name and said: "You are not to give your daughters in marriage to their sons, nor are you to take their daughters in marriage for your sons or for yourselves."
>
> Nehemiah 13:25

We would identify Nehemiah as a driven leader! His vision of a restored people moved him to action.

Thus Nehemiah developed a two-phased vision: phase 1—a restored city accompanied by restored dignity for its Jewish inhabitants; phase 2—a restored people serving the Lord and walking according to the Law of Moses.

Re-envisioning pastoral ministry requires the same type of true grit that characterized Nehemiah. Opposition outside the church, corruption and self-centeredness within all plague turnaround efforts. Church renewal comes at a price. Our efforts to re-envision a church consisting of transformed worship, godly Christians, and new believers must drive us relentlessly. Re-envisioning a church may also require a second phase in vision. After reaching two-, five-, and ten-year objectives, we of necessity need to retool for the next steps.

Paul

The apostle Paul, perhaps better than any other human in the New Testament, defines the character of vision-driven leadership. God used him as a catalyst for change. Many accounts in the New Testament describe his life. We would like to focus on a few key passages that describe his vision and passion for his ministry. The bullet points below contain a sampling of truths about this mighty man of faith.

- A chosen vessel to bear the name of Christ before Gentiles and kings (Acts 9:15–16).
- He vehemently defended the gospel (Acts 15:2; Gal.1:6–9).
- He became so impassioned with his mission that he left all hindrances behind (including John Mark in Acts 15:36–40).
- In his theology the gospel is the power of God for the salvation of everyone who believes (Rom. 1:16).
- The apostle's passion extended especially to "regions beyond" (2 Cor. 10:16) where Christ was not yet named (Rom. 15:20).
- His passion not only extended to those who did not know Christ, but he greatly desired to build mature believers and leaders. He charged Timothy, "And the things you have heard me say in the presence of many witnesses entrust to reliable people who will also be qualified to teach others" (2 Tim. 2:2).
- His objective was to glorify God in all things (1 Cor. 10:31).

Here's a summary statement of Paul's vision for his ministry: To glorify God by reaching a growing number of unreached people groups with the gospel through (1) preaching the gospel, (2) planting churches, and (3) developing an ever expanding leadership base who would in turn (1) preach the gospel, (2) plant churches, and (3) develop an ever expanding leadership base! And so it continues.

Pastors who desire to re-envision churches must, in like manner, keep the main thing the main thing. Successful ministry reproduces the same patterns: evangelism, church planting, and leadership development. Anything less fails to capture Christ's design for his church.

Our Lord Jesus Christ

It is obvious that the Lord Jesus Christ is the supreme Agent of Transformation for all time. He changes individuals, churches, leaders, kings, and nations. His ultimate triumph over sin and death was achieved at the cross and through his subsequent resurrection and ascension. Listed below are a few passages that hint at his purpose, mission, and vision.

- Genesis 3—the fall and the promised redemption after the fall (v. 15).
- Genesis 12—fulfilling Abrahamic and attendant covenants, including the promise to become a blessing to the nations.
- Matthew 16:18—He came to launch the church, a movement of redemption.
- Mark 1:38—He came to preach the gospel.
- Mark 10:45—He came to serve and to give his life a ransom for many.
- Luke 9:51—Christ did not avoid the cross, but "resolutely set out for Jerusalem" where his cross awaited him.
- Luke 19:10—Jesus came to seek and to save the lost.
- John 1:1, 14—He, the Word, came to tabernacle (live) among us.
- John 1:17—He portrayed grace and truth.
- John 19:30—He wrote "paid in full" across the sin of humanity, a gift of forgiveness that must be appropriated by faith.
- 1 Corinthians 15:55–57—He destroyed our enemies: sin and death.
- 2 Corinthians 5:18–20—He instituted the ministry of reconciliation and endowed believers with that ministry.
- 2 Corinthians 5:21—He became a substitute on the cross for sinners.
- Galatians 3:13—He redeemed us from the curse of the law by becoming a curse for us.
- Ephesians 1:20; Hebrews 8:1—He returned to heaven to be seated at the right hand of the Father.
- Philippians 2:5–11—The humbled Christ is now exalted so that all should bow and confess that he is Lord, to the glory of God the Father (see also Rev. 5:13).
- Hebrews 2:10—To bring many sons [disciples, followers] to glory.
- Revelation 21–22—He will restore paradise lost.

Many of these passages speak to his purpose and his mission in life. But his vision is greater yet. We believe that in his high priestly prayer in John 17, we have an even greater glimpse of his vision, which includes being glorified through the cross (v. 1), giving life to as many as the Father had given him (v. 2), glorifying the Father through his finished work (v. 4), and returning to his pre-creation glory (v. 5). Hebrews 12:2 instructs us to look "unto Jesus, the author and finisher of *our* faith, who for the joy that was set before Him endured the cross, despising the shame, and has sat down at the right hand of the throne of God" (NKJV). Jesus's vision included not just time but beyond time to eternity.

Though words can never adequately comprehend him and his work, we believe the following statement captures the essence of the vision of our Lord Jesus Christ on his mission of redemption. His vision was, in accordance with his covenants and promises, to bring an innumerable company of believers to glory from every nation, tribe, people, and language (Heb. 2:10; Rev. 7:9) through his finished work, resulting in the thunderous ovations of praise, honor, and glory due the Triune God from all creation for all eternity.

We can say with the hymn writer, "Hallelujah, what a Savior!"

Re-envisioning pastors need to have the same mindset as the Savior. Our work is not just temporal, for our time and place, but we gaze beyond our time into eternity. It's not about building a large congregation; it's about making an impact that outlasts time. This reality became apparent to me (Gordon) in a most unusual way in the early 1980s.

Frustration stalked me as a young pastor on Memorial Day weekends. I noticed that people stayed away from church in droves. However, something happened Memorial Day weekend in 1984 that proved to be an eye-opening time in my life. I walked into the auditorium my first Memorial Day weekend in my second pastorate, and there were more people in the pews than any Sunday during the year. I was shocked. It turns out that the community loved class reunions, and those reunions took place Memorial Day weekend. Year after year our largest services normally fell on that weekend. We hosted more guests than regulars that Sunday. Finally it dawned on me that our church was a "missionary sending church." That is, young people came to Christ in the church, grew, developed in the faith, and then moved on to other churches across the country. Nearly all the people who attended from out of town on Memorial Day weekend had significant responsibilities in their own churches. I realized that the ministry of our church extended far beyond our average Sunday crowd. Over the years the church trained and sent hundreds of people who, in turn, were making a difference for Christ in the communities where they resided. So as a church we began to re-envision our ministry. It stretched from here to eternity. We intentionally concentrated on developing the next generation of leaders, regardless of whether they stayed in town or moved to another part of the country or the world. The church never grew large (we resided in a small, shrinking community), but the ministry influence continues to this day all around the country while stretching into eternity. This, of course, is Christ's vision for the church. To revision, we must first see clearly Christ's vision.

In addition, no genuine turnaround occurs without new birth. Our Lord Jesus came to establish the New Covenant and the attendant result, new birth. Re-envisioning pastors recognize that outreach and evangelism must occupy a huge place in ministry. As they do so, they begin to capture the Lord's vision for his church. And nothing will revitalize a church faster than lots of new believers!

Pastors and Revitalization in the New Testament

PASTORS AND REVITALIZATION IN THE NEW TESTAMENT
Recognition
Response
Refresh

How does the Lord Jesus Christ deal with his pastors? The only place in the New Testament where the Lord actually interacts directly with them is in Revelation 2 and 3. As we explained in chapter 1, the "messengers" of the seven churches in Revelation 2 and 3 are the pastors of the seven congregations. In these seven letters to the seven churches, we find the Lord's assessment of his pastors and his churches. This passage offers us a penetrating look into the Lord's designs for revitalizing his pastors, who in turn revitalize the churches. These leaders and churches, for the most part, needed a midcourse adjustment, a re-envisioning of both leader and congregation.

Note the maturity of these churches; most were likely forty to forty-five years old. No longer fresh and vibrant, these congregations evidenced elements of decline and a growing tolerance of sinful practices. Leaders and congregations alike needed renewal, a revisioning.

Theologian Charles C. Ryrie notes the following pattern in the assessment of each church:

- Destination of the Epistle
- Description of the Lord from Revelation 1
- Commendation
- Condemnation
- Exhortation
- Promise[3]

The commendation, condemnation, and exhortation provide the basis of evaluating each pastor and corresponding church. For convenience, these commendations, condemnations (we will call them criticisms), and exhortations are catalogued in the following table.

The Assessments of the Seven Churches of the Revelation[4]

Church	Commendation	Criticism	Exhortation
Ephesus	Good works, patience, endurance, discernment in rejecting false apostles, and a hatred of Nicolaitans.	They had left their first love.	Remember, repent, and return to your first love.
Smyrna	Works, tribulation, poverty (yet true riches).	None.	Fear not, for I will give you the crown of life.
Pergamum	You dwell where Satan's throne is; you hold fast my name and my faith.	Some hold the doctrine of Balaam and the doctrine of the Nicolaitans.	Repent or else the Lord will fight against you with the sword of his mouth.
Thyatira	Works, love, service, faith, and patience.	They allow Jezebel to commit sexual immorality and idolatry.	To the faithful: hold fast what you have until I (Christ) come.
Sardis	The church as a whole failed. The few faithful are commended.	Lifeless profession. ("You have a reputation of being alive, but you are dead!" 3:1)	Remember what you have received and heard in the beginning. Watch for the Lord's coming.
Philadelphia	Using opportunities, little power (small in number), keeping God's Word, and separation.	None.	Five promises, no exhortations.
Laodicea	None.	Gross indifference, self-deception.	Find in Christ true riches, purity, and sight.

As noted in chapter 1, these messages are addressed to the church spokesmen and to "Whoever has ears, let them hear what the Spirit says to the churches."[5] In other words, the messages were not written exclusively to those seven pastors and seven churches in the late first century. The messages target all churches of all times.

How can these seven epistles to the seven churches help us in re-envisioning ministry? Several key truths can be mined from this text. Three key steps are discovered: recognition, response, and refreshing.

Recognition

The Lord Jesus himself assessed the life and vitality of each pastor and, through the pastor, each church. The Lord caused each church to recognize its spiritual condition. When church assessment occurs, we must follow the same pattern: first evaluating the pastor, then pastoral staff, church leadership, membership, church ministries, and the local community setting. Of prime importance is reconnecting the pastor and church to Christ, our living Head. Some pastors and churches are capable of self-assessment but most need fresh pairs of eyes from the outside to help them see clearly.

The church where I (Gordon) currently serve had endured a 40-year slide toward oblivion. From 1965 until 2005 the church declined from 272 members to 70 members and from over 200 to 85 in worship attendance. There were no major fights, no major blowups, or major doctrinal issues, just a slow, almost imperceptible, decline of an average of 5 people per year for 40 years. The church simply lost its way, oblivious to their peril. The church could possibly have existed for another 10 to 15 years max before it closed.

At the beginning I was called to serve as an intentional interim pastor to help prepare the church for its next steps. During that time I provided an assessment of the church before they called me as pastor. My initial evaluation led to prescriptions that developed into a five-year vision.

- Rediscover the purpose, mission, vision, and core values of the church. These ceased to exist in any recognizable form.
- Restructure the constitution and bylaws so the pastor is empowered to lead the congregation.
- Revitalize the worship service and begin a second, contemporary service with the primary objective of reaching young people eighteen to thirty years of age. This age group was missing in action.
- Develop a ministry to young families, as young families were scarce in the church. The community as a whole is quite young.
- Replace the aging building with a new one that was handicap accessible and functional for the church's ministry. Make the new facility and grounds useful and useable by the community. Build debt free.
- Restructure the current budget to make room for a pastoral intern or staff member. Train him to eventually assume the role of pastor in the church.
- Join Gordon in Fresh Start Ministries by allowing him eight weeks each year to minister to other churches and pastors.

Remarkably, the church agreed to the prescription and vision. In six years the vision is virtually complete. We are now in phase 2, revisioning for the next five years.

Response

Pastors and churches must respond to the Lord as he requires us to do. Examine the exhortations in the text in light of the life of your church. If there's sin, repent. If there is doctrinal error, correct it. Immorality? Face the brother(s) or sister(s) and deal with it. If there is no repentance, remove the offending parties from the body. If you have church bullies, deal with them. If people are divisive, remove them permanently, following the pattern of Titus 3:10–11. *Remember, return,* and *repent*. These are action verbs found in Revelation 2–3 and they demand a response.

Refresh

Two key passages stand out when we consider the need for refreshing in a church, Revelation 2:5 and 3:20. Revelation 2:5 instructs the pastor at Ephesus to "do the things you did at first." The Christian life can be likened to a ship at sea. After years of service, barnacles attach themselves to the hull of the ship causing it to lose sailing efficiency. The ship needs to be in dry dock where the hull is scraped, repainted, and repaired, enabling it to return to its intended purpose—efficient sailing. A similar thing can happen to believers. Over the years the joy of the Lord and passion for souls are overshadowed by the cares of the world. Bible reading and prayer become routine. The Lord desires to reinject us with life and vitality. Allow the Lord, the King, to knock off the barnacles of sameness, the debilitating effects of sin, and attitudes of indifference and boredom. When this occurs, times of refreshing return.

Perhaps the most telling passage in these two chapters is Revelation 3:20. Here we find the Lord outside his own church seeking entrance. It's his church, his body, his people, but he is not welcome in their presence. Self-reliance and self-importance have overshadowed the reign of Christ. God forbid this should happen, but it does! Churches torn by conflict and strife have effectively removed Jesus Christ from their equation. These churches need to confess their sin collectively, to bow humbly before the King and, as a body, invite him to enter the fellowship and once again rule as Lord of the church. When this occurs, the church will discover a fresh start.

Mentoring and Revitalization

Mentoring is not mentioned directly in the biblical discussion of transformational leaders. For that matter, the term *mentor* is not found on the pages of Scripture. The term originated in ancient Greece. However, the concept of mentoring is certainly evident in Scripture. Moses and Joshua, Elijah and Elisha, Jesus and the Twelve, Paul and Timothy, and Paul and Titus are just a few portraits of leaders passing the mantle of their leadership to and empowering the next generation of leaders.

Moses and Joshua are prime examples of a mentor/protégé relationship. Moses mentored Joshua throughout the wilderness sojourn. Here are some examples of that relationship. Joshua commanded the army under Moses (Exodus 17). As an aide, he journeyed to the mountain with Moses, who received instructions for constructing the tabernacle (24:13). Joshua was one of the twelve spies picked to survey the Promised Land. Then as the time drew near for Israel to enter the Promised Land, the Lord instructed Moses saying, "But your assistant, Joshua son of Nun, will enter it. Encourage him, because he will lead Israel to inherit it" (Deut. 1:38). Can you imagine the chaos trying to enter the Promised Land had Moses not prepared a strong leader in Joshua?

The relationship between teacher and pupil or mentor and protégé is clear. Moses groomed Joshua, the son of Nun, as his successor. Leadership and management instructor Peter Wiwcharuck makes a simple but profound statement: "Success without a successor is failure."[6] Because of God's instruction, Moses understood the critical need for a successor. Joshua was an indispensable piece of the vision to lead an enslaved people from Egypt to the freedom of the Promised Land. Mentor/protégé; leader/successor—result: vision accomplished.

Turnaround works best when a re-envisioning pastor is followed by another re-envisioning pastor. That way the ministry is not just "one and done." Before he departed for heaven, Jesus initiated the ministry that his disciples would continue. Paul took the gospel to the Gentiles; Timothy, Titus, and others took it farther. Successful transformation requires a successor! The mini-bio of chapter 2 is a perfect, current example of the process. Les Magee intentionally passed the leadership baton to Roy Gruber. The ministry continues to flourish.

This is a brief introduction to mentoring. A much broader discussion of the concept of mentoring and coaching and re-envisioning leadership is found in chapter 12.

Mini-Bio: A Re-Envisioned Church

Timberline Church was "a happy family church, a warm, loving community."[7] The church had grown from 126 when the pastor first arrived to 600 in average attendance. Everything ran smoothly—until Nikki arrived. Nikki, a beautiful, young stripper, discovered a friend in hair salon owner Larry Baker.

In Nikki's own words, "Larry shared Jesus and the woman at the well story with me at lunch one day after I had thanked him for being such a good friend. (Larry did not care what other people thought about him hanging out with me, getting to know me without an agenda. I had known my 'type' back then was not in his general circle.) He then proceeded to share that very story with me, and I said, '*That* story is in *the Bible*?!' Larry said yes it was in the Bible. I told him I wanted a Bible right away to check it out myself. He got my first Student NIV version. I asked Larry, 'Where do I start?' He thought that the New Testament would be good, starting with Matthew. I read nonstop for a week, sometimes until 2:00 or 3:00 a.m. I even called Larry a few times to come over so I could chat with him more about it. After that week or so I asked Larry if I could go to 'mass' with him."[8]

Larry Baker picks up the account. "It was summertime and Nikki, as usual, wasn't wearing much. Knowing we'd soon be at the church, I persuaded her to sit in the balcony with me, for two reasons besides lack of clothing. One was so I could explain the service as it went on; the other was that the only woman my church had seen with me was my wife. I did not want to cause a commotion. Plus, if we sat down front, people might pay more attention to Noticeable Nikki than to the preacher.

"After about two minutes in the balcony, she said, 'I don't want to be way up here; I want to go down where I can see better.' Since I knew there was no winning with Nikki, we headed for the front of the sanctuary. She plopped down Indian style on the first pew."[9]

Nikki continues the saga. "At that August 1994 service, Pastor Dary spoke on how some of us build walls around us to protect ourselves, sealing everyone out so we won't get hurt, and so on, and in doing so we also shut the things of God out as well. Therefore He cannot bless us or show Himself to us because of those walls. At the end of service, I gave my life to Jesus, changing my entire world from black to white."

Larry writes, "I looked over at Nikki and here was the worldly wise, tough little stripper with her hand in the air and tears running down her face. She made a commitment that morning that changed both our lives."[10]

Nikki adds, "The baptism came not long after my salvation. I also invited several people from my workplace at that time and about three or four people came to my baptism. I remember a couple later asking us more about Christ and who He was, as well as what happened to me, because I really went from a party college girl (extreme partying not the normal 'get a little crazy at college' partying) to never wanting to leave my new church family, never partying or stripping again."

Pastor Dary relates, "That Sunday became a turning point in the life of the church. Nine people came to Christ in that service. We realized that we had to change the way we approached people who were not believers. We recognized that we had to become more culturally relevant without compromise." Nikki was the catalyst of a whole new vision, an entirely different way of being the church.

Since that fateful Sunday, the church has grown to well over 5,000 in average attendance. Of the new people who have joined the church, 44 percent are new believers. The church's vision, based on the Great Commandment, is simply, "Let love live." This passion has driven the church for nearly twenty years.

The Great Commandment became the new driving force at Timberline. As in any church setting, a biblically based vision is where we must begin.

Questions for Reflection, Discussion, and Application

1. Do you have a clear, compelling, biblically directed vision? Can you state it or write it out clearly and distinctly? Re-envisioning pastors can. If not, why not try!
2. Have you fulfilled your original vision for your church or in your ministry? If so, what will you need to do to retool and begin to develop the next step or steps for your ministry?
3. Have you failed in ministry? If so, how? What have you learned through the process? What did you not learn that you should have learned?
4. Which description(s) of the seven leaders of the seven churches best fits you? Which exhortation(s) applies to you? How should you respond?
5. Should your church consider an assessment by an outside church consultant? Why or why not?
6. Do you agree or disagree that "success without a successor is a failure"? Why or why not?
7. Are you developing a new leader or leaders to take your place? If you do not have a plan in place, try to establish one. Pray for a protégé. Pick a date when you ought to begin and put it on your calendar.

4

Design, Direction, and Development

The purpose of this chapter is to introduce you to the three *D*s that provide you with a background and the information you will need to best understand our exploration of re-envisioning pastors in the following chapters. The three *D*s provide us with a context or backdrop for how leaders lead and do ministry in general and revitalize churches in particular.

The first *D* stands for *design*. Your divine design enables you to understand how God has uniquely, intentionally wired you for ministry. Job says, "Your hands shaped me and made me. . . . Remember that you molded me like clay" (Job 10:8–9). If God has shaped you, and Job says he has, what is your shape? The question for pastoral leaders in the context of this book is, Has God designed or shaped you to re-envision his church?

The second *D* refers to our ministry *direction*. It addresses what God wants you to do with your unique design. The question here is, Is God pointing you toward church revitalization and how would you know?

The third *D* is our *development*. It explains how you prepare for this ministry. At this point, you know your design and direction. The question becomes, How do pastoral leaders prepare to re-envision the church? The answer will range anywhere from individualized self-instruction on the one hand to attending a school or seminary on the other or both. With this brief introduction in mind, let's investigate each *D* in more detail.

Divine Design

DIVINE DESIGN
God's Call to Vocational Ministry
Prior Life Experiences
Current Life Circumstances
Natural and Spiritual Gifts
Passion
Temperament

The great assumption in America is that anyone can do or be whatever he or she wants. I can recall hearing former President Bill Clinton say this to a group of inner-city kids. His goal was noble; he wanted to encourage these kids to pursue their dreams and make something of their lives. The only problem is that it's simply not true. Everybody can't do or be whatever they want. Similarly, the great assumption of pastoral ministry is that any Christian can be a pastor. And in some circles the view is that every Christian can be a re-envisioning pastor. That's not true either, as it flies in the face of how God has designed us. God has not wired every Christian with the potential to pastor or lead a church.

God's Call to Vocational Ministry

Another assumption is that God calls men and women into vocational pastoral ministry. Those who hold this view warn against going into vocational ministry without such a call. Otherwise when the going gets tough, those who aren't called will likely drop out, while those who are called will hang in there. If you are a leader who strongly believes in such a divine call, then please hear us out on the following. Read on! As we've explored this concept, we've discovered that the understanding of God's call is very subjective and deeply involves one's emotions. In reality, one pastor's experience is different from another's. And very little Scripture is used to support the concept of being called to vocational ministry. Some point to Isaiah 6 as describing Isaiah's call to ministry. However, the passage is descriptive and not prescriptive. Those who claim this passage as support of the need for a call find it difficult to argue that Isaiah's purpose for writing Isaiah 6 is to show us what is involved in a call to ministry either back then or today. At the same time, I (Aubrey) would be the last person to argue that God can't or doesn't call some people to vocational ministry. However, I suspect that a call to ministry is strongly impacted by one's passion for a particular ministry. I equate a person's call to ministry with his or her passion for that particular ministry. I'll say more about passion below.

A more objective and biblical approach to ministry than waiting on a special call from God is to investigate one's divine design for ministry right now. God has made us the way we are and specifically gifted the members of his body for ministry. This consists of various natural and spiritual gifts and abilities that make up one's divine design. The question is whether you have a divine design suited for pastoral ministry and for re-envisioning churches. With this in mind we're ready to pursue this design concept.

Prior Life Experiences

PRIOR LIFE EXPERIENCES
Heritage
Heroes
High points
Hard times

One's divine design consists of his or her prior life experiences from birth to the present. What do you learn about yourself from your past? What is your life story? Bill George writes, "The leaders' life stories are unique to them and more powerful than any set of characteristics or leadership skills they possess."[1] For example, have you experienced leading an organization such as a business through a revitalization? Or perhaps you've experienced much success as a Bible teacher in your church. These kinds of past experiences speak volumes about how God has wired a leader, and how he or she might use these experiences in the ministry world.

As you look at your past experiences, consider your heritage, heroes, high points, and hard times.[2] These have all helped to shape you into the person you are today.

Heritage

Your heritage focuses on your family and its influence on your design. Has a parent attempted to influence you to move in a particular vocational direction? For example, my (Aubrey's) mother-in-law repeatedly informed her son as he grew up that he was going to be a medical doctor. Despite his mom's efforts, the medical profession was not to be his destiny. How many times have we heard someone say he or she is in vocational ministry because of the influence of his or her mother, father, or grandparents? Though largely unexplored, genetics could have an influence here as well.

Heroes

Your heroes are those whom God has brought into your life to impact your life's direction. They are individuals whom you've looked up to in some way. Often they're wired a lot like you are, and you intuitively recognize this. At Dallas Seminary we have some students who are wired like our former president Chuck Swindoll, and their similar ministry design has attracted them to his ministry. For them he is a hero.

I (Aubrey) played high school football where I grew up in Gainesville, Florida. And though I wasn't a believer, I was attracted to a player on another team because of his Christlike character. The way he treated others on the field of play impressed me, and he became what I refer to as a hero from a distance. I wanted to be like him someday in terms of my character.

High Points

Your high points in this context are the pleasurable or successful events in your life. They may reveal to some degree your design. These events include successful ministries, such as preaching and teaching, or when people recognized and appreciated your abilities, perhaps complimenting you on them. When people benefit from your work or ministry and let you know about it, you begin to realize that God was at work specifically using you and your abilities through these times of ministry in the lives of his people to accomplish his goals.

Hard Times

Your hard times are those difficult events that have brought you pain but nonetheless have put you in contact in some way with your design. These could include sickness, a loved one's death, failure, and disappointment. A key verse to claim in hard times is Romans 8:28: "And we know that in all things [bad as well as good] God works for the good of those who love him, who have been called according to his purpose." Many leaders confess that while no one invites hard times, it's during the hard times that we learn our greatest lessons in life and ministry. We learn how we respond to difficulty and we learn things about ourselves that will help us lead better next time.

Current Life Circumstances

Your current life circumstances work along with divine design to show you what God wants you to do now. They include such things as your age, marital status, gender, ethnicity, education, health, finances, a second occupation, and ministry experience. You need to consider these as you look to ministry in the body of Christ. Let's examine some of these circumstances in more detail.

CURRENT LIFE CIRCUMSTANCES
Age
Marital status
Gender
Ethnicity
Education
Health
Finances
Second occupation
Ministry experience

Age

Based on our research for this book, we believe that one is never too young or too old to pursue ministry. Churches and parachurch ministries tend to retire pastors and leaders too early. On the other hand, some tend to stay too long. One pastor of a large, prominent Dallas church stayed too long and the church lost a large number of the congregation to another church in the suburbs. There are some ministries that look only for younger pastors for their ministry positions. Their stance seems to be that older pastors and leaders don't have much wisdom to offer them. This is misguided and unfortunate.

Marital Status

Marital status is also important. Most churches prefer their pastors to be married as opposed to single. While this is understandable in terms of ministering to the whole church family, we must keep in mind that both Jesus and Paul were single. Another point to be aware of is that, for some people, a divorce will limit what you can do, especially in leading or pastoring a church.

Gender

Gender is an important issue to some degree in all churches, especially the role of women. The critical question is, Can a woman pastor a church or be an elder on a church board? Those who hold the complementarian view believe that the Scriptures don't allow women to assume these roles. Currently they are in the majority. Those who hold the egalitarian view feel that a woman can do anything a man can do in ministry, which includes being the senior pastor of a church or sitting on a governing board. Willow Creek Community Church in Chicago is known for being egalitarian. However, they don't have a woman in the position of senior pastor. They do have women on their elder board.

Ethnicity

Ethnicity isn't a big issue in most churches because birds of a feather tend to flock together. And many, especially older believers, have come to accept this over the years, regardless of their ethnicity. Today younger believers have begun to challenge this stereotype and many prefer a multiethnic church. If this is accurate, then perhaps the birds of a feather mentality will change as younger people become leaders and exert more influence on their churches.

Education

For a long time a leader's education has been an issue in some churches, especially in the more liturgical churches and some denominational wings of the church. The former will limit your ministry without the proper credentials, which include seminary training. Some people will go to the other extreme and play down the importance of seminary or college training, especially if they don't have such training themselves. Regardless, seminaries in general are changing their agendas and are now including online training and other venues that make a seminary education more possible.

Health

Health is an important factor to ministry. Poor health can certainly limit one's ministry. Pastoring a church has become a twenty-four-hour-a-day job that can drain a leader emotionally as well as physically. Thus if you're attempting to pastor while dealing with poor physical or mental health, you'll find that you won't last long in ministry. You would be wise to seek some kind of ministry that doesn't demand so much of your time and energy.

Finances

Most of those who have been involved in ministry for any length of time will acknowledge that ministry will not provide a lot of money. With few exceptions, ministry in general and pastoral ministry in particular don't pay a lot by today's standards. Many in ministry, perhaps the majority, are bi-vocational. Those who pursue ministry will need to examine their motives carefully, and a good salary can't be one of them.

The biblical principle regarding a pastor's salary is found in 1 Timothy 5:17. The elders referred to in this passage were first-century house church pastors. The principle here is the pastor who leads well is worthy of "double honor." But what does that mean? We believe that the passage is telling churches to take good care of their leaders.

A Second Occupation

There are some occupations that naturally sync well with ministry. The functions required for a profession may be similar to that of a pastor or staff person. Teaching in a public school would obviously be such a function, because pastors and staff people spend much time in teaching and communication. Another is the world of business. Much like business leaders, CEOs, and managers, pastors and parachurch leaders find themselves strategically leading and developing their ministries. This includes such crucial roles as developing and casting a mission and vision, designing a strategy to accomplish the mission and vision, and caring for staffing, facilities, and so forth.

Ministry Experience

If you apply for a position in a church or parachurch ministry, somewhere in the application process an interviewer will ask about your prior experience. Most feel that the more experience an applicant has, the better. This assumes that the past ministry experience has been positive. When a person has bounced around from church to church, never finding a good fit, it probably signals that he or she should not continue in ministry.

Natural and Spiritual Gifts

In addition to one's prior life experiences and current life circumstances, divine design consists of the believer's natural and spiritual gifts or abilities. Believers and unbelievers alike have natural gifts. God in his grace has given gifts to unbelievers. Matthew quotes Jesus, "He causes his sun to rise on the evil and the good, and sends rain on the righteous and the unrighteous" (Matt. 5:45). Thus we're not surprised when a non-Christian can sing well, excel in sports, write good fiction, lead a school board, and so on. And believers may also have these God-given natural gifts and abilities.

God gives Christians spiritual gifts or abilities as well, most likely at the point of conversion. I use the term *gifts* because it's the biblical term and people associate it with the Scriptures. However, I like to use the term *abilities* because it captures how the gifts function. *Gifts* implies the biblical origin and *abilities* implies ministry action. Paul writes more about spiritual gifts than any other biblical author of the New Testament. He addresses them in Romans 12:3–8, 1 Corinthians 12:1–31, and Ephesians 4:7–16. Peter also addresses spiritual gifts in 1 Peter 4:10–11. One of the issues we will address in chapter 6 as part of our research is whether re-envisioning pastors have gifts distinct from those of non–re-envisioning pastors. Is there any distinction between the two based on gifting alone?

As a further extension of his grace, God has given us the Holy Spirit who helps us implement our gifts. First, we have been indwelt by his Spirit (1 Cor. 6:19). And the purpose for that indwelling is to empower us to do ministry (Eph. 3:16, 20). We are not left alone with our gifting; we have the Holy Spirit and his power to make our gifts operational.

Passion

God has provided each of us with a unique passion or passions that direct and excite our gifts. Passion is our God-given capacity to attach ourselves emotionally to something or someone over an extended period of time to meet a need. Passion provides a person both with motivation to do their ministry and the focus that directs that ministry. Your passion is what you feel strongly about, what you care deeply about that touches your emotions. It has such an impact on you and your ministry that should a church or parachurch ministry not be able to hire you in your area of passion, you would be willing to pursue it for free.

Discovering one's passion may relate to what some describe as a call to ministry. Perhaps the call to ministry is the same as discovering one's passion for ministry. A call to ministry or "surrendering" to such a call can be a very emotional experience. Regardless of what you believe about a call to ministry, the important question for every pastor reading this book is, Do you have a passion for re-envisioning Christ's church?

Temperament

Along with our gifting and passion, God has given each of us a unique temperament with which to do ministry. I suspect God does this at birth, since children display temperament very early in life. And if it takes place at birth, then God by his grace has blessed lost people with a temperament with which to live and do life. What exactly is temperament? We define temperament as one's unique, God-given (inborn) behavioral style. It relates to how we behave or do ministry as well as life. It addresses the unique, personal behavioral characteristics and tendencies that deeply impact ministry. This brief section is meant to introduce you to temperament and its importance to leadership and ministry as well as to show that it fits naturally with our gifting and passion. In the next chapter, we will focus entirely on the concept of temperament, and one of the questions that we'll explore in chapter 7 is whether re-envisioning pastors display a particular temperament that is different from that of non–re-envisioning pastors.

Divine Direction

Divine design addresses how God has wired us for ministry. Some even refer to it as one's divine thumbprint. (Everybody has one, and some are similar, but none are exactly the same.) Divine direction introduces a new factor into the discussion. It has to do with what God wants a person to do with his or her life. In short, we ask, What is God's will for my life and ministry?

To understand direction, you must look back at how God has designed you. Design dictates direction. If you have a gift of leading, then it's obvious that he wants you to lead. If you have a passion for working with adults, it's obvious he wants you to lead adults. We use the term *obvious*. Actually, it's not always that obvious to the individual. Often it can be more obvious to another person who has the opportunity to observe us. This stresses the importance of inviting others (a friend, spouse, coach, mentor, pastor) to provide input. They bring an element of objectivity that's vital to one's discovery of one's direction. Rarely do we see this happening in our churches.

Observing what people with gifts, passions, and temperaments like yours are doing in ministry can be very helpful. For example, some pastors of large churches, such as Rick Warren, Bill Hybels, and my (Aubrey's) pastor Steve Stroope (pastor of Lake Pointe Church in Rockwall, Texas), have three gifts in common: leadership, preaching, and evangelism. They also tend to be DIs or IDs on the Personal Profile or DISC. (People with these two similar temperaments have strong people skills balanced with a goal-orientation to ministry.) If you have these same gifts and temperaments, God may be directing you to serve as a senior pastor of a large church. One Dallas Seminary graduate wired like the three pastors above confided in me that he intuitively sensed that God planned to use him as the pastor of larger churches. And that's exactly what happened.

Do pastors who can re-envision the church have certain gifts, passions, and temperaments in common that point them in the direction of church revitalization? Remember, design dictates direction! If so, then knowledge of self will make a huge difference in ministry placement and ultimate satisfaction. We'll return to and address this later in the book.

Determining your ministry direction involves your personal mission and vision in addition to your gifts, passions, and temperament. Discovering and understanding your unique divine design will guide your life's ministry direction. Envisioning what that will look like in the next five or more years determines your personal vision for ministry. You must ask, Based on my ministry direction, what do I see myself doing in the near future that touches me deeply, that excites me, that could even keep me awake at night? We believe that your ministry direction includes your church's mission and vision. God would have us be part of a local church ministry, and that church should have an organizational mission and vision. The mission is to make disciples (Matt. 28:19), and the vision is what that will look like in the next few years. That becomes a part of our mission and vision as well.

Divine Development

Through development we get better at what God has designed us to do. We grow and improve. God molds and shapes us to use the design and accomplish the direction he prepared for us. This is the third *D* and the order here is important. I (Aubrey) have observed at the seminary level that we attract a number of students who are trying to discover what God's will or direction is for their ministry (the second *D*), but this is entering the process at the end rather than at the beginning. For example, in the medical or legal profession, this would be much like going to medical school to see if you want to be a doctor or going through law school to see if you have what it takes to be an attorney. It doesn't make sense. The third *D* assumes you know your design and direction and asks, How do I best prepare to pursue my divine direction? How does God want me to prepare? Should I go to school? Should I pursue an internship at a church or parachurch ministry? Should I do both? And what else might God want me to do so that I will be best prepared to serve him specifically as a leader? Two questions will help us determine how development should take place: Where are leaders developed? How do leaders develop?

Where Are Leaders Developed?

WHERE ARE LEADERS DEVELOPED?
Churches
Seminaries
Denominations

Who develops or should play a role in developing pastoral leaders in general and church re-envisioners in particular?

Churches

The local church is one place where leaders are developed. Perhaps local churches are most responsible for leader and people development. Many of the larger churches either put on their own leader development conference or send their people to various conferences of this type throughout the year. This can be helpful, but the effects of such training tend to wear off several months after the event. However, there are other experiences they can support, such as learning clusters, coaching, internships, residencies, and so forth. We at the Malphurs Group (TMG) have found it most productive to put on workshops for leader training. Rather than presenting a series of lectures alone, we walk leaders through a process so they will leave with what we call "a plan in hand." For example, we help churches craft a leadership development process for every level of their church. And our approach is to present a certain amount of material and then have the attendees actually begin the process at the event. By the time the day is over, they have accomplished the goal—they will have "a plan in hand." The idea is they return to their churches not to come up with a plan but to implement the plan. We have also discovered that implementation is more likely to happen if several people are involved in the training.

Seminaries

Seminaries are also in the leader development business. They must play a role in leadership development along with the churches. They can provide a re-envisioning pastor with knowledge of the Bible and theology and training in homiletics. Today our concern is that we see a number of emergent or young pastors who are wonderfully gifted to plant and re-envision churches but who don't know the Bible or theology well. Consequently, their teaching and preaching may come across as shallow or simply not be truth. They can be seen as a mile wide and an inch deep. As we stated earlier in this book, seminaries are doing a good job at some things. They're developing thinkers who know the original languages, the Bible, and church history, and that's important. It's what they aren't doing that troubles us, and that's training leaders in how to lead or develop other leaders.

Denominations

In addition to churches and seminaries, denominations, networks, and judicatories at the association and state levels can play an important role in developing leaders. In fact we believe that this is a new day for them and their ministry to their constituencies. But in the recent past some of these organizations seem to have lost their way. They're not doing much in the way of providing training for their constituents, but they appeal to them for their support based on filial obligations. A growing number of emergent pastors see through this and no longer attend or support these organizations. I (Aubrey) was invited to speak to an association located in south Texas. When I asked what they were doing to serve their constituent pastors, their answer was most revealing. They were there to support financially some long-term, faithful missionaries in the area. That's it! My response was patiently to point out to them that this is the churches' job, not theirs, and their job was to serve their pastors.

LEADERSHIP DEVELOPMENT
Character development
Knowledge development
Skills development
Emotional development
Physical development

How Do Leaders Develop?

How do leaders develop? The answer is to draft a personal leadership development plan (an LDP) that addresses the following: character competencies, knowledge competencies, skills competencies, emotional competencies, and physical competencies. The following questions are critical to forming such a plan:

- What kind of character is necessary for me to lead at the level where I am in my ministry, whether I'm a senior pastor or staff person? What do 1 Timothy 3:1–7 and Titus 1:5–9 present as character qualifications for leading a ministry?
- What do I need to know to best minister at my leadership level? Do I need to know the Bible and theology? Do I need training in the original languages and church history? Do I need to know and understand people better? Do I need to know how to preach and teach the Bible? Do I need to know how to lead a ministry?
- What do I need to be able to do, or what skills do I need, to lead well at my leadership level within the ministry? Do I need stronger people skills? Do I need stronger task skills? Do I need to be skilled at listening, communicating, collaborating, problem solving, conflict resolution, team building, budgeting, networking, and so forth?
- What should I feel in leading at my leadership level? In what ways do I need to become emotionally competent and mature, and what do I need to correct to be emotionally healthy? (It's my [Aubrey's] view that it's in the area of the emotions that we're losing the battle in protecting those in ministry leadership from sexual and legal entanglements. Too many pastors bring with them into the ministry serious dysfunctions from their childhood.)
- What are the physical requirements for leading as a senior pastor or staff person? How important is my health to my ministry and what can I do to be physically healthy?

I (Aubrey) have written *Building Leaders*[3] to help leaders develop a churchwide leader development plan that culminates with a personal leader development plan (LDP). The purpose for that book is to help you craft such a tool.

Finally, a developmental question that we'll need to ask and answer is, Can a non–re-envisioning pastor develop and become a REP? Is this possible? And, if so, how, when, and where? We will address these and similar critical questions later in this book.

Mini-Bio: A Costly Misunderstanding of Design

The call came about 9:30 in the morning. Angst filled the regional director's voice. His straightforward request explained the urgency in his tone. One of the churches in the association had reached critical mass. Noxious spiritual gases simmering just below the surface needed only a small spark to ignite into a full-blown church conflagration. Would it be possible for me to meet with the church to help calm the issues and settle the disputes? I (Gordon) hesitated because of a scheduled trip. A departure for a teaching assignment in Ukraine loomed on my horizon.

He called back an hour later with greater urgency in his voice. "If we don't intervene today, the church will be ripped apart and the ministry may end. We will have to close the church!" The problems had led the church to the boiling point. We needed to begin an intervention process that day. My wife, Beth, and I packed our bags to make the six-hour journey to this church.

We arrived for a hastily called meeting on Wednesday night. As we walked up to the double glass doors at the front of the building, we observed people standing in groups of two or three, heads down, arms folded, whispering to one another. I turned to Beth and said, "This 'cain't' be good!"

This could be labeled "The case of a terrible mismatch." The pastor, though a great person with a wonderful family, did not fit in this ministry setting. Misunderstanding abounded on both sides—the church and the pastor. God's design and direction for both entities had been ignored. The pastor's disposition did not fit with the majority of the congregation. This resulted in a seething caldron of discontent on the part of both the pastor and the church.

When a mismatch occurs in church ministry, catastrophic results normally follow. Broken relationships, broken individuals, destroyed families, and weakened or dead churches litter the landscape. Unfortunately, many pastors, pastors' wives, their children, and churches never recover. To be more effective in ministry and limit the damage to churches and individuals, pastors and churches must better understand and implement the concepts of divine design, divine direction, and divine development.

Questions for Reflection, Discussion, and Application

1. Do you find the concept of the three *D*s helpful? How so? Is this a biblical concept; that is, does Scripture seem to support the concept? What passages support it?
2. Do you agree with the authors' concept of divine design? Do you really believe that God has designed us the way we are to serve him? If so, why? If not, why not? How might this concept be helpful in ministry?

3. Do you agree with the assumption that anyone can do or be whatever he or she wants? If so, why? If not, why not? How might this assumption impact one's ministry?
4. Do you believe in a "call to ministry"? Why or why not? If so, how would you respond to the authors' viewpoint on a call? Is Isaiah 6 a good proof text for a divine call to vocational ministry? Why or why not?
5. How might your prior life experiences affect your leadership? How might your current life circumstances affect it? Is there anything in your past or present that might disqualify you from or make it difficult to pursue vocational ministry?
6. Does the authors' view that design dictates direction make sense? Why or why not? If design does dictate direction, what might be your possible ministry direction or directions? What ministries are people who are wired like you doing? How might this concept help you discover and know God's will for your life?
7. Assuming you know what God's will is for your vocation, what are some ways that you could pursue development for ministry? What are some options, and what are some non-options? Why?
8. Do you have a personal leadership development plan? Why or why not? If not, what will you do about it, assuming you should have one?

5

The Leader's Behavior

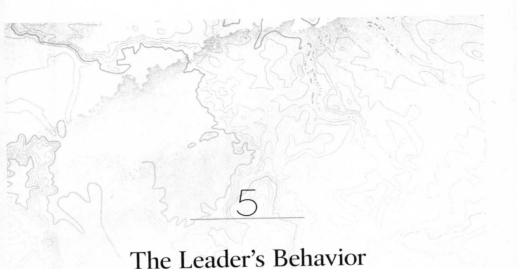

Temperament is a vital piece of the divine design puzzle and ultimately of pastoral turnaround as you will see later on. It addresses the visionary leader's behavior. Therefore, we have included this chapter to familiarize or refamiliarize you with the topic of temperament and type so that you'll be clear in the chapters that follow as to the role temperament played in our exploration of re-envisioning leaders and their ministries. In short, its role in our exploration was *huge*.

What Is Temperament?

Temperament or type is your unique, God-given (inborn) behavioral style. Your temperament is the combination of preferences that you choose when you take the Personal Profile (DISC) and/or the Myers-Briggs Type Indicator (MBTI). It's up to you to determine what temperament or type you really are. The tools are only as accurate as the information you put in them when responding to them. The first time that I (Aubrey) took the DISC I scored high as an "I." However, I discovered that I didn't know myself as well as I thought. Thus I became more observant of my actual behavior and learned that I clearly wasn't an "I."

There are no good or bad temperaments. Each temperament may express some good and bad qualities. No temperament preference is any more spiritual or carnal than another. For example, there are times when an extrovert is controlled by the Spirit and times when he or she is controlled by the flesh. And the same follows with the other temperaments.

While we may prefer and express a particular temperament or two, all of us use all the temperaments at some point or other. For example, while extroverts prefer to be around people, there are times when they need to be by themselves. We may be a high C temperament on the DISC with very little S, but may function as an S in certain rare situations that call for that type of response. Also your temperament is not an excuse for your doing or not doing something. For example, being an introvert is not a reason to ignore or not spend time with people.

Why Is Temperament Important?

First, when we understand temperament, we can learn a great deal about the people with whom and to whom we minister. We can also learn a lot about ourselves. We learn why people behave the way they do. Most important to this exploration is the fact that leaders who do well at a particular kind of ministry often pattern alike on the temperament tools. For example, church planters tend to be ENTPs on the Myers-Briggs Type Indicator and an ID on the Personal Profile. Therefore, a leader who scores as an ENTP or ID needs at the very least to ask whether he might function well as a church planter. Thus temperament can play a vital role in vocational ministry placement. We specifically used the Personal Profile and Myers-Briggs Type Indicator to help us look for behavior patterns shared by re-envisioning pastors.

What Are Some Temperament Tools?

PERSONAL PROFILE (DISC)
D-Dominance
I-Influence
S-Steadiness
C-Conscientiousness

The Personal Profile (DISC)

The Personal Profile is based on an historic four-temperament model that goes as far back as the Greek physician Hippocrates (460–370 BC). Later Galen (AD 131–200), who was a physician and a philosopher, came up with the terms *choleric, sanguine, phlegmatic*, and *melancholy,* which are still used today to describe temperament. The current tool that reflects Galen's model is the Personal Profile or DISC, an acronym for the four behavioral temperaments: dominance, influence, steadiness, and conscientiousness. The following provides a brief look at these four temperaments. As you read through them, make note of any that describe you.

Dominance Temperament

The following are some characteristics of the D or dominance temperament. A person's orientation to life reflects whether he or she is goal-oriented (purpose) or people-oriented. Those with D temperament believe that accomplishing goals is more important than relating well to people. Thus they'll get the job done but may alienate some people in the process.

Pacing has to do with the speed at which one moves through life both mentally and even physically. (Some refer to this as capacity.) The D temperament is fast-paced and moves through life quickly, while other temperaments move more cautiously. Ds are motivated by a challenge. It's important that supervisors challenge them regularly in the ministry or workplace to realize their potential.

The environment is where one's ministry takes place. It may include actual space, such as an office, and may include other people who make up the ministry team in some way. The most favorable environment for Ds is one that provides lots of challenges and opportunities. In addition, they like to be in control of their circumstances and prefer freedom from the control of others.

Ds tend to be visionaries so it's important that their environment be vision-oriented and open to innovation. When a D is under pressure he or she becomes aggressive and takes charge of the situation. Ds tend not to listen well as they're preoccupied with what they feel are more important matters, such as getting things done. With exceptions, Ds tend to be open to change as long as change accomplishes the ministry's goals. Ds display a number of strengths, several of which are productivity, decisiveness, persistence, and firmness. Their weaknesses include being too busy, insensitive to others, impatient, inflexible, and too quick to take control.

Summary: Dominance Temperament

- *Orientation to life:* goal or purpose
- *Pacing/capacity:* fast-paced
- *Motivation:* a challenge
- *Environment:* lots of challenge and opportunity, freedom from control while being in control, innovative, and visionary
- *Under pressure:* aggressive, autocratic

- *Would benefit from:* listening
- *Response to change:* open to change
- *Strengths:* productive, decisive, persistent, firm
- *Weaknesses:* too busy, insensitive, impatient, inflexible

Influence Temperament

In contrast to the D temperament, the I or influence temperament favors being with and building relationships with people. Like the Ds, they too are fast-paced and move through life quickly. That which motivates them is recognition. It's important that we recognize their accomplishments if we want them to reach their full potential under our ministry. They prefer an environment that is inspirational, optimistic, and fun-loving. They are party people. Chuck Swindoll has the I temperament, and while he was the president of Dallas Seminary, he would always show up whenever there was a birthday party on campus because he so enjoyed interacting with people. A warning is needed, however. Because they are so friendly, it is a surprise to know that under pressure they can attack.

People with the I temperament tend to start a number of different projects but quickly lose interest and leave them in an unfinished state. They need to learn to finish what they start. Like the Ds, they are open to change, especially if it makes for building up people. In terms of strengths, they may be described as optimistic, inspiring, personable, and enthusiastic. However, they tend to exaggerate and are impatient, manipulative, and impulsive.

Summary: Influence Temperament

- *Orientation to life:* people/relationships
- *Pacing/capacity:* fast-paced
- *Motivation:* recognition
- *Environment:* friendly and fun-loving, optimistic, opportunities to inspire people
- *Under pressure:* attack
- *Would benefit from:* finishing what they start
- *Response to change:* open to change
- *Strengths:* optimistic, inspiring, personable, enthusiastic
- *Weaknesses:* exaggerate, impatient, manipulative, impulsive

Steadiness Temperament

Like the I temperament, the person with the S or steadiness temperament is oriented to life through people and relationships. They are very interested in people and their welfare. When they ask how you're doing, they aren't simply saying hello, they really want to know. Unlike the D and I temperaments, the Ss move through life more slowly. They're simply not in a hurry and prefer not to be rushed. Good relationships with people motivate them.

They prefer security in their ministry positions and really like when people show appreciation for them. Under pressure they are likely to give in to others' wishes. They tend not to initiate but follow the initiatives of others. Thus they would benefit from at times being the initiator. They are slow to change, because they're concerned that change may hurt people or their relationships with people. If it can be demonstrated that change won't affect people adversely, they are more likely to accept it. Their strengths are that they are agreeable, loyal to a fault, and supportive of the ministry's initiatives. Their weaknesses are that they are nonconfrontational when they need to be confrontational, they miss advancement opportunities due to their loyalty, and they are too conforming when they need to provide pushback.

Summary: Steadiness Temperament

- *Orientation to life:* people/relationships
- *Pacing/capacity:* slow-paced
- *Motivation:* relationships, security, appreciation
- *Environment:* consistent and stable, relational, little conflict, working with people
- *Under pressure:* give in, acquiesce
- *Would benefit from:* initiating
- *Response to change:* slow to change (depending on how it affects relationships)
- *Strengths:* agreeable, loyal, supportive
- *Weaknesses:* nonconfrontational, missed opportunities, conforming

Conscientiousness Temperament

Like the D, the C's orientation to life is more goal or purpose oriented. At the end of the day, the C evaluates the day by what goals they accomplished, not by the relationships they established. Like the S they tend to be slow-paced. They're in no rush to get things accomplished but are motivated by accuracy and quality, which take time. They prefer to minister in an environment where things are planned out and predictable with few surprises. They also want privacy and tend to be somewhat risk aversive. They minister best where there are clear policies and procedures.

When Cs are under pressure, their natural reaction is to withdraw emotionally. This tendency to withdraw can be a problem and they must learn to communicate at these times with teammates and family, especially their spouse.

The Cs, like the Ss, respond slowly to change. While they're not exactly opposed to change, they are concerned about how it will affect the quality of the ministry. If the change promotes ministry quality, they'll support it.

Finally, the Cs' strengths are their desire for accuracy and quality of ministry, their thoroughness, and their sincerity. Their weaknesses are fussiness and perfectionism, which make their relationships with others difficult. Also they are stuffy, lacking a sense of humor.

Summary: Conscientiousness Temperament

- *Orientation to life:* goal or purpose
- *Pacing/capacity:* slow-paced
- *Motivation:* accuracy, quality
- *Environment:* planned and predictable, private, low risk, established policies and procedures
- *Under pressure:* withdraw
- *Would benefit from:* communicating
- *Response to change:* slow (concerned with how it affects quality)
- *Strengths:* accurate, thorough, sincere
- *Weaknesses:* fussy, perfectionistic, stuffy

One of these four temperaments is most like you. And chances are good that two and in some rare cases even three will characterize you in various ministry situations.

The Myers-Briggs Type Indicator (MBTI)

MYERS-BRIGGS TYPE INDICATOR (MBTI)
Extroversion versus Introversion
Sensing versus Intuitive
Thinking versus Feeling
Judgment versus Perception

Katharine Briggs and her daughter, Isabel Myers, developed the Myers Briggs Type Indicator during World War II. The MBTI takes a different approach than does the Personal Profile. It helps us discern our inborn preferences in four key functional areas of life: how people focus their attention (extroversion versus introversion); how they acquire information (sensing versus intuition); how they make decisions (thinking versus feeling); and how they relate to the world of people and things (judgment versus perception). The following provides a brief explanation of these four types. Note which best describe you.

Extroversion versus Introversion

Determining if one fits the extroversion or the introversion type means answering this question: Where in the world of people and things does the person focus his or her attention? The answer depends on how one is energized. Extroverts and introverts are like batteries. Extroverts charge their batteries when they are around people. They focus their attention on the outer world of people and things. Introverts, however, charge their batteries when by themselves. People tend to drain them of energy. The result is they focus their attention on the inner world of ideas and concepts.

In terms of their orientation to life, extroverts are after-thinkers. Their natural approach to life is to act first and think later. Thus they come across as impulsive, at least to introverts. While extroverts prefer to explore the world to understand it, introverts prefer to know or better understand their world before exploring it. Consequently, they think first and then act. Extroverts view them as "plodders."

Extroverts prefer a ministry environment where they're with others. They like to have people around them, preferably a team, and appreciate the verbal interaction, whereas introverts gravitate to quiet environments where they are mostly alone. In effect, they are loners and may not be good team people unless they work at it. Again, where they get their energy strongly affects how they do or don't relate to people.

The extroverts' strengths are their ability to remember names and faces and greet well. They handle interruptions well and are easy to get to know. Introverts are able to use times of quiet for concentration and relaxation. They are good ideas people who are insightful.

The extroverts' weaknesses include talking too much. They say what is on their minds, which isn't always appropriate to the situation. They are impatient when a ministry is involved in a process such as strategic planning.

Unlike extroverts, introverts don't remember names and faces well, due largely to their task orientation to life. And they tend to be very private, keeping much to themselves.

So which are you?

Summary: Extroverts and Introverts

- *Questions*
  Where do you prefer to focus your attention?
  What energizes you—other people or being alone?

- *Focus*

  Extroverts: Prefer to focus attention on the outer world of people and things. This is what energizes them.

  Introverts: Focus on the inner world of ideas and concepts. The inner world energizes them.

- *Orientation*

  Extroverts: After-thinkers, they act first and then think.

  Introverts: Fore-thinkers, they think first and then act.

- *Ministry Environment*

  Extroverts: Like to be with others, seek verbal interaction.

  Introverts: Like to be alone, seek quiet.

- *Communication*

  Extroverts: Talkers.

  Introverts: Writers.

- *Strengths*

  Extroverts: Remember names and faces, greet people well, like variety and action, handle interruptions well, easy to get to know.

  Introverts: Use quiet for concentration, can work on a single project for a long period of time, good ideas people, observant.

- *Weaknesses*

  Extroverts: Impatient with "process," talk too much, say what's on their minds, impulsive.

  Introverts: Don't remember names and faces, don't greet people well, not team people, private, slow to act.

Sensing versus Intuitive

Determining if one fits the sensing or the intuitive type means answering this question: How do you obtain information, learn about, or find out about things? The answer depends on your focus. The sensing type person gains their information through one or a combination of the five senses (hearing, smelling, seeing, tasting, or touching). So their focus in life is more on the facts. In a discussion, they will often ask for factual information. The intuitive person acquires information through what some refer to as a sixth sense—intuition. They may explain a decision with these words: "It just felt right." Their focus is on future possibilities and what could be.

In terms of one's orientation to life, the sensing types view life as it is. The phrase "you get what you see" describes their outlook. "Seeing" includes tasting or touching or any of the other senses. The intuitive types view life as it could be, not necessarily as it is. They tend to be born visionaries who see into the future and articulate what is out there for a church or ministry.

The sensing types prefer to minister in an environment that focuses on the facts and provides detailed information. They also depend heavily on the skills they've developed through past experience. The intuitive types prefer to see the big picture. They believe that it's good to have the facts but want to know how they fit into the big picture or the grand scheme of things. They enjoy developing new skills along the way rather than depending solely on current skills.

A strength of sensing persons is their focus on the facts. We do need to know the facts surrounding a situation before making a decision, and most often the sensing type will know them. They are also very practical and rely heavily on what their common sense tells them. Other strengths are their ability to apply what they've learned to everyday life and their living and enjoying each day as it is rather than living for tomorrow.

The intuitive types also have a number of strengths, such as their focus on fresh, new ideas as opposed to the "same old same old." They also tend to be more theoretical than practical and challenge us to consider what could be more than what is. This is only enhanced by their constant challenging of the status quo. In addition, they thrive on new challenges and opportunities and are big ideas people whose focus is on tomorrow and what it will bring.

Both the sensing types and the intuitive types display a number of weaknesses that we should be aware of. Sensing types can make a task more simple than it is and may be surprised when a project falls through or isn't completed on time. They prefer maintaining rather than challenging the status quo, and leaders may find it difficult to inspire them. They need to learn to look beyond the facts from what is to what could be.

Intuitive types need to focus more on the facts, because they tend to leap to conclusions, even when the evidence indicates otherwise or they don't have the facts right. They would also benefit by learning from the past as well as focusing on today's new ideas. They must understand that to learn from the past doesn't mean living in the past. Finally, they tend to be always in a rush and are impatient with people who take up their time.

Are you sensing or intuitive?

Summary: Sensing and Intuition

- *Questions*

  How do you acquire information?

  How do you find out about things?

- *Focus*

  Sensing types: Acquire information through the five senses, focus on the facts or what is there.

  Intuitive types: Gain information through a sixth sense (intuition), focus more on the possibilities or what could be.

- *Orientation*

  Sensing types: Live life as it is.

  Intuitive types: Pursue life as it could be.

- *Ministry Environment*

  Sensing types: Want to know the details, use current skills to accomplish tasks.

  Intuitive types: Want the big picture, prefer to develop new skills to accomplish tasks.

- *Strengths*

  Sensing types: Focus on facts, use common sense, are good at applying what they learn, very practical, enjoy today more than contemplating tomorrow.

  Intuitive types: Focus on new ideas, are more theoretical than practical, love to challenge the status quo, look for new challenges and opportunities, think about tomorrow instead of today, are new ideas people.

- *Weaknesses*

  Sensing types: Often oversimplify a task, aren't easily inspired, prefer the status quo, focus only on the facts, can be too patient.

  Intuitive types: Focus only on new ideas, leap to conclusions too soon, may not get the facts right, never seem to have enough time, easily become impatient.

Thinking versus Feeling

Determining if one fits the thinking type or the feeling type means answering this question: Do you make decisions by analyzing acquired information or do you use your senses, even a sixth sense—intuition—to make decisions? Thinkers are logical people who make decisions based on their rational abilities. They are objective decision makers who first analyze a situation and then come to a conclusion based on that information. As far as decision making is concerned, we think of them as a head. Feelers, however, make their decisions not based on logic and analysis of a situation but on their feelings and their values. They decide matters subjectively based on person-centered values. As far as decision making is concerned, we see them as a heart.

The thinkers' orientation to life is mostly based on facts and so they are more objective. For example, they seek an objective standard of truth for people, which for Christians is the Bible. They are thinkers who rely much on their logic. They are justice-based. If they observed a car run a red light, hit another car, and then leave the scene, their first thought would be to attempt to get the car's license plate or even pursue the fleeing driver. The feeler would stop first to render aid and not worry about getting a license number or pursuing the guilty driver. The feeler is more grace-based.

In regard to their ministry environments, thinkers prefer to deal with the facts, such as impersonal data, and analyze such information. Feelers prefer to work with people and their beliefs and personal values and they are quick to sympathize with others rather than just look at the facts or analyze impersonal data.

Thinkers display a number of strengths. It's no surprise that they think logically and are good at analyzing and solving problems. They are firm and tough-minded and will reprimand people when necessary. Feelers are slow to reprimand people, are more sympathetic, and are sensitive to people's feelings. To them people are more important than any job.

Both thinkers and feelers have their weaknesses. On the one hand, thinkers act tough and can come across as insensitive and terse. They may struggle with personal relationships and may overanalyze situations. Feeling types, on the other hand, have a tendency to want to please people and dislike delivering bad news. Often they are too chatty and illogical and put values ahead of thoughts.

Which best describes you—the thinker or feeler?

Summary: Thinking and Feeling

- *Question*

  Do you make decisions by analyzing the facts or by following your feelings, even your intuition?

- *Focus*

  Thinkers: Make decisions after thinking through the facts, rely heavily on logic, focus on the head not the heart, decisions objectively based on an analysis of the situation.

  Feelers: Make decisions based more on feelings (values), weigh values and needs, focus on the heart not the head, make decisions subjectively based on person-centered values.

- *Orientation*

  Thinkers: Objective, are facts-oriented, seek an objective standard of truth to live by, are justice-based.

Feelers: Subjective, people-oriented, seek harmony between people, grace-based.

- *Ministry Environment*

  Thinkers: Deal with the facts and impersonal data, prefer analyzing information to working with people.

  Feelers: Deal with people and personal values, quick to sympathize with people.

- *Strengths*

  Thinkers: Logical, analytical, can reprimand people when necessary, firm, tough-minded, good at convincing people of their position on an issue.

  Feelers: Work for harmony, sensitive to people's feelings, believe that people are more important than a job.

- *Weaknesses*

  Thinkers: Insensitive, struggle with relationships, overanalyze situations, act tough.

  Feelers: People pleasers, chatty, put values ahead of thoughts, may not share bad news when necessary.

Judgment versus Perception

Determining if one fits the judgment type or the perception type means answering these questions: How do you relate to the outer world of people and things? What lifestyle do you adopt to deal with the world around you? The judgment types prefer living in a planned, organized world that involves their being in control of that world and thus able to regulate it and what happens to them. They are purposeful and desire to shape their world even if they don't understand it. Everything has a purpose and place, and they want things to be in their proper place. They tend to be quick decision makers who like to reach closure soon, because they don't need or take lots of time to think through situations.

Perceptive types prefer to live in a flexible, spontaneous world and this means they may not be in control of their world and even their own lives. However, they don't have a problem with this. Unlike judgment types, perceptives are adaptable and slow to make decisions because they like to keep their options open and gather as much information as possible, believing this will help them make the best decisions.

In terms of their preferred ministry environments, judgment types can't understand why perceptives aren't ready to make decisions and move on with ministry. Their mantra is, Take what information you have and act on it. They argue, "What we really need around here is not more information but more deadlines or we may not accomplish much of anything." Perceptives object and want to keep their options open so they have time to make more discoveries about their world.

The judgment types make good managers because they are skillful at planning and then following those plans. To them it's important to dot every *i* and cross every *t*. Because they are purposeful, they are deliberate people who manage their time well.

The perceptive types understand that they live in a world of constant, chaotic change and are able to adjust better than the judgment types to that world. They are more spontaneous people, reacting to situations and the moment. Whereas judgment types "live on the plan," perceptives "live on the fly."

Because of their desire for closure, judgment types can make decisions too quickly. They don't do well when they're not in control of their world. Occasionally judgment types need to take some time off to relax and play a little.

Perceptive types will struggle with and prefer to postpone unpleasant jobs or decisions. While good at starting a number of projects, they aren't so good at completing them. Finally, unlike the judgment people, they are poor planners and don't follow plans well. Which best describes you—the judgment type or the perception type?

Summary: Judgment and Perception

- *Question*

  How do you relate to the world of people and things?

- *Focus*

  Judgment types: Live in a planned, organized world; seek to regulate and control the world; make decisions quickly; reach closure.

  Perceptive types: Live in a flexible, spontaneous world; seek to understand and respond to that world; make decisions slowly; like to keep options open; are information gatherers.

- Orientation

  Judgment types: Planners, purposeful, able to explain why they do what they do.

  Perceptive types: Not planners, adapt to the world around them, may not be able to explain why they do what they do.

- *Ministry Environment*

  Judgment types: Seek closure, complete tasks, quick decision makers, meet deadlines, left-brain people.

Perceptive types: Slow decision makers, explore tasks, keep options open, need time to make discoveries, right-brain people.

- *Strengths*

Judgment types: Good at planning and following plans, deliberate, manage time well.

Perceptive types: Spontaneous, adapt well to changes, able to relax and play.

- *Weaknesses*

Judgment types: Make decisions too quickly, don't handle interruptions well, need to feel in control, little down time, tend to ignore events that aren't scheduled.

Perceptive types: Postpone unpleasant tasks, not good at planning and follow-through, start too many projects that never get finished, put off making decisions, don't manage time well.

The Keirsey Temperament Sorter (KTS)

The Keirsey Temperament Sorter is a self-assessed personality questionnaire designed to help people better understand themselves and others. It was first introduced in the book *Please Understand Me* by David Keirsey and Marilyn Bates. The KTS and KTS II are closely associated with the Myers-Briggs Type Indicator (MBTI). This is because Keirsey drew on the views of several predecessors, Isabel Myers being one of them. While there are practical and theoretical differences between the two and their associated different descriptions, Keirsey divided his four temperaments into sixteen types that correlate with the sixteen personality types of Myers and Briggs.[1] We focused on eight that proved to be most helpful to our research.

As a tool, we prefer to use the KTS II over the MBTI because it is self-assessed, easier to obtain, and ultimately gives you the same results as the MBTI. We used the KTS II to help discern how leaders pattern on the MBTI and what that means for ministry in general and church re-envisioning in particular as we shall see in the next chapter.

Is Temperament Biblical?

So far in this chapter we have asked and answered three questions: What is temperament? Why is temperament important? And what are some temperament tools? At this point the Christian reader should be asking one final question:

Does temperament or type square with the Bible? In other words, What is the biblical-theological justification for temperament as we have described it in this chapter? Should Christians be hesitant to assess or be assessed by tools such as the Personal Profile and the Myers-Briggs Temperament Indicator that have been influenced by so-called modern psychological principles? These tools have been developed by those who don't necessarily profess to be persons of faith. Therefore, could such tools be based on unbiblical presuppositions? In short, are such tools biblical, that is, do they square with God's revelation of truth? Our answer to this last question is yes, based on God's general and special revelation, the fact that all truth is God's truth, and the wisdom literature in the Old Testament.

General and Special Revelation

Evangelical theologians recognize two domains of revelation. One is special revelation, which refers to God's knowledge as found in Christ (John 1:18) and the Scriptures (1 John 5:9–12). The other is general revelation, which refers to God's knowledge as found in his creation: nature, science, and history (see chart on p. 84). Special revelation is the domain of the theologian; general revelation is the domain of both the scientist and the theologian. Christians have no problems with knowledge based on the former. Most accept the Bible as God's trustworthy, authoritative Word. The problem lies in knowledge based on general revelation. Our understanding of general revelation may or may not be compatible with Scripture. Based on our repeated use of these tools over the years, our stance is that temperament tools fall legitimately under the category of general revelation.

All Truth Is God's Truth

While all the content of the Bible is true (2 Tim. 3:16), not all truth is found in the Bible. For example, scientists have discovered the truth that if people brush and floss their teeth on a regular basis, they will have fewer cavities. They have also found that cigarette smoking is harmful to your health. Both truths are not found in the Bible, yet few would challenge their validity. We could cite numerous other examples. The point is that all truth is ultimately God's truth. The problem lies in discerning truth from error in the domain of general revelation. When Scripture addresses a topic, we have God's truth on the matter. But how do we discern God's truth in matters that Scripture does not address, such as the brushing and flossing of our teeth, smoking cigarettes,

Figure 5.1

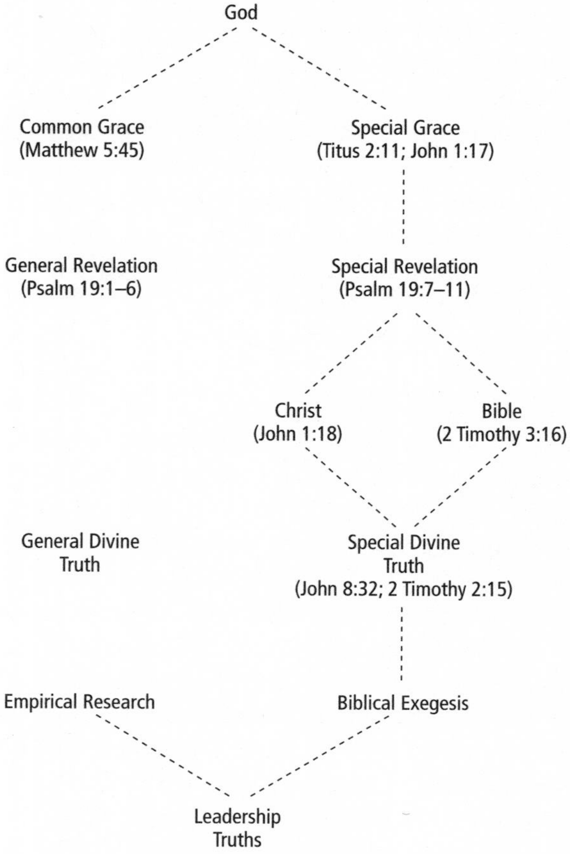

Divine Revelation

or matters of temperament? When dealing with knowledge based on general revelation, the Christian must proceed cautiously.

The key to the truthfulness of any temperament or psychological profile is its degree of accuracy in correctly measuring what it purports to measure, in this case behavioral styles. Those that prove accurate over time are most likely based ultimately on God's truth regardless of their source, but those that do not prove accurate are not based on divine truth. Consequently, the validation of a temperament tool is important to the Christian who is seeking God's truth in the domain of natural revelation. As Christians, we must not forget that many people who may not profess faith in Christ are just as concerned with accuracy and arriving at truth as we are.

The Personal Profile and the Myers-Briggs Type Indicator have demonstrated high reliability, as based on professional studies of their validity. The Personal Profile has been through a rigid validation process, and the results are available in *The Kaplan Report*.[2] Katharine Briggs and Isabel Myers as well as others have submitted the MBTI to rigorous standards of validity.[3] That is why it is used so widely today in the general population as well as the psychiatric profession. Those of us who have worked with these tools over the years have found from personal experience that they accurately detect behavioral styles.

Wisdom Tradition

The Old Testament contains several books classified as Hebrew wisdom literature. The books are Proverbs, Job, Ecclesiastes, and certain psalms that deal specifically with the topic of wisdom.[4] The Hebrew concept of wisdom was essentially practical. The Old Testament writers did not distinguish between the intellectual and the practical or the religious and the secular. For them the whole of life was to be viewed from the religious experience, and wisdom was relevant to every area of man's existence.[5]

According to scholars, biblical wisdom literature reflects more influence from the ancient Near East than the other literature in the Bible. Old Testament scholar Roland Harrison writes, "It would seem clear, therefore, that not merely was Hebrew wisdom far from being an isolated literary or didactic phenomenon, but that in fact it was part of a large cultural heritage common to the whole of the ancient world."[6] However, Harrison is careful to point out that the Hebrew writers did not depend entirely on other ancient Near Eastern wisdom sources for their contribution.[7] In his commentary on Proverbs, Derek Kidner adds that parallels with the book of Proverbs show that Israel's wise men sifted through and assimilated some of the wisdom tradition of the Near East.[8] Former Dallas Seminary student and faculty member David Ward explains this process and how it interacts with inspiration:

> Under divine inspiration, Solomon and others sometimes took wise lessons from life captured in proverbs composed by pagan wise men, and reoriented their advice under the proper frame of reference. Namely, the fear of the Lord. Wisdom living had more to do with successful living in this world than it did with any redemptive vision of a future heaven. Therefore when wise insight was seen to help live for the true God more effectively, it was adopted as God's truth anyway. So it was not as much a case of being unoriginal and borrowing as it was a case of recovering truth for the believer's use that was God's truth in the first place.[9]

The point is that God's inerrant, authoritative Word under divine inspiration drew on lessons of truth and wisdom from the surrounding cultures. Again the reason is that all truth is God's truth regardless of where it is found. Therefore the careful use of insights from validated, reliable temperament tools closely parallels the wisdom process of Israel's sages.

What Is Your Temperament?

Our last question is, What is your temperament? At this time you need to take the DISC and the MBTI or KTS II. Since these tools are copyrighted, we can't provide them for you in this book. We ask that you obtain copies and take them on your own. Most likely you can locate and request them online. However, we don't want the time needed to obtain one of these tools to impede your progress, so we have provided two similar tools that should help you discover your temperament. Temperament Indicator 1, though not the same, is most like the DISC; Type Indicator 2 is most like the MBTI. You will find the first in appendix A and the second in appendix B. We also want you to know that the two indicators have not been formally validated, so we strongly encourage you to follow up by taking the DISC and MBTI or KTS II as soon as you are able.

Mini-Bio: Fitting Ministry Temperament to Ministry Need

Recently I (Gordon) taught in a doctor of ministry cohort at Biola University in the Talbot School of Theology. We worked through a section of the class that dealt with the DISC Profile. I had just completed a section on the DISC when we took a break. The last slide that I showed remained on the screen. It showed the fruit of church planters who exhibited each of the DISC characteristics. The slide is printed below.[10]

The chart shows plainly that the I profile leads the pack in church planting. However, during the break, Dave Page, church-planting director of the Evangelical Free Church West, came up and pointed at the screen. He made a remarkable, clarifying statement. He pointed at the planter who had thirty-eight people in his first year. "I'll bet those thirty-eight people are thankful for that church planter." Even people who don't fit the standard profile of a church planter (high D or high I) can be successful, and the people touched by their ministry would be grateful.

Figure 5.2

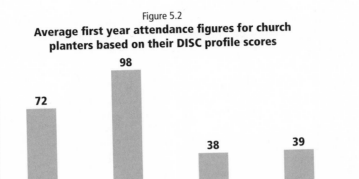

Average first year attendance figures for church planters based on their DISC profile scores

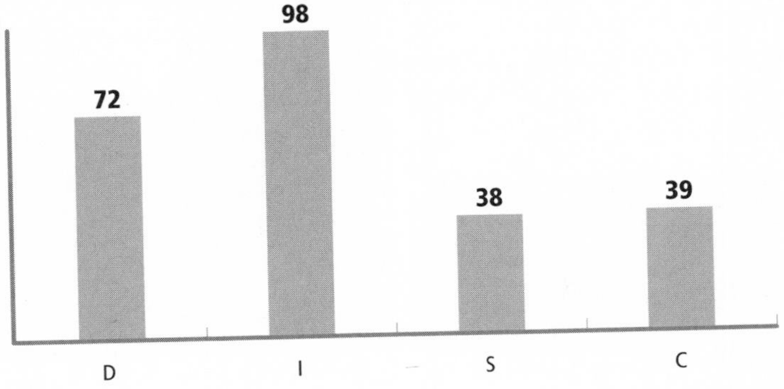

George Klippenes, director of church planting for the Evangelical Free Church, added, "When you have a large core group to organize a large daughter church, we have had success with C planters. Also in rural and urban areas where resources are small, growth is slow, and you need a plodder—C planters work."

These two statements brought great clarity for me. The point is this. The body of Christ consists of many members. The Lord does not want to use just the Ds and Is. His design is to use every member of the body for his glory. Part of our responsibility is to discover where we fit best, work there, and enjoy the ride.

Questions for Reflection, Discussion, and Application

1. Prior to reading this chapter, do you believe that you had a good knowledge of people? Why or why not? Do you understand them and why they behave a certain way? Do you find that a knowledge of temperament helps you understand better the people you come into contact with? Why or why not?
2. Prior to this chapter, do you believe you had a good understanding of yourself and why you behave the way you do? Why or why not? Does the information on temperament help you understand yourself and your behavior better? Why or why not?
3. Which temperament tool do you find most helpful in understanding yourself and others, the Personal Profile (DISC) or the Myers-Briggs Temperament Indicator (MBTI)? Why?

4. Have you taken either of these tools before? If so, do you sense that you've changed or are you basically the same person? If you sense that you've changed, is it just a little or a lot? How would you explain any change?
5. Do you have a problem theologically with using temperament tools? Why or why not? Did the material that addressed whether temperament is biblical help? If yes, how? If not, why not?

PART 2

Process of Discovery

Now that we have completed our preparation, we need a process and practice for re-envisioning Christ's church. Chapters 6–8 provide the process while chapters 9–14 provide the practice. The process portion presents our exploration of the characteristics of re-envisioning pastors and concludes with a section that addresses four critical questions that summarize our discoveries. The practice portion presents what re-envisioning pastors must do to lead their churches in a turnaround.

6

Our Initial Exploration

This chapter details the discoveries we made about re-envisioning and non–re-envisioning pastors. We made two discovery expeditions. This chapter provides the first discovery expedition that we are calling Discovery 1. It was born out of my (Gordon's) initial research that explored the reasons some pastors go into a plateaued or declining church and lead it in a successful turnaround and others pursue the same success but see only further numerical decline. In this chapter I will present the initial exploration, followed by the results or what I discovered on the journey.

Discovery 1

DISCOVERY 1
The Exploration Question and Assumptions
Exploration Tools

The problem facing the future of the church is the need for church revitalization as well as church planting. We need healthy established churches to plant healthy churches. The most important finding of this exploration is that it seems to take a turnaround pastor to lead a turnaround church. We use the term *turnaround pastor* (TAP) in Discovery 1 and will switch to the term *re-envisioning pastor* (REP) in Discovery 2 (presented in the next chapter) because of our shifting emphasis to vision.

For the sake of clarity, it's critical that we pause and define the term *turnaround pastor*. My working or operational definition is that a turnaround pastor is a leader whose current ministry (or last ministry) has demonstrated an average annual growth rate (AAGR) in worship attendance of at least 2.5 percent per year for five years. We base this on a statement from Gary McIntosh, a professor at Talbot Seminary, who says that if a church keeps all of its biological growth, it will grow an average of 2.5 percent per year over a five-year period.[1]

The Exploration Question and Assumptions

The exploration question I (Gordon) was asking and attempting to answer in my initial research was: Are there identifiable characteristics of TAPs among evangelical churches that will help to discern between who is and isn't a TAP?

An exploration question assumes an audience. I chose to explore the topic with churches and judicatories in the Rocky Mountain States. In 2009 to 2011, I sampled evangelical pastors from Colorado, Utah, Wyoming, Montana, and Idaho. I also sought help from certain judicatories and denominations, such as Conservative Baptists, Baptist General Conference (Converge), the Evangelical Free Church, the Evangelical Church, Southern Baptists, Presbyterian Church in America, the Wesleyan Church, the Christian and Missionary Alliance, the Assemblies of God, and the Nazarene Church.

My primary assumption or "educated guess" going into this exploration was that turnaround pastors exhibit significant differences in their leadership style, spiritual gifting, interpersonal relationship skills, and "visioneering" skills when compared to non-turnaround pastors (NTAPs). I assumed that a variety of characteristics is found in TAPs that isn't found or that would exist to a lesser degree in NTAPs. As happens with most so-called educated guesses, some of this was true and some didn't pan out.

In addition to my primary assumption, there were nine additional assumptions that surfaced in process.

- Church growth is good. The Savior promised to build his church (see Matt. 16:18). Therefore, I assumed in Discovery 1 that church growth is good.
- Not every church is able to grow. Often there are mitigating circumstances that make church growth impossible.
- The majority of churches can grow given the right leadership.
- Worship attendance is the best indicator of growth, plateau, or decline. There are certainly other strong indicators of church health and growth,

but, for this study, I chose worship attendance as the most accurate measure of church growth.[2]

- The responses of the pastors and lay leaders were representative of pastors and lay leaders found in the Rocky Mountain States.
- Pastors and lay leaders answered their surveys truthfully. Some of the information from the pastors and others may be exaggerated and in some cases incorrect. This may surprise some but shouldn't. Pastors, like the rest of us, are subject to various temptations, one of which is to over-report their attendance, which for many is a mark of their success.
- There would be exceptions to some of the findings, which would simply be just that—exceptions to the norm.
- There is no perfect turnaround pastor. No one has all the qualities listed in the research.
- Other factors can affect our exploration, such as the church's geographic location, weather, demographics, physical health, and so on.

In addition to the nine assumptions listed above, I recognize the sovereignty of God. God is sovereign (Ps. 24:1–2; 135:6; Dan. 4:32, 35; Acts 4:24, 28; Eph. 1:11). Thus he chooses to bless some churches with growth and others who meet all the turnaround criteria with little to no growth. We must let God be God. If we had all the answers, we might think we don't need him. He does what he does for reasons that he may never reveal. In a real sense, we are simply observing him as he exercises his sovereignty.

Exploration Tools

Some would call exploration tools "methodology." If so, then there's a method to my madness. The exploration tools that I chose to work with consisted of a Pastoral Survey and a Lay Leaders Survey. I used the Performax DiSC profiles in this study.

The Pastoral Survey

The purpose of the pastoral survey was to try to determine if there are any significant differences between turnaround and non-turnaround pastors. The following eight areas were included in the survey.

1. Results of the pastors' Personal Profile or Performax DiSC profiles.
2. Their spiritual gifts mix, using the Modified Heights Spiritual Gift Survey.

3. Their history of pastoral leadership. (I was trying to determine if TAPs have a consistent history of turnaround ministry and NTAPs have a consistent history of non-turnaround ministry.)
4. Their clarity in communicating the purpose/mission of the church.
5. Their clarity in communicating the church's vision.
6. Their interpersonal relationship skills with multiple generations.
7. Two questions about having coaches or mentors now or in the past.
8. Their pastoral leadership style.

The Lay Leader's Tools

The lay leader's tools included questions 4–6 and 8 of the Pastoral Survey above. This survey was to be completed by three lay leaders in each church. It compared the pastor's perception of his ministry with that of his lay leadership with the purpose of validating or invalidating the pastor's responses. It is interesting to note that in virtually every case pastors viewed themselves less favorably than did their lay leaders.

The Results

The important question after the initial exploration was, What information did Discovery 1 yield?

First, I contacted a number of mid-level judicatory leaders to secure names of turnaround and non-turnaround pastors in their judicatories. This led to forty-nine pastoral contacts. Twenty-eight pastors completed and returned the surveys, so the results given below were based on these twenty-eight contacts.

Concerning the eight questions on the pastoral survey, there were four areas where no measurable differences were found between turnaround and non-turnaround pastors. First was their spiritual gifts mix (Modified Heights Spiritual Gift Survey). I expected significant differences in gifting but was surprised at the conformity of the TAPs and NTAPs in their gift mix.[3]

The second area where there was no measurable difference was their history of pastoral leadership, which included their tenure or length of ministry at a church and the age or number of churches served. Length of tenure was not a determining factor in turnaround or non-turnaround. TAPs had tenures ranging from two to twenty-five years. NTAPs had tenures ranging from three to twenty-six years. Long tenure did not guarantee growth and short tenure did not necessarily result in lack of growth. It should be noted that this section was used to determine whether a pastor was a turnaround or non-turnaround pastor.

The third area was their clarity in communicating the purpose/mission of the church to the church, and the fourth was their interpersonal relationship skills with multiple generations.

There were four areas where I found significant measurable differences between the two groups. Their Performax Leadership (DiSC) profiles were distinct. The TAPs tended to score mid to high D and i. The NTAPs scored high in the S and C temperaments. Also their clarity in communicating the church's vision was distinct. The TAPs communicated the church's vision with much greater clarity and passion than their NTAP counterparts. The third difference was that the TAPs had coaches or mentors more often than the NTAPs—62 percent of TAPs have had and continue to have coaches and mentors today, while 57 percent of NTAPs had coaches at the beginning of ministry but only 14 percent still do today. Finally, their leadership styles were distinct. See appendix C for a list of these distinctions.

Results of the Eight Questions on the Pastoral Survey in Discovery 1

Significant Measurable Differences	No Significant Measurable Differences
Performax Leadership (DiSC) Profiles	Spiritual gifts mix
Communicating the church's vision with clarity and passion	Effect of tenure on turnaround or non-turnaround pastors
Use of coaches and mentors	Clarity in communicating purpose/mission
Leadership style distinctions	Interpersonal relationship skills with multiple generations

Exploration Summary

Following are the summary findings for Discovery 1 regarding the characteristics or attributes of turnaround pastors:

- Score of mid to high D or i or D/i combination on the DiSC personal profile.
- Passionate and visionary.
- Have a mentor/coach more often than not.
- More outgoing with good people skills.
- More innovational than traditional.
- More energetic (this is essential).
- "Young in ministry," regardless of their biological age.

- Better team players.
- Better at delegating.
- Better at training new leaders.
- Focused and determined.
- Able to embrace necessary change and willing to pay the price to do so.
- Good conflict resolution skills.
- Better than average communicators (vision and direction as well as preaching).
- Passionate use of their primary spiritual gifts and ability to empower others to use theirs.

Other Observations

In addition to the above information, there were several other significant findings.

- The length of pastoral tenure and its impact on numerical growth differed for TAPs and NTAPs. Long tenure of a TAP produces steady and continuous growth. However, long tenure of an NTAP at best produces a plateau and in most cases steady decline.
- Though researcher George Barna says the age limit for a TAP is the midforties or younger,[4] I found that seven of twenty-one TAPs began their last turnaround at age forty-eight or older.[5]
- Barna says these pastors normally experience only one turnaround in an entire lifetime.[6] I found that seven pastors have led two or more churches in a turnaround, while two pastors have led four churches through a turnaround.
- TAPs are in short supply. This is what others are saying about the number of TAPs. Gary McIntosh says that TAPs make up about 5 to 7 percent of all church leaders.[7] Church consultant Paul Borden estimates that 10–15 percent of pastors are TAPs.[8] Wayne Wager, district superintendent of the Central New York District of the Wesleyan Church, identified 9.8 percent of his pastors as TAPs (5 of 51 pastors).[9] David Bowman, the executive director of the Tarrant Baptist Association, says that in his association around 12.4 percent of pastors are TAPs (that's 42 of 338 pastors).[10] I interviewed three judicatory leaders who believed that the number of TAPs in their judicatories was 23.7 percent of the pastors (64 of 270).[11] I suspect this figure is inflated. In the association where I serve and have done considerable research, only 11.9 percent of the pastors qualify as TAPs. Bob Dean, the executive director of the Dallas Baptist

Association, placed the number of TAPs in Dallas County churches at 6.1 percent or 30 of 492.[12] Daryl Thompson, district superintendent of the Northern Plains District of the Evangelical Free Church of America, observed that 14 percent of the pastors in his district would be seen as TAPs (5 of 35).[13] See table below for a summary.

The Number of TAPs among Various Denominational Groups

Sources of Statistics	Re-envisioning Pastors/Total Churches	Percentage of Pastors
Gary McIntosh		5–7%
Paul Borden		10–15%
Wayne Wager	5 of 51	9.8%
David Bowman	42 of 338	12.4%
Rocky Mountain CBA	8 of 67	11.9%
Three districts	64 of 270	23.7%
Bob Dean	30 of 492	6.1%
Daryl Thompson	5 of 35	14%

As you can see, the percentage of TAPs ranges from 6 to 24 percent in the judicatories studied. The small number of turnaround pastors is a challenge. This small percentage of pastors cannot turn around the large percentage of churches in need of transformation.

The fact that 80–85 percent of churches are plateaued or in decline would seem to indicate that a great number of these churches are led by NTAPs. The table above indicates that 5–24 percent of pastors in your denomination or association are TAPs. That means 76–95 percent are NTAPs. This raises a critical question. When we send an NTAP into a plateaued or declining church, are we setting them up for failure?

Mini-Bio: A Re-Envisioning Leader

Re-envisioning pastors come in a great variety of shapes and temperaments and they serve in varied settings all across America. This story ought to encourage us toward re-envisioning leadership regardless of our location.

The voice on the other end of the line certainly sounded like a turnaround pastor. After interviewing dozens of pastors since 2008, we recognized the unmistakable tones, attitudes, excitement, and energy.

Marty Rostad's background was not unlike Amos's in the Old Testament. Marty was raised in rural Montana and had spent a great deal of his life working on farms that raised hogs, cattle, and buffalo. It turned out that he had worked for a number of years for a prominent family in the church that I (Gordon) currently pastor in Colorado! Rural America can be a very small place.

At age 45 Marty began pastoral ministry. He moved from hog farms to a buffalo ranch to the pulpit. And what a move it was! He landed in Clearmont, Wyoming, population 114, and Clearmont Community Church, a flatlined church with a membership of 15. A pretty inauspicious beginning, or so it seemed—not much of a congregation in a wide spot in the road in the ranchlands and sagebrush of northeastern Wyoming. But the Lord had *big* plans for this community and this church. Turnaround began immediately. In 8 years the church grew from an average attendance of 15 to 75. On resurrection Sunday 110 people crammed into the church building. That's a whopping 97 percent of the community's population! Later the church sponsored a "Someday" Sunday. Folks had said to Marty, "We'll come to church someday." Marty advertised that "Someday is next Sunday." "Someday" arrived, and 135 people gathered from the community and the surrounding ranches.

Much of their growth in Clearmont was conversion growth with 51 people responding to the gospel and being baptized. That is turnaround.

After concluding the ministry in Clearmont, Marty became a church planter in Torrington, Wyoming. The other churches in the community did not want this church to begin. "After all," they said, "there are enough churches in Torrington, Wyoming."

Marty and his wife, Nancy, anticipated that both of them would need to work, but the Lord miraculously supplied their needs and both plunged full-time into the ministry. The church has grown from ten souls to seventy-five in two and a half years. They continue to reach people that other churches disdain.

Although the church was in Torrington, folks began to visit from neighboring Fort Laramie. Two and a half years after Lifeway Community Church was planted in Torrington, the church launched Lifeway Community in Fort Laramie. Fort Laramie is a community of 230 people where spiritual darkness reigned unmitigated. No longer. After only three weeks, the church is averaging 25.

Marty and Nancy prove that it does not matter where you live, how large or small the mission field, God wants to use you to accomplish his mission, the Great Commission. Some would look at Clearmont, Wyoming, and say, "There's not much need for a church or work to be done here." Others, like Marty, look at the field and say, "Look at how many people in this community need the Savior!" He had a vision to reach a community and the Lord blessed his ministry. Not only that, but the turnaround continues in Clearmont under the leadership of its current pastor. And the beat continues in Torrington and Fort Laramie.

Questions for Reflection, Discussion, and Application

1. How large is your mission field? What does God want to do through you in your mission field? Do you see lost people as problems or as potential? Your perception will, to a large extent, determine your effectiveness!
2. Do you understand how God has gifted you spiritually? The better you understand yourself, the better you can serve the Savior. The tool we prefer is the Modified Heights Spiritual Gift Inventory. The reason is that three people who know you well also complete the survey. That provides a way for you to see if your perception of your giftedness aligns with the perception of those who know you well.
3. If you are a turnaround pastor, what are you doing to invest in others? Perhaps the Lord would direct you to be a mentor or a coach for a young pastor or ministerial colleague who is desperately seeking direction.
4. If you are a non-turnaround pastor now, are you coachable? Would you be willing to seek out a mentor or coach who can help you in areas of need in your ministry? Are you willing to do so for the sake of the testimony of our Lord and his gospel?
5. Are you a non-turnaround pastor? Look at the Exploration Summary on page 95. Where are areas of weakness in your life and ministry? Make a list of changes you would like to see. Make these the focus of prayer and study. Pick one or two areas you need to address and work on them for a year. Reevaluate your progress at the end of a year.
6. Score yourself on the traits found in appendix C. Cover the answers supplied from the research and honestly evaluate yourself on the characteristics listed in the chart. Ask three or four leaders in your church to evaluate you. Compare your responses with theirs. Ask them what areas they feel you need to address in your ministry.
7. Remember that there are no perfect pastors. Take courage knowing that the Lord can use you. Continue, as long as you have breath, to "grow in the grace and knowledge of our Lord and Savior Jesus Christ" (2 Peter 3:18).

7

Our Follow-up Exploration

In the last chapter, we donned the hat of the explorer and initially presented what Gordon discovered about re-envisioning and non–re-envisioning pastors. We made two discoveries. This chapter presents Discovery 2 that was the result of and a continuation of Discovery 1.

Gordon presented his findings in a paper at a gathering of pastors, professors, and some church growth researchers in California. I (Aubrey) happened to sit in on his presentation and was quick to realize what this could mean for the body of Christ in general and struggling churches and their pastors in particular.

Having done some thinking and writing along these lines, particularly related to church planting, I challenged Gordon to join me in further work, exploring revitalizing pastors and their churches. This chapter is the result of our work together and primarily follows the same outline and topics as Discovery 1. Thus we begin by presenting our follow-up exploration, followed by what we discovered.

We want to make you aware that in this chapter we present a large number of statistics. We are well aware that this can be mind-numbing for some people but most important to others. We suggest that those of you who struggle with statistics skim over them, stopping at any that flag your attention. Regardless, you will likely benefit the most by reading the results and not so much the statistics. You will see what the statistics tell us, what their message is for us

as we explore re-envisioning and non–re-envisioning pastors. The numbers can tell us much about them.

Discovery 2

DISCOVERY 2
The Churches' Need
The Exploration Question
THE SAMPLING OF CHURCHES
Assumptions
Exploration Tool

For Discovery 2 we combined our exploration skills and knowledge. We built Discovery 2 on Gordon's foundational work in Discovery 1, making the following seven adjustments.

- We wanted a larger sample or population than the twenty-eight pastors; we aimed for at least one hundred participants.
- We narrowed the number of years that a pastor needed to have served a church to be in a turnaround situation. As you may recall from chapter 6, Gordon used Gary McIntosh's definition of a turnaround pastor, which stated that a pastor needed to be in a church that experienced 2.5 percent growth per year in worship attendance for five years. However, we felt that with the average pastoral tenure in America at 3.5 (see this discussion in the Introduction) a two to three year time span was more realistic than five years. Also we noted that for some pastors a turnaround was already in evidence between two and three years.
- We broadened the geographic representation from the Rocky Mountain States to all of America and beyond. We involved pastors who served churches in all fifty states, Washington, DC, and ten Canadian provinces.
- We used the Myers-Briggs Type Indicator (MBTI) as well as the Personal Profile (DISC).
- We adopted the terms *re-envisioning pastor* (REP) and *non–re-envisioning pastor* (NREP) rather than turnaround pastor (TAP) and non-turnaround pastor (NTAP). This was due primarily to our recognition of the huge role that vision plays in leading churches and their people through a turnaround. We did use the other terms as synonyms.
- We adjusted the questions in Gordon's Pastoral Survey, What Are Defining Characteristics of Turnaround Pastors? and developed a second survey, the Pastoral Leadership Survey. This included refining a number of the questions on Gordon's Leadership Style Survey (appendix C) and replacing it with the Pastoral Leadership Audit (appendix G).
- We implemented a twofold approach. First, we distributed a detailed questionnaire—our Pastoral Survey—to the pastors who agreed to be a part of this study (a quantitative approach). Next, as much as possible,

we met one-on-one with pastors in the field or over the phone and posed questions directly to them (a qualitative approach).

We didn't base our quantitative and qualitative work on reams of statistics, comparison analysis, and finely crunched data. Some would argue that it's not as reliable this way. However, Patrick Lencioni, who wrestled with this same issue, quotes top researcher Jim Collins of *Good to Great* fame concerning this issue: "Qualitative field research is just as reliable as the quantitative kind, as long as clients and readers attest to its validity."[1]

The Churches' Need

The problem in Discovery 2 is much the same as for Discovery 1. There is a need in America for church revitalization along with church planting. Church planting alone will not stem the tide of church decline. To add to this problem, often a pastor will take a church that is plateaued or declining only to see it remain on a plateau or go into further decline. The results are that some of these pastors become discouraged, feel like failures, and may even leave the ministry.

As in Discovery 1, we needed a working or operational definition for a re-envisioning pastor. We used the same definition, changing the five-year requirement to two and one half to three years, which we believe is more realistic. So our definition for Discovery 2 is the following: A re-envisioning pastor is a leader who has transitioned a church from a plateau or numerical decline in worship attendance to a positive average annual growth rate (AAGR) of 2.5 percent for a minimum of 2.5 years regardless of the church's size. In the exploration process, we discovered that turnaround may begin at the outset of a new ministry and the direction a church will take is quite apparent after two or three years.

The Exploration Question

The primary exploration question was essentially the same as Discovery 1: Are there identifiable contributing factors or characteristics of re-envisioning pastors (REPs) that set them apart from non–re-envisioning pastors (NREPs)?

The Sampling of Churches

As in Discovery 1 we focused on a number of churches, some of which belonged to a denomination and others that didn't. I (Aubrey) live in the

Dallas–Fort Worth Metroplex, which is the proverbial "buckle on the Bible Belt." While our study was not limited to this area, the location provided me with a number of denominational and nondenominational sample churches and pastors within driving range. And this added much to our qualitative approach and validation of our findings. Gordon, likewise, has met a growing number of pastors through his boot camps, pastor gatherings, and teaching in doctor of ministry programs that has afforded him both face-to-face and phone interviews.

We worked with the following churches: Southern Baptist, Church of the Nazarene, Missionary Baptist, Fellowship Bible Church, Lutheran Church (ELCA), Pentecostal, Conservative Baptist, Baptist General Conference (Converge), Assemblies of God, Evangelical Free Church, Christian and Missionary Alliance, Independent Bible Church, United Methodist Church, American Baptist Church USA, Presbyterian Church in America, Presbyterian Church USA, Christian Church (Disciples of Christ), Wesleyan Church, Church of God Anderson Indiana, Evangelical Covenant Church, Christian Methodist Episcopal Church, Congregational Christian Churches of Canada, Mennonite Brethren, Baptist World Alliance, Evangelical Fellowship of Baptist Churches of Canada, and several nondenominational churches.

Assumptions

Our primary assumption or "educated guess" (what some call a hypothesis) going into this exploration was threefold, focusing on where we thought TAPs would score on the DISC, MBTI, and Pastoral Leadership Survey.

We believed that on the 7–point range of the Personal Profile (DISC), re-envisioning pastors would score in the mid to higher range on either the D or I or both temperaments.

- Low range: 1–3
- Mid-range: 4
- High range: 5–7

We assumed that re-envisioning pastors would likely score one of the following on the MBTI or the KTS II: ENTP, ENTJ, or ENFP.

Finally, we guessed that re-envisioning pastors would score in the 25 to 62 range on the Pastoral Leadership Audit, found in the Pastoral Leadership Survey.

Our additional assumptions are essentially the same as for Discovery 1.

- Church growth is good. The Lord Jesus promised to build his church (see Matt. 16:18). Therefore, we assumed that church growth is good.
- Not every church is able to grow. Often there are mitigating circumstances that make church growth impossible.
- The majority of churches can grow given the right leadership.
- Worship attendance is the best indicator of growth, plateau, or decline. There are certainly other strong indicators of church health and growth, but, for this study, we chose worship attendance as the most accurate measure of church growth.[2]
- The responses of the pastors were representative of pastors and lay leaders found across America and Canada.
- Pastors answered their surveys truthfully. Some of the information from the pastors and others may be exaggerated and in some cases incorrect. This may surprise some but shouldn't. Pastors, like the rest of us, are subject to various temptations, one of which is to over-report their attendance, which for many is a mark of their success.
- There will be exceptions to some of the findings, which would simply be just that—exceptions to the norm.
- There is no perfect turnaround pastor. No one has all the qualities listed in the research.
- Other factors can affect our exploration, such as the church's geographic location, weather, demographics, physical health, and so on.
- And we must include in this the sovereignty of God. God is sovereign (Ps. 24:1–2; 135:6; Dan. 4:32, 35; Acts 4:24, 28; Eph. 1:11). Thus he chooses to bless some churches with growth and others who meet all the turnaround criteria with little to no growth. We must let God be God. If we had all the answers, we might think we don't need him. He does what he does for reasons he may never reveal. In a real sense, we are simply observing him as he exercises his sovereignty.

Exploration Tool

The primary exploration tool that we developed and used was the Pastoral Leadership Survey. It consists of three parts.

Church Ministry Experience

Part 1 of the Pastoral Leadership Survey asks pastors to provide a brief résumé of their church ministry experience. This may also involve their experience in more than one church. We followed this up with an interview of pastors that addresses their ministry information (our qualitative approach).

For example, we asked if the church was plateaued or in decline when they first arrived on the scene. Re-envisioning pastors come into churches that are plateaued or declining and see them turn around. We also asked the same question about the church when they left it. Re-envisioning pastors leave a growing church. We did not use growing churches or church plants, because they fell outside our re-envisioning parameters.

Scores on the Personal Profile (DISC) and Myers-Briggs Type Indicator (MBTI)

Part 2 asks pastors to take the DISC Personal Profile or a similar DISC profile (Temperament Indicator 1 in appendix A). Some are familiar with and have taken this tool and some haven't. If they've not taken this tool in the past, we recommend that they find it online and take it as soon as possible. A similar version of the tool was available with expanded information about it (see appendixes A and D). These were provided so that the pastors didn't have to wait until they could locate a copy of the DISC.

Part 2 also asks the pastors to take the MBTI or the Keirsey Temperament Sorter II that will provide them with the necessary MBTI scores. The Keirsey Temperament Sorter is much easier to obtain online and to score. However, if this would cause an unnecessary delay in their response, we encouraged them to take Type Indicator 2 (see appendix B) and to read appendix E, which provides additional help in discovering and validating one's MBTI score.

Score on the Pastoral Leadership Audit

Finally, part 3 of the Pastoral Leadership Survey asks the pastors to take the Pastoral Leadership Audit. It consists of twenty-five questions (using a four-part Likert scale) that deal with the characteristics of re-envisioning pastors.

The Results

DISCOVERY 2 RESULTS
The Number of Participants
Results of the Pastoral Leadership Survey
Results of the Personal Profile (DISC)
Results of the Myers-Briggs Type Indicator (MBTI)
Results of the Pastoral Leadership Audit (PLA)

As we look at the results of Discovery 2, we'll address the number of pastors who took the surveys and the results from their church ministry experience. We'll examine the scores on the Personal Profile (DISC) and the Myers-Briggs (MBTI). Finally, we'll examine the pastors' scores on the Pastoral Leadership Audit.

The Number of Participants

In Discovery 1, Gordon made 49 pastoral contacts that resulted in 28 pastors who actually completed and returned his surveys. In Discovery 2, we contacted well over 200 American and several Canadian pastors. There were 146 pastors who responded to and participated in some way in Discovery 2. Not all of the contacts took all the tools that we asked them to take. For example, some took the DISC but not the MBTI, and some didn't take the Pastoral Leadership Audit but took the other tools and so forth. This isn't uncommon when attempting a project such as this, but the response exceeded overwhelmingly the 28 responses in Discovery 1.

Number of Discovery Participants

Discovery 1: 28 participants in 58 churches in the Rocky Mountain States.

Discovery 2: 146 participants in 285 churches in every state in America and ten provinces in Canada.

129 pastors served American churches only.

10 pastors served Canadian churches only.

4 served in both the United States and Canada.

3 pastors served in other situations.

Results of the Pastoral Leadership Survey

Church Sizes and REP to NREP Ratios

Life is fluid and situations are constantly changing. The results of the discovery process represent a snapshot in time. We gathered the statistics on a day in the life of the pastor and the church. Hence, these figures represent ministry realities on the day they were given.

Distribution of Church Sizes and the REP to NREP Ratios

Average Worship Attendance	Number of Pastors	Percentage of Total	REPs/ NREPs
0–99	60	41.1%	37/23
100–199	28	19.1%	20/8
200–499	31	21.2%	28/3
500–999	13	9.0%	11/2
1000–1999	9	6.2%	8/1
2000+	5	3.4%	4/1
Total	146	100%	108/38

The table shows the average church worship attendance, ranging from 99 and under to 2,000-plus, and the number of pastors in each range. It includes the number of REP and NREP pastors as well.

- The churches in the survey had an average weekly worship attendance ranging from 15 up to 5,500. The number of REPs increased in the larger churches, and the larger churches scored higher on the number of total REPs.
- The largest group of churches was in the 0–99 average attendance range and made up 41 percent of the churches.
- REP and NREP churches were found in each category. However, there was a higher percentage of NREPS in the lower 0–99 range and a greater percentage of REPs in the higher ranges.
- It would appear from this that REPs lead and grow larger churches.

Ministry Experience

Ministry Experience

Category	REP (in years)	NREP (in years)
Pastors with the most ministry experience	40.2	42.5
Pastors with the least ministry experience	0.5	.75
Pastors with the least ministry experience who have served a minimum of 2.5 years	2.5	2.5
Average ministry experience as a solo or senior pastor	14.6	14.7

We examined several areas of the Pastoral Leadership Survey. One was the pastors' total years or amount of ministry experience. Here's what we discovered. The pastor with the most experience served four churches for a period of 42.5 years. He was a non–re-envisioning pastor. The pastor with the next most experience was a REP who served for 40.2 years. The pastor with the least experience had served one church for only 6 months. He appears to be a re-envisioning pastor.[3] Two pastors tied with the least experience, having served their churches for the minimum of 2.5 years. One was a non–re-envisioning pastor and the other was a re-envisioning pastor. Thus our range of ministry experience was from 6 months to 42.5 years.

Summary of Ministry Experience

6 months to 42.5 years

One pastor (an NREP) with most experience: 42.5 years

One pastor (a REP) with least experience: 6 months

Re-envisioning pastors as a whole averaged 15 years of ministry experience and non–re-envisioning pastors averaged 15 years. The average tenure per church, including pastors who served less than 2.5 years, is 7.4 years. This was encouraging to us, because of the typical pastoral tenure being 3.5 years as discussed in the introduction to this book. We found that there was no distinction between NREPs and REPs regarding the length of ministry experience. However, long tenure with a re-envisioning pastor produces steady continuous growth, while long tenure with a non–re-envisioning pastor results in decline.

Average Tenure of Ministry Experience

15 years

REPS averaged 15 years of ministry experience

NREPs averaged 15 years of ministry experience

(Typical pastor's tenure is 3.5 years)

Chronological Age

The Chronological Ages of the Pastors

Category	REP (in years)	NREP (in years)
Oldest pastors still serving their churches or at retirement	70	76
Youngest pastor serving at present	27	27
Youngest age at the beginning of ministry	19	26
Average age of participating pastors	48.2	52.4

The oldest pastor was 76 and the youngest was 27. The oldest REP was 70 and the youngest REP was 19. The oldest NREP was 76 and the youngest was 26. The average age of REPs was 48.2 and the average age of NREPs was slightly older at 52.4. Thus the chronological ages weren't statistically significant.

The table below provides us with the age distribution of the pastors and how that distribution relates to REP and NREP pastors.

Distribution of Church Sizes and the REP to NREP Ratios

Pastor's Current Age	Number of Pastors	Percentage of Total	REPs/NREPs
20–29	5	3.5%	4/1
30–39	18	12.4%	15/3
40–49	45	31.0%	36/9
50–59	55	37.9%	38/17

Pastor's Current Age	Number of Pastors	Percentage of Total	REPs/NREPs
60–69	19	13.1%	12/7
70+	3	2.1%	2/1
Total	145	100%	107/38

Note that the majority of pastors (69 percent) were 40 to 59 years old. And 22 (15 percent) ranged from 60 to 70+. Only 5 pastors (3.5 percent) were in their twenties and 23 pastors (16 percent) were between 20 and 39. On the one hand, this should be a cause for rejoicing in that older pastors in general are able to pastor into their 50s and beyond. On the other hand, this should be a cause for concern over a dearth of younger pastors. We need to recruit more young REPs as well as NREPs or we'll experience a severe shortage of pastors in the future.

Next we addressed the ages at which young and old re-envisioning pastors began their ministries at their established churches. How young might a re-envisioning pastor be when he takes a church and how old might he be when he takes his last church? Are there any age limits? NREPs began their last ministries between the ages of 26 and 60. Thus age isn't a determining factor for being a non–re-envisioning pastor.

Must we limit pastoral ministry to younger pastors if we expect a revitalization? Four REPs were 60+ when they began their ministries at their churches. The oldest was 67, one was 65, and two were 60. The youngest was 19 and the next youngest was 21.

One NREP was 60 when he began his ministry. Two of the REPs were 60, one was 67.5, and one was 65. And two pastors were the youngest at 26. We weren't surprised that pastors as young as 19, 21, and 26 pastored established churches. However, we were somewhat surprised to discover that pastors in their sixties and older were taking churches and leading them in a turnaround. One of the reasons for our surprise is that George Barna writes that in his research, REPs were 45 years or younger.[4] We discovered that in a sense one is never too old to join a church and lead it to re-envision itself. (An exception might be the 76-year-old NREP.) If you are older than 45 and you're a REP, then you shouldn't use age alone as a reason to rule out leading a church to re-envision itself.

Age at Ministry Beginning

Beginning age range for REPs: 19 to 67

Four oldest REPs: 60(2), 65, and 67.5 years old

Two youngest REPs: 19 and 21 years old

Beginning age range for NREPs: 26 to 60

Five oldest NREPs: 54, 56(2), 57, and 60 years old

Two youngest NREPs: 26 years old

Average Annual Growth Rate

We calculated the churches' average annual growth rates (AAGR) to see how many in the study scored 2.5 or above. The answer was 213. Seventy-two churches scored below 2.5 percent AAGR. The highest AAGR for a church was 220 percent; the church went from 25 to 80 people in one year. The lowest was –29 (29.3) percent; the church went from 85 to 15 people in 5 years. Appendix F contains the comparison for pastoral tenure, growth, percentage of growth, and AAGR.

Average Annual Growth Rates

2.5 percent and above: 213 churches

Highest AAGR: 220 percent (church grew from 25 to 80 people in one year)

2.4 percent or below: 72 churches

Lowest AAGR: –29 percent (church declined from 85 to 15 people in five years)

Multiple Church Turnarounds

In our exploration of the church world, we noted, much to our surprise, that fifty-three pastors had led multiple churches in a turnaround. Twenty-four pastors had led their churches in two turnarounds. Twenty-five had led their churches in three reversals. Three had led their churches in four turnabouts, and one had led churches in seven turnarounds. The latter began his ministry at age nineteen and at the time of our exploration was sixty years old. His average tenure was six years per church. It's interesting that Barna writes that the average turnaround pastor will lead only one church through a reversal.[5] Our work indicated that this isn't correct. REPs shouldn't be too quick to step down after leading one church in a turnaround. Allow God to use you repeatedly.

Multiple Turnarounds

24 pastors: 2 turnarounds

25 pastors: 3 turnarounds

3 pastors: 4 turnarounds

1 pastor: 7 turnarounds

Results of the Personal Profile (DISC)

Gordon asked the pastors involved in Discovery 1 to take the Personal Profile (DiSC). We did the same for Discovery 2, and 139 pastors out of 146 (95 percent) followed through. Before reading any further, you might want to return to chapter 5 and briefly review the material in that chapter on the Personal Profile (DISC) or look up various temperament combinations as you encounter them in this chapter.

Re-Envisioning Pastors' Scores on the DISC

First, we examined the scores of the re-envisioning pastors—those who were able to go into a church that was plateaued or in decline and see it begin to grow numerically. Our exploration discovered that 75 of the total 103 re-envisioning pastors (73 percent) patterned as some combination of the D or I temperament on the Personal Profile. Of the 75, 22 were DIs, 14 were IDs, 7 were Ds, and 13 were Is. We discovered 19 additional REPs who patterned DS, DC, CD, and IS. In terms of the S or C temperaments, 8 of the pastors were SCs and 4 were CSs for a total of 12. Based on the evidence above, these are exceptions. The remaining 13 REPs not listed in the table exhibited varied profile combinations with no patterns representing more than three pastors. By far the most prevalent profiles of the re-envisioning pastors were DI, ID, D, or I or some other combination with D or I.

Selected Leadership Profiles of REPs and NREPs

Profile Type	REP	NREP	%
DI	22	1	16.5%
ID	14	2	11.5%
D	7	2	6.5%
I	13	4	12.2%
DS	4	1	3.6%
DC or CD	4	2	4.3%
IS	11	3	10.1%
SI	0	3	2.2%
SC	8	5	9.4%
CS	4	4	5.8%
S	2	2	2.9%
C	1	3	2.9%

The Primary Patterns Discovered for Re-Envisioning Pastors

75 Re-envisioning pastors (D, I, or D and I combinations)

DI—22 pastors	DS—4 pastors
ID—14 pastors	DC or CD—4 pastors
D—7 pastors	IS—11 pastors
I—13 pastors	

12 Re-envisioning pastors (SC or combination)

SC—8 pastors (exceptions)

CS—4 pastors (exceptions)

Non–Re-Envisioning Pastors' Scores on the DISC

Next, we focused on the non–re-envisioning pastors' scores. As you recall, they are the pastors who find it most difficult to lead a plateaued or declining church in a turnaround. It usually doesn't happen. Of these thirty-six pastors, one of them was a DI, two were Ds, two were IDs, and four were Is. Six pastors exhibited strong S tendencies coupled with the I. The remaining four NREPs not listed in the table exhibited varied profile combinations with no patterns representing more than one pastor. Listed below are the primary patterns discovered among the NREPs.

The Primary Patterns Discovered for Non–Re-Envisioning Pastors

9 Non–re-envisioning pastors (D or I or combination)

DI—1 pastor	D—2 pastors
ID—2 pastors	I—4 pastors

14 Non–re-envisioning pastors (S or C or combination)

SC—5 pastors	S—2 pastors
CS—4 pastors	C—3 pastors

6 Non–re-envisioning pastors (IS or SI)

IS—3 pastors

SI—3 pastors

The DISC Profile differences between the re-envisioning and non–re-envisioning pastors are significant. Consequently, you should carefully and prayerfully consider these differences if you believe that God is leading you to be a senior pastor of a church, or you are coaching someone who desires to be a pastor. Pastors must understand their divine design in order to improve their ability to serve the body of Christ.

Results of the Myers-Briggs Type Indicator (MBTI)

Gordon didn't use the Myers-Briggs Type Indicator in Discovery 1, but we agreed to use it along with the Personal Profile in Discovery 2. We wanted to see if we might glean similar significant information from the MBTI as we did with the DISC. Thus we asked our sample pastors to take both the Personal Profile and the Myers-Briggs Type Indicator. As with the Personal Profile, you may want to turn back to chapter 5 and briefly review the material on the MBTI before you begin this section.

As you recall, 139 out of 146 pastors or 95 percent took the DISC. In addition, 131 out of the 146 or 90 percent also took the MBTI. As with the Personal Profile, we believe this was an excellent response on the part of these pastors.

Following are the number of re-envisioning pastors for each type (extroverts, introverts, and so on) on the MBTI:

Extroverts	Introverts
68	31

Sensing	Intuitive
54	45

Thinking	Feeling
47	52

Judgment	Perception
68	31

Following are the number of non–re-envisioning pastors for each type on the MBTI. Note the differences between them and the REPs.

Extroverts	Introverts
17	15

Sensing	Intuitive
18	14

Thinking	Feeling
18	14

Judgment	Perception
28	4

The scores on the MBTI for the REPs in general are significant. REPs are clearly extroverts as they score more than two to one over the introverts. They are more sensing than intuitive. They are slightly more feeling than thinking. And they score significantly higher on judgment over perception (more than two to one).

The distinctions between the REPs and NREPs are also telling. Unlike the REPs, they tend to be more introverted. Like the REPs they are more sensing than intuitive. Unlike the REPs they are slightly more thinking than feeling, and like the REPs judgment exceeds perception by a wide margin.

The most common patterns for REPs are: ESTJ (15), ENFP (12), ESFJ (11), or ISTJ (9). Those patterns for the NREPs are INTJ (6) or ISFJ (4), or ESFJ (4). This is most significant. It would appear that if you are an ESTJ, ENFP, ESFJ, or ISTJ on the MBTI, you are likely a pastor who can lead plateaued or declining churches to re-envision themselves and should strongly consider this when taking a church.

Results of the Pastoral Leadership Audit (PLA)

There were 135 pastors who took the Pastoral Leadership Audit. We asked pastors to respond to 25 characteristics with one of the four following options: true, more true than false, more false than true, and false (Likert Scale). The 25 items are characteristics of re-envisioning pastors, based on Discovery 1. Somewhat as expected, no REPs manifested all 25 characteristics. We did have one pastor (REP) that manifested 24 of the 25.

Scoring the PLA

We asked each leader who took the tool to total their score and then we plotted that score within the following three ranges:

Range 1: 25–47. You likely have what it takes to be a re-envisioning pastor/leader. Chances increase the lower your score. Thus God may have wired you to revitalize struggling churches.

Range 2: 48–57. You may or may not be a re-envisioning pastor/leader. Chances increase the lower your score. Note areas with high scores. You may want to attempt to improve in these areas if possible.

Range 3: 58–100. You probably aren't a re-envisioning pastor or leader and that is okay. (The higher your score the less likely God has designed you to revitalize an organization.) Assuming this is true, God seems to have wired you to thrive and serve best in some other ministry.

PLA Scores and Church Size

Total number who took the PLA: 135

Average Worship Attendance	REPs Average Score	REPs Typical Range of Scores	NREPs Average Score	NREPs Typical Range of Scores	REPs/ NREPs
2000+	36	26–41	50	50	6/1
500–1999	38	27–48	48	47–48	19/2
200–499	39	30–54	43	35–52	28/4
100–199	43	34–54	51	42–65	20/7
0–99	48	31–56	52	32–73	29/19
Total	—	—	—	—	102/33

Results from the ranges:

- 97 pastors (the majority) scored within the 25–47 or range 1 as likely re-envisioning pastors.
- 32 pastors scored between 48–57 or range 2 as possible re-envisioning leaders.
- 6 pastors scored between 58–100 or range 3. They are not likely re-envisioning pastors.

Results from information in the table above:

- Based on worship size, the larger the church, the lower and thus the better the score. REPs seem to be attracted to and thrive in larger churches.
- The average number of REPs scored between 36 and 44 on the PLA, which was lower and better than the NREPs, who ranged between 43 and 52 on the PLA.
- The REPs ranged between 26 and 56 on the PLA, which was lower and better than the NREPs, who ranged between 32 and 73 on the PLA.

Results of the PLA

Range 25–47: 97 pastors
Range 48–57: 32 pastors
Range 58–100: 6 pastors

Summary of Discoveries 1 and 2

So What's the Big Picture?

There is much information here and in chapter 6 from our exploration of churches. Our fear is that you might get lost in all this information. Some people really appreciate lots of information including statistics, and others prefer to get to the results without crunching all the numbers or wading through all the details. Therefore we have reserved this last section of the chapter to give you the "big picture"—to summarize our findings through a series of twenty-four discoveries or observations of re-envisioning pastors, using as few numbers as possible. Not all of these discoveries are true of all re-envisioning pastors, but the majority will be. (Note that we have used a number of synonyms for re-envisioning pastors such as revitalizers, turnaround pastors, renewal pastors, and re-envisioners.)

Twenty-four Discoveries

Discovery 1: Re-envisioning pastors are passionate and visionary. They have a clear vision and cast it well.

Discovery 2: More often than not, re-envisioners have a mentor or coach who supplies wisdom and counsel to help them through the good times as well as guide them in the difficult times.

Discovery 3: Renewal pastors have good people skills and thus get along and work well with people.

Discovery 4: Re-envisioning pastors tend to be more innovational than traditional.

Discovery 5: Turnaround pastors seem to have more energy to expend on ministry than the NREPs.

Discovery 6: Re-envisioners are young in ministry, regardless of their chronological age.

Discovery 7: Pastors who revitalize churches are good team players. They get along well with people (see Discovery 3) and work well with them on teams.

Discovery 8: Re-envisioning pastors are delegators. They realize that they can't re-envision churches alone. They know that if they fail to delegate the re-envisioning process, it won't happen.

Discovery 9: Turnaround pastors are good at training new leaders. They realize that leadership is the hope of the church—everything rises or falls with leadership. Thus they are committed to leader development.

Discovery 10: Revitalizers are focused and determined. They realize what is most important, focus on that, and push until it gets done.

Discovery 11: Turnaround pastors embrace necessary change and are willing to pay the price that change brings with it.

Discovery 12: Re-envisioning pastors have good conflict resolution skills. Conflict is part of the process of leading a church to re-envision itself, and REPs are skilled at handling such conflict.

Discovery 13: Re-envisioners are better than average communicators. This includes not only preaching and teaching but casting the church's vision and direction as well.

Discovery 14: Turnaround pastors passionately use their primary spiritual gifts and empower those under their ministry to do the same.

Discovery 15: The long tenure of re-envisioning pastors grows churches. In our study sample, pastors stayed an average of 7.4 years. However, for REPs this means steady, continuous growth, whereas with NREPs long tenure at best results in a plateau and in most cases steady decline.

Discovery 16: The age of a revitalizer isn't a major factor in re-envisioning a church. While the average age is forty-nine, a number have led a church in a turnaround up into their sixties. If there is an age limit, it's probably when they reach their seventies.

Discovery 17: Re-envisioning pastors are capable in their lifetime of leading multiple churches (two or three on average) through a turnaround.

Discovery 18: Turnaround pastors score a DI or ID or a D or an I on the Personal Profile (DISC).

Discovery 19: Re-envisioning pastors' scores are considerably more extroverted than introverted and their judgment (living in a planned, organized world) far exceeds their perception (living in a flexible, spontaneous world) on the Myers-Briggs Type Indicator (MBTI). You may want to review these types in chapter 5. Their most common patterns on the MBTI are ESTJ, ENFP, ESFJ, or ISTJ.

Discovery 20: Most renewal pastors score between 25 and 62 on the Pastoral Leadership Audit.

Discovery 21: Turnaround pastors are leaders. They influence people toward behavioral change.

Discovery 22: Re-envisioning pastors exert a strong influence on their churches.

Discovery 23: Turnaround pastors are future focused. They learn from the past but have learned not to live in or lead from the past.

Discovery 24: Renewal pastors may have already led a church to re-envision itself.

Questions for Reflection, Discussion, and Application

1. If you are a pastor or have been a pastor, how many years have you spent in pastoral ministry? How does your ministry experience stack up next to that of the re-envisioning and non–re-envisioning pastors? Which are you, based on your experience?

2. What is your age? How do you think your age will affect your ministry of turning around churches? If you are in your sixties, should you attempt to lead a church in a revitalization? Why or why not? How about if you are in your seventies?
3. What is your church's average annual growth rate (AAGR)? Is it 2.5 percent or above? Have you maintained this percentage for three or more years? If so, are you a re-envisioning pastor? Is it 2.4 or below? If so, what might this seem to indicate?
4. If you are a re-envisioning pastor, how many churches have you led in a turnaround? What is a reasonable expectation?
5. What is your score on the Personal Profile (DISC)? Are you a DI, ID, D, or I? What might this indicate regarding your re-envisioning a church?
6. What is your score on the Myers-Briggs Type Indicator (MBTI)? Are you an extrovert? Did you score fairly high on the judgment factor? What was your pattern on the MBTI? Are you an ESTJ, ENFP, ESFJ, or ISTJ? What might all this indicate about your ability to lead a church in a revitalization?
7. If you're not a re-envisioning pastor, what should your response be? If you are currently pastoring a church, is it plateaued or in numerical decline? If so, why? Does this mean that you're a failure as a pastor? Why or why not? If you feel like a failure or that you should get out of ministry all together or you're very discouraged, then it's imperative that you read chapter 8 in general and question three in that chapter in particular, which addresses the so-called failure mentality.

8

Four Critical Questions

Now that you have seen the results of our exploration of re-envisioning and non–re-envisioning pastors, what should you do with this information? Where should you go from here? We have four critical questions that we believe will help you wrestle intelligently with the results of Discovery 1 and 2 and capture God's direction for your life. The four questions are What if I'm a re-envisioning pastor? What if I'm a non–re-envisioning pastor? Can a non–re-envisioning pastor become a re-envisioning pastor? And finally, if that is possible, should a non–re-envisioning pastor become a re-envisioning pastor?

What If I'm a Re-Envisioning Pastor?

FOUR CRITICAL QUESTIONS
What if I am a re-envisioning pastor?
What if I am a non–re-envisioning pastor?
Can a non–re-envisioning pastor become a re-envisioning pastor?
Should a non–re-envisioning pastor become a re-envisioning pastor?

If you discover that God has designed you to be a re-envisioning pastor, your church will have been experiencing 2.5 percent growth or better for at least the last three years, if not more. We would strongly encourage you to continue in church re-envisioning as opposed to some other ministries, because we desperately need re-envisioning leaders in our churches, as we discovered in chapter 6.

How might you make a difference? We have several suggestions.

- You could make a major contribution to church revitalization if you serve as a mentor, coach, or model to other pastors, interns, and residents in and beyond your area. Offer internships and residencies.
- If you are part of a denomination, judicatory, network, or some similar organization, volunteer to work with the directors of missions, executive directors, superintendents, bishops, and so on. Carve out some time for them.
- If you've not pursued it already, get involved in planting church-planting churches. Make sure it's on your "ministry drawing board." The best and most successful church plants are those who partner with a spiritually healthy, growing, established church, and that probably describes yours.
- Capture a vision for a movement that promotes and casts a broad, exciting vision for church renewal. The need for such a movement is evident. What could you do and who could you enlist to get the ball rolling for a re-envisioning movement?

What If I'm a Non–Re-Envisioning Pastor?

What if you discover that you are not a REP? What does this mean? In far too many cases, it means that as a senior or lead pastor, your church most likely will plateau or go into a decline if it hasn't already. And this isn't good for you as a pastor or your local body of Christ.

The critical question here is, how does this make you feel? Many feel like a failure, are discouraged, question whether they're leaders, question their call to the ministry, and consider dropping out of ministry altogether. We hear, "Maybe I should go back to the business world where I came from. I'm not sure that I have any business being a pastor. Maybe it's time to throw in the ministry towel." We experienced this when we invited pastors to be a part of our exploration. The re-envisioning pastors were quick to respond, whereas the non–re-envisioning pastors were slow to respond if they did at all.

A Blessing in Disguise

It's imperative that you realize that what you may believe is failure is a wonderful blessing in disguise. It's likely that God has specially designed you *to pursue some other ministry* (missionary, youth pastor, counselor, worship, teacher, for example). Therefore, don't become depressed, give up, or drop out of ministry. Instead, discover the ministry or ministries—there probably are several—that God has designed you for and pursue them.

Andy Stanley says it well:

> Change requires vision. Sustained vision requires leadership. If you have it, Paul would tell you to *lead diligently*. If you don't, discover the gifts God has blessed you with and lean into them with all your heart. Find a staff position that allows you to operate from your strengths. That is the biblical model. Churches and church leaders who organize and operate around that premise do well. Those who don't, don't.
>
> So, as you contemplate the changes you feel need to be made in your current context, first determine whether or not you are the one to lead the change. Take a personal inventory. An honest inventory. . . . If you are more comfortable problem solving than vision casting, you're going to have a difficult time of it. . . . If you are conflict—or risk—averse, there's no need to start a process that you probably won't finish. You are better off managing what's been handed to you and praying that God will raise up a leader who will challenge the status quo and introduce change. Your observations about what needs to change may be spot on. You just may not be the one to drive the process.[1]

An Objection

A common objection that we hear, and one you may be articulating this very moment is, "But what if I believe that God has called me to be a pastor?" This is a most important objection, and a question that many of the readers of this book are asking.

The Concept of a Call to Ministry

Many use the concept of the calling of God as an indispensable factor in determining God's will for the believer's life in general and the believer's pursuit of a vocation in particular. Many of those who hold this view see a call to ministry as a higher calling for Christians than a call to other professions, such as that of a lawyer or a banker. For some, it is the highest of calls. Therefore we want to take some time in this section to wrestle with this important concept.

In general, the idea behind this view is that God issues a special higher call for a lifetime of vocational ministry to certain individuals whom he has chosen. God is active in choosing, while the person is passive and receives. Most often the call is to the vocational ministry of pastor or missionary. He accomplishes this call in a variety of ways, most of which are described as a subjective "inner call." For example, the Holy Spirit may call people through such experiences as a special inner conviction, an unusual urge to preach the gospel, a particular passage of Scripture that is impressed on one's mind, and so on.

Is a Call Supported by Scripture?

Regardless of what constitutes a special call to vocational ministry or how that is accomplished, the real issue is whether or not the concept is scriptural. And what we mean by that is whether it is found in or mandated by the Bible. Those who believe it is, cite certain examples, such as Moses, Isaiah, Jeremiah, Paul, and the commissioning of the apostles. But the classic text is Isaiah 6:1–13, where God calls Isaiah the prophet. Some believe that this particular call has all the classic elements that are common to the experience of those who have obeyed God's call to minister: a vision of God's holiness, recognizing our unholiness, the forgiveness of sin, and obedience.

Six Reasons a Call Is Not Dictated by Scripture

SIX REASONS A CALL ISN'T DICTATED BY SCRIPTURE
1. It is not biblically normative for all pastors.
2. It was not a qualification for first-century pastors (elders).
3. The term *call* is used of the call to salvation, not pastoral ministry.
4. The analogy between the body of Christ and the human body doesn't allow for a special "called" body part.
5. The priesthood of believers applies to all believers, not just pastors.
6. God has called all believers to the ministry.

Further examination of the Bible indicates that the concept of a special divine call is not found in or mandated by the Bible, nor is it normative for all believers of all ages, and those who argue that it is are skating on scriptural thin ice. There are several reasons for this. First, to argue for this concept on subjective grounds alone raises all kinds of problems and questions, which most who hold this view will acknowledge. Its validity rests mostly on the scriptural evidence used to support it.

To argue for a special, inner call, those who embrace the concept must demonstrate that the experiences of Moses, Isaiah, Jeremiah, and Paul are normative experiences for all who pursue vocational ministry in all ages. The simple fact that these Old Testament prophets and some apostles had a special call from God does not necessarily mean that others must as well. This is a non sequitur argument. Also it's hard to believe that Isaiah recorded his call to be a prophet as an example to all pastors who follow him, expecting that they are to look for and have the same kind of experience. That was not his purpose for writing his book nor this section of his book. We believe that such an interpretation would surprise Isaiah.

Isaiah and the others were prophets who spoke God's word and prophesied future events (Isa. 1:1; 7:14; 9:6; Jer. 1:7–9). Paul was an apostle with apostolic authority who was involved in recording divine revelation. These responsibilities would not be equivalent to the contemporary pastoral office.

A second reason a call is not normative for all believers is that the office or position of elder in the New Testament most approximates today's office of pastor. The elders were first-century house church pastors. In light of the significant size of the early first-century churches, the elders spent a lot of time with their ministries and were compensated for their work (1 Tim. 5:17–18; 1 Pet. 5:2). Much of that ministry involved shepherding God's flock (Acts 20:28; 1 Pet. 5:1–2) as well as preaching to and teaching God's people (1 Tim. 5:17). The qualifications for elders are listed in 1 Timothy 3:1–7 and Titus 1:5–9. Of the fifteen or more qualifications, a special, inner call is not among them nor implied. First Timothy 3:1 indicates that a person could "desire" or set his heart on being an elder/pastor. This clearly teaches personal proactivity on the part of the believer, which contradicts the idea that God is active in the divine call while the person remains passive.

Third, the New Testament uses the term meaning a *call* or a form thereof more than 150 times. However, a study of that usage reveals that it is primarily used of the divine call to salvation (Rom. 8:30, for example), never to vocational Christian ministry as described above.

Fourth, the New Testament also makes an analogy between the church, the body of Christ, and the human body (1 Corinthians 12). In this analogy, no body part is separated out for special or separate ministry. While mention is made of the head, there is no indication that it was a special or divinely "called" body part separate from and higher than the rest.

Fifth, the New Testament teaches the priesthood of all believers (1 Pet. 2:9–10; Rev. 1:6). There is no mention of a special priestly caste or a hierarchy of the few who are set aside for any ministry, such as pastoral or missionary service.

Sixth, in a sense, God has called all believers, not some, into the ministry regardless of their profession, whether a pastor, missionary, businessperson, and so on. He has equipped every believer with spiritual gifts and the empowering of the Holy Spirit to accomplish his ministry.

The Conclusion

The conclusion of this brief study is the same one reached earlier in this chapter—all believers are to be involved in ministry. The key to the exact nature of that ministry is not necessarily some special, inner call from God but a person's divine design. Therefore people who desire the pastoral office in particular do not need to wait for a call to that office but need to determine if their design best suits them for the position. And this is fully supported by Scripture as reflected above. Often this pastoral design consists of such gifts as leadership, administration, teaching, pastoring, and so on.

Now, having said all this, please understand that we are not saying that God can't come into your life in such a way that you believe he wants you to pursue pastoral ministry. So don't get upset with us and toss this book in the trash. We all agree that God is sovereign and we must let him be God. If you have read this section and still believe that God has called you to be a pastor, then pursue that. However, if your ministry is plateaued or in decline, and you are overwhelmingly frustrated, you may want to reconsider. Again, he may have something much better in mind for you.

One Last Question

One question that you must consider is, Why? Why do you want to be a pastor? This is a question that will probe your motives and the validity of your desire for the pastoral position. I (Aubrey) know a number of people who were told early in their Christian experience that God wanted them to be a pastor. This counsel came from well-meaning people, such as Christian parents, their pastor, their friends. I know one young man who went to Dallas Seminary because the pastor who led him to faith pushed him to go into the ministry to be a pastor. I am sure the pastor meant well but I wonder about that pastor's motives. He may have liked the idea of developing a disciple. After a year of seminary, the young man realized he wasn't cut out to be a pastor and he dropped out. I believe the body of Christ in general and the pastoral ministry in particular are better off for it.

Another example is my brother-in-law. For much of his life, his mother told him that he was going to be a medical doctor. She too meant well, but we suspect that this had more to do with motherly pride than her knowing what was best for her son. Not only was he not interested in the medical field, but God had wired him to move in another direction. I mention these things for your consideration. You may have had similar experiences that influenced you to pursue pastoral ministry. Check your motives. Probe why you want to be a pastor. Is it because you have a servant's heart and you love and want to serve people? Then the next question is: Can you become a re-envisioning pastor?

If you're a non–re-envisioning pastor who still wants to be a senior pastor, you need to consider the next question.

Can a Non–Re-Envisioning Pastor Become a Re-Envisioning Pastor?

Can an NREP become a REP or at the very least embrace enough qualities of a REP so as to stand a better opportunity of leading a church to re-envision itself?

This takes us back to the age-old nature versus nurture debate. Are leaders born or made? Are leaders and their capabilities a matter of nature or nurture? This has always been a matter for debate in leadership circles, especially academic circles. No one knows for sure, and knowledgeable people land on both sides of the issue. For example, on one side, leadership guru Peter Drucker believes that leaders are born. Thus leadership is a God-given capability. On the other side, leaders such as James M. Kouzes and Barry Z. Posner (coauthors of the *Leadership Challenge*) argue that the art of leadership can be learned, and thus leaders are made. Our view is that one may or may not be a born leader, but all leaders have the potential to grow and nurture their abilities to lead. And one who is born with an ability to lead or a leadership gift and chooses to develop that gift will be extraordinarily adept at leadership. We suspect that most non–re-envisioners are not gifted leaders but can certainly develop as leaders. And this means that one can learn how to re-envision churches. So what is needed for this to happen?

A great number of the re-envisioning skills of REPs are by nature teachable and learnable. Some examples of these reproducible skills are vision casting, delegating, problem solving, leader development, preaching, communicating. However, there are several problems that surface as one attempts to embrace and hone these characteristics.

Temperament

One problem may be temperament. Since temperament is an inborn trait, it's only natural for a person to behave according to his or her temperament. You can learn to mimic a temperament's behavior. For example, I (Aubrey) find that in my leadership role at Dallas Seminary, I need to behave like the I temperament. And because I've been a student of temperament for fifteen years or more, I find that I can do it, though I'm not an I. It's kind of like handwriting. You are either right- or left-handed. Few people can write with either hand. Mimicking a temperament other than your own is much like trying to write with the wrong hand. Some can do it better than others, and some can hardly do it at all. With practice, most can improve, but it's not natural and that's where the problems lie.

A problem with trying to behave with a temperament that is not you can be called temperament default. In my case, while I tend to behave like a High I temperament at the seminary, whenever stress or pressure comes my way and I need to be at my best, I naturally default to my true God-given temperament.

Authenticity

Another problem with trying to hone REP skills is authenticity. Can you be comfortable with being who you aren't? Being who you aren't directly addresses one's authenticity. Am I unauthentic when behaving like one with an I temperament? For some this is a problem. The cry of the day especially among young people is for authenticity—be true to yourself. Can a non–re-envisioning pastor become a re-envisioning pastor? As we've seen, the answer is yes, but should you? This is the next question.

We are not through addressing how one can change and become a re-envisioning pastor, so we will return to this topic in depth in chapter 9.

Should a Non–Re-Envisioning Pastor Become a Re-Envisioning Pastor?

Should a non–re-envisioning pastor even try to become a re-envisioning pastor? It seems like the answer should be no, that it would violate a person's authenticity or the person God made them to be—their divine design. And would someone who is ministering outside their design be effective?

The Need

We desperately need re-envisioning pastors who can re-envision churches. In chapter 6 we discovered that re-envisioning pastors are in short supply. The collective evidence is that re-envisioning pastors make up anywhere from 5 to 20 percent of established pastors. Thus 75 to 90 percent of pastors are non–re-envisioning pastors. Why is this the case? Does God make more non–re-envisioning pastors than re-envisioning pastors? The answer is we just don't know. However, my (Aubrey's) thinking is that a lot of our younger, talented, gifted leaders are going into the business world and aren't really interested in pastoring churches. The problem is that many are turned off by what they've seen in churches—the politics, xenophobia, and stubborn people who simply want their way. Why put up with all that?

It bears repeating, to be most effective, you need to discover your divine design (gifting, passion, and temperament) and minister accordingly. Then you will be most effective at what God has wired you to do, whether it's a high- or low-profile ministry position.

For the Sake of the Gospel

In 1 Corinthians 9:19–24 Paul teaches us an important principle that relates to our ministry. He relates that at times we have to make sacrifices for the sake of the gospel if we're to move a ministry forward. He writes, "Though I am free and belong to no one, I have made myself a slave to everyone, to win as many as possible" (v. 19). Then he summarizes: "I have become all things to all people so that by all possible means I may save some. I do all this for the sake of the gospel, that I might share in its blessings" (vv. 22–23). The same can be the case in leading a church through a revitalization. Though a person may not be wired to re-envision churches, he might take up the challenge to do so for the sake of the gospel—doing what he's not best wired for that he might save some.

A great illustration of this principle is the ministry of Chuck Swindoll. Chuck moved from Fullerton, California, to Dallas, Texas, in the early 1990s for the purpose of planting a church. At that time the Dallas Seminary board of which he was a member asked him to put aside that dream and become the fourth president of Dallas Seminary. The school was experiencing a downturn in finances and student enrollment, and the board felt that Chuck was the right person to address this. He accepted the challenge and was president for seven years from 1994 to 2001. The point is that God wired Chuck as a church planter and now an established church pastor, not the president of a theological seminary. His passion for ministry didn't include fund-raising and seminary vision casting. Yet he did it, and God blessed him and the seminary by using Chuck to turn the situation around and help make the seminary what it is today.

Questions for Reflection, Discussion, and Application

1. Do you believe that God has wired you to lead your church and possibly others through a turnaround? If so, are you pursuing this or are you involved in other ministries? In light of the dearth of re-envisioning pastors, would you be willing to change course and consider a ministry of re-envisioning churches? Why or why not? If not now, when?

2. If you're a re-envisioning pastor, are you training others to become or function as re-envisioning pastors? Does your church offer an internship or residency for training these pastors? If not, why not? Are you a mentor or coach to some pastors or future pastors? Why or why not? If you are part of a denomination, association, network, or judicatory, are you willing to help it re-envision its pastors? Why or why not?
3. If you're a re-envisioning pastor, have you planted any churches or do you have church planting on your ministry drawing board? If not, why not?
4. If you consider yourself a non–re-envisioning pastor, how do you know? Is your church plateaued or declining? Why? Are you discouraged and about ready to throw in the ministry towel? Have you thought about pursuing another ministry or vocation that is more in line with your divine design?
5. The authors question the concept of a call to vocational ministry. Do you agree or disagree or are you somewhere in between? Why? What is your argument for your view? Can you support it with Scripture?
6. If you're a non–re-envisioning pastor, do you have any desire to function as a re-envisioning pastor? If so, why? If not, why not? How would you go about this? Do you view this as a challenge to your authenticity? Why or why not?
7. If you're a non–re-envisioning pastor, are you willing to attempt to become a re-envisioning pastor? Why or why not? Do you recognize the need for such a change in role? Do you agree with the authors' interpretation of 1 Corinthians 9:19–24?
8. Sometimes pastors can be the loneliest people in the church. Do you have someone in your life who can come alongside you and give you objective input as to your divine design and your abilities to envision or re-envision churches? Who might be such a person? What will you do about this, if anything?

PART 3

Practice of Discovery

If you desire to be a re-envisioning pastor, how might you pursue this? What curriculum might you follow? There are no less than five essential answers or lessons that make up the re-envisioning curriculum found in chapters 9 through 14, the practice portion of this book. The first is to discipline oneself to embrace the characteristics of re-envisioning pastors. This is the topic of chapter 9. The second is to learn how to develop and cast a clear, compelling vision. Re-envisioning pastors are good at this. This is the content of chapter 10. The third is to become an agent of cultural change who leads his church culture through the change process. We will address this in chapter 11. The fourth is to draft a mentor or coach who can help you through the process. We cover this in chapter 12. The fifth we cover in chapter 13. Finally, we challenge you as the reader to make application of the results. We cover this in chapter 14.

9

Embracing the Characteristics of Re-Envisioning Pastors

In the last chapter, one of our questions for pastors was, Can a non–re-envisioning pastor become a re-envisioning pastor? The purpose for putting the question there was to introduce the idea of changing to become what one isn't. Our assumption and conclusion were that becoming a re-envisioning pastor is possible but depends much on the individual who desires to move in that direction. With that in mind, this chapter addresses in depth how to go about making such a move.

The three tools that we have discovered are so critical to divine design and personal discovery are the Personal Profile (DISC), the Myers-Briggs Type Indicator (MBTI), and the Pastoral Leadership Audit (PLA). These make up three phases of the transformation process that we'll walk through in this chapter. We assume that you are a re-envisioning pastor who wants to sharpen and further hone his tools as a re-envisioning pastor or that you are a non–re-envisioning pastor who sincerely desires to become as much of a re-envisioning pastor as possible. You might find it beneficial to return to chapter 5 and briefly review what that chapter teaches about temperament.

Phase 1: The Personal Profile (DISC)

What does the DISC teach us about becoming a re-envisioning leader? More specifically, how does the Personal Profile (DISC) help us become re-envisioning pastors? The answer is to take the following five steps that will lead you through the first of three phases of the discovery process.

PHASE 1: THE PERSONAL PROFILE (DISC)
Step 1: Discover Your DISC Temperament
Step 2: Confirm Your DISC Temperament
Step 3: Understand Your DISC Temperament
Step 4: Compare Your DISC Score to That of a Re-Envisioning Pastor
Step 5: Apply Your DISC Results to Your Ministry

Step 1: Discover Your DISC Temperament

To begin with, take the Personal Profile or DISC. If you've taken it prior to reading this book, we suggest that you take it again. Sometimes we don't get it right the first time, but that initial experience causes us to become more aware of and focused on our temperament with the result that we truly discover it a second or even a third time. You should be able to locate the tool online, or there may be a representative in your area who can sell it to you directly. The advantage of taking this tool is that it's been well validated. If you have trouble locating it or want to move ahead now and not wait to purchase it, we have provided you with a similar tool in Temperament Indicator 1 located in appendix A. In addition to that, a tool labeled the Expanded Temperament Indicator is in appendix D. Both the Personal Profile and Temperament Indicator 1 present a limited number of descriptors for each profile. The Expanded Temperament Indicator presents a larger number of descriptors as options to help you better identify your temperament. This tool includes both the strengths and weaknesses of each profile.

Step 2: Confirm Your DISC Temperament

It almost goes without saying that discovering your temperament depends on your getting an accurate read of who you are on the Personal Profile or any of the other tools. Taking such a tool depends on the information that you put into it and the tool itself. This is commonly referred to as validation. We believe that validation is twofold. First, there is the validation of the tool itself. Does it truly measure what it claims to measure? Most good tools will address the validation issue somewhere in the description of the tool. The Personal Profile, for example, is a well-validated tool and readily provides this information.

Also the tool is only as accurate as the information one contributes in taking it. If the person doesn't know him- or herself well, it's unlikely that the tool will provide an accurate reading of his or her temperament. This was my (Aubrey's) experience the first time I took the DISC. I didn't really know myself all that well and my responses reflected that lack of self-knowledge. However, the very experience of taking it raised questions about my temperament with the result that I began to pay more attention to my behavior.

Validating Your Results

How might you validate your results on the DISC? Here are four suggestions.

- Take the Expanded Temperament Indicator 1. The additional characteristics will help you hone and refine your temperament.
- Ask someone who knows you well, such as a spouse, parent, child, best friend, mentor, coach, or pastor if they agree with your assessment of your temperament. If not, why not? What would they change or correct?
- You might have them assess your temperament using one of the tools and then you could compare their findings with your own.
- Take the tool periodically (once a year) and see if it confirms your initial findings.

Can One's Temperament Change?

An issue that can affect validation relates to whether or not one's temperament changes over time. We've heard from some who swear that they're not the same person who took the Profile initially. They're convinced that they've changed, and in some cases for the better. Our view is that you don't change that much. What is more likely is that you, like me (Aubrey), have begun to pay more attention to who you are and you've been able to correct some false observations or assumptions about yourself. There's no change for the better, because no temperament is superior to or better than another. God gave you the temperament you are and that is good.

Step 3: Understand Your DISC Temperament

This step assumes that you have taken the Personal Profile or some similar tool and validated the results so that you know your temperament. At least one if not two of the descriptions of the temperaments will be true of you. Now the question isn't who you are so much as so what? What does it mean to be a D or I or S or C on the DISC? We addressed this question in chapter 5. A brief review of that information should suffice.

Dominance Temperament

The letter D represents the dominance temperament. The profile suggests that one with this temperament may be somewhat strong and controlling. The

D's orientation to life is that they're more goal oriented than people oriented. They are also fast paced as they go through life as opposed to operating at a slower pace. The way you motivate a D is with a challenge. They function best in an environment that provides lots of challenges and opportunities and freedom from control while being more in control. Under pressure a D will be aggressive as well as autocratic. They like to take charge. Ds would benefit from listening first and acting later. Ds tend to be open to change, especially when that change brings challenges with it, which is normally the case. Their strength is that they're productive. They get things done. They're also decisive and firm. However, their weaknesses are that they come across as too busy, insensitive, and inflexible.

Influence Temperament

The letter I represents the influence temperament. The profile sums up this temperament as characteristic of one with a natural ability to influence or lead others.

The I's focus in life, unlike the D, is people and forming relationships with them. Like the Ds, Is are fast paced and move through life quickly. And you motivate them through recognizing them and their accomplishments. They function best in an environment that is friendly and fun loving and where they can inspire and relate to people. Under pressure, though, they may surprise you by attacking you. Although Is benefit by finishing what they start, this can be a problem for them, so in leadership positions, they need assistants who will do this for them. In general, most Is tend to be open to change, especially if it promotes relationships with people. Their strengths are their optimism, their ability to inspire, and their enthusiasm. Their weaknesses are that they exaggerate, are impatient, and can be manipulative.

Steadiness Temperament

The letter S represents the steadiness temperament. An S is emotionally steady and calm. Like the Is, they value people and relationships. Unlike the D or I, they move through life more slowly so you don't benefit by rushing them. They prefer to minister in more secure situations with little risk. Ss are motivated by relationships and security. They also like to be appreciated for what they contribute to a ministry. They function best in a context that is consistent and stable and appreciate working with people where there is little conflict. In pressure situations, they tend to give in to whoever is applying the pressure. Ss would benefit most by initiating and being more proactive as opposed to passive. They tend to be slow to change in contrast to the Ds and Is. However, they'll support change if convinced that it won't hurt people and their relationships. Their strengths are that they're agreeable, loyal, and supportive. Their weaknesses are that they are nonconfrontational when they need to confront, miss opportunities often due to their loyalty, and are too conforming.

Conscientiousness Temperament

The letter C represents the conscientiousness temperament. Like the D, a C is goal or purpose oriented. Like the S they tend to be slow paced. Accuracy and quality motivate Cs. They are into the details and live a scheduled life, preferring an environment that is planned and predictable—they don't appreciate surprises. They also enjoy privacy and prefer to follow policies and procedures. Under pressure, they may withdraw emotionally and at times physically. They would benefit by communicating more. It's not so much that they don't communicate well as that they don't communicate at all. Like the Ss, Cs are slow to change. The issue for them is accuracy and quality control, but if they can be assured that change won't adversely affect accuracy and quality control, they will agree to change.

Step 4: Compare Your DISC Score to That of a Re-Envisioning Pastor

In chapter 7 we unwrapped re-envisioning pastors' responses to the Personal Profile. To an overwhelming degree, their temperaments were a combination of the D and the I (DI and ID) or a lone I or D. We did have several combinations of the S and C profiles (SC and CS), but they were the exception, not the norm. Thus you can compare your validated score with that of the re-envisioning pastors. Have you proved to be a DI, ID, D, or I? The closer you are to these profiles, the greater the chances you are a re-envisioning pastor. The further away you are (a C or S or combination), the less likely you are. But don't stop here. When you get to the discussions of the MBTI and the Pastoral Leadership Audit in this chapter, you will further understand where your temperament fits best in ministry.

Step 5: Apply Your DISC Results to Your Ministry

Now you need to know how you can apply your DISC results to your life and ministry. What can you learn that will help you to re-envision churches? Following are several applications.

If you are a DI, ID, D, or I, you may need to review the strengths and weaknesses of this temperament. To refresh your thinking, read over the description of the D and I temperaments in chapter 5. Then look at the characteristics in the Temperament Indicator 1 to see which characteristics of the D and I are true of you. We have listed the D and I characteristics below. The positive D characteristics are usually the following: decisive, competent, competitive, persistent, productive, and self-reliant. It's possible that some could be negative in the wrong situation. For example, team-reliant might be better than self-reliant and being competitive could be problematic, depending on the situation. The negative D characteristics are usually the following: controlling, blunt, competitive, callous, and volatile. The positive I characteristics are the following: outgoing, expressive, influential, enthusiastic, persuasive, personable, animated, and articulate. The negative characteristics are impulsive and manipulative.

The D Temperament	The I Temperament
___Decisive	___Outgoing
___Controlling	___Expressive
___Competent	___Influential
___Blunt	___Enthusiastic
___Competitive	___Persuasive
___Callous	___Impulsive
___Volatile	___Manipulative
___Persistent	___Personable
___Productive	___Animated
___Self-reliant	___Articulate

As you look at the characteristics, both positive and negative, that are and are not true of you, it can be most instructive. Place a check by those above that are not true of you. Study them, even memorize them. Then begin to focus on embracing as much as possible the positives and eliminating the negatives from your behavior.

Make the positive characteristics that aren't true of you a part of your personal leadership development plan and discipline yourself to apply them in your life and ministry. Don't attempt to implement all of them at once. Instead, start with a few and focus on them. You would be wise to put them in priority order. Which would result in the biggest gains for you in being or becoming a re-envisioning pastor? Then add others to your list as you find you're able to embrace them. Finally, be sure to review them periodically.

Make a point of being around or spending some time with and observing people who are DIs, IDs, Ds, and Is, especially pastors. They can be your models; it's similar to Paul's inviting the Corinthians to imitate him in 1 Corinthians 11:1. This might involve you in an internship or residence in a church. In particular focus on staff in general and pastors in particular who are wired accordingly and are re-envisioning people. What do you observe? What can you learn from them, both good and bad? Another suggestion along similar lines is to work on this area with a coach or mentor.

Phase 2: The MBTI

PHASE 2: THE MBTI
Step 1: Discover Your MBTI Type
Step 2: Confirm Your MBTI Type
Step 3: Understand Your MBTI Type
Step 4: Compare Your MBTI Type to That of a Re-Envisioning Pastor
Step 5: Apply Your MBTI Results to Your Ministry

Now we look at the Myers-Briggs Type Indicator (MBTI) to discover what it can teach about becoming a re-envisioning leader. How might it play a part in your becoming a re-envisioning pastor or if you are a re-envisioning pastor, how can it be a refresher course for you? We've given you five steps below to follow in this process.

Step 1: Discovering Your MBTI Type

To begin with, take the Myers-Briggs Type Indicator (MBTI). As with the DISC, if you've already taken it in conjunction with this book or at some other time in your life, you would benefit from taking it again. We believe that each time you take it or the DISC, you increase your knowledge of what these tools are teaching you and what they're telling you about your design. You should be able to locate the tool online. Also, a number of counselors, psychologists, and educators would be able to provide you with the tool as a part of their services, which entail some cost. Another option is the Keirsey Temperament Sorter II (KTSII), which is similar to the MBTI. This instrument is in David Keirsey's book *Please Understand Me II* or can be found online.

Should you have trouble finding the MBTI or if you do not want to pay a psychologist or educator for their services, we have provided you with a similar tool in Type Indicator 2 located in appendix B. In addition, we have provided you with a tool we call the Expanded Type Indicator 2 in appendix E. Both the MBTI and Type Indicator 2 present a limited number of descriptors for each profile. The Expanded Type Indicator 2 will provide you with a larger number of descriptors as options to help you better identify your type. These tools don't necessarily surface one's strengths and weaknesses but a person's preferences on a number of factors, such as extroversion and introversion, thinking and feeling, and so forth.

Step 2: Confirm Your MBTI Type

The MBTI is a well-validated tool. It accurately measures what it purports to measure—your unique type. Thus the only way not to get a proper reading of your type is if you enter the wrong information when taking it. The problem isn't the tool itself; the problem is understanding yourself well enough to be able to respond to each question truthfully and accurately.

Validating Your Results

What are some ways to validate your results on the MBTI? They are much the same as with the Personal Profile.

- Take the Expanded Type Indicator 2 in appendix E. It will provide you with a number of additional characteristics beyond what is in the MBTI or KTSII.
- Ask someone who knows you well if they agree with your assessment of your type. If not, ask them for what specifically isn't accurate or true of you.
- Invite the person who knows you well to assess your type by taking the Type Indicator 2 or the KTSII and then share their results with you.
- Take the tool annually and see if it confirms your initial identity. If not, note the changes.

Can Your Type Change?

An issue that addresses validation is whether one's type can change over the years due to any number of factors. Our view is that, as with the DISC, your type doesn't change regardless of the factors, barring some kind of brain injury. A member of my (Aubrey) family is seizure-prone and did experience a change in temperament due to several violent seizures. I believe that the seizures affected this person's brain chemistry. Most people do not have this problem and, as we've said, if there are changes in your results, they are most likely because you have become more aware of your temperament over the years, not because your temperament has changed.

Step 3: Understand Your MBTI Type

This step assumes that you have both taken and validated your type and you know what it is. But what does it mean? How can you understand your type? How does or will this affect your behavior? And most important, how will it help a non–re-envisioning pastor operate to some degree as a re-envisioning pastor? Since we addressed this in chapter 5, we will give a brief summary here of that information.

Extroverts versus Introverts
How do you energize?

	Extroverts	Introverts
Energy	People energize them Quiet drains them	Quiet energizes them People drain them
Focus	Focus on the outer world of people and things	Focus on the inner world of ideas and concepts
Orientation	Act first and then think	Think first and then act
Ministry Environment	Work with others	Work by themselves
Communication	Talkers	Writers
Strengths	Good with people	Good with ideas
Weaknesses	Impulsive	Private

Sensing versus Intuition
How do you acquire information?

	Sensing	Intuition
Focus	Acquire information through the five senses	Acquire information through intuition
Orientation	Live life as it is	Live life as it could be
Ministry Environment	Use current skills to do ministry	Develop new skills to do ministry
Strengths	Very practical	Visionary
Weaknesses	Prefer the status quo	Leap to conclusions too soon

Thinking versus Feeling
How do you make decisions?

	Thinking	Feeling
Focus	Make decisions based on thinking	Make decisions based on feeling (values)
Orientation	Objective, facts oriented	Subjective, people oriented
Ministry Environment	Analyze the facts	Sympathize with people
Strengths	Logical and analytical	Serve people
Weaknesses	Insensitive	Too sensitive

Judgment versus Perception
How do you relate to the world of people and things?

	Judgment	Perception
Focus	Live in a planned, organized world	Live in a flexible, spontaneous world
Orientation	Control the world around them	Adapt to the world around them
Ministry Environment	Seek closure and complete tasks	Stay open and explore tasks
Strengths	Scheduled and good at planning	Flexible and adapt well to change
Weaknesses	Make decisions too quickly	Put off making decisions

Step 4: Compare Your MBTI Type to That of a Re-Envisioning Pastor

In chapter 7 we explored the re-envisioning pastors' responses to the MBTI. To an overwhelming degree, their types were the ESTJ, ENFP, ESFJ, and/or ISTJ. Though not a primary type, the ENTJ or ENFJ leader should theoretically be good at re-envisioning churches due to their intuition and natural focus on the future as opposed to the present. What was also important to note was that as signaled above the re-envisioning pastors were overwhelmingly both extroverts and judgment types (more than two to one). Compare your validated score with that of the re-envisioning pastors. Have you patterned to be one of the four above? Which? The closer you are to these profiles, the greater the chances of your being or becoming a re-envisioning pastor. The further away you are, the more difficult it becomes, but not impossible. Look back to your DISC score. What did it reveal when compared to that of a re-envisioning pastor?

Step 5: Apply Your MBTI Results to Your Ministry

Now you need to think about how you can apply your MBTI results to your ministry. What can you learn that will help you re-envision churches? Following are several applications.

You would be wise to review the description of your type in chapter 5 to refresh your memory. What do you learn about your type? Then focus specifically on the strengths and weaknesses of the Extroverts and Introverts and the Judgment and Perceptive types in descriptions and the summaries. Which strengths of the Extrovert and Judgment types are true of you and which aren't? Which of their weaknesses are true of you? Using the lists below, place a check by the strengths and weaknesses of those that apply. Study them and become familiar with them. There are two goals: one is to focus on embracing as much as possible the strengths and eliminating the weaknesses from your behavior. The other is to begin to embrace the strengths that aren't true of you but are key to being or becoming a turnaround pastor.

Don't attempt to implement all of these at once. Instead, start with a few characteristics that are not true of you but are characteristic of re-envisioning pastors and focus on them. You would be wise to put them in priority order. Which one, two, or three would result in the biggest gains for you in being or becoming a re-envisioning pastor? Make them a part of your personal leadership development plan, and discipline yourself to apply them in your life and ministry. Add others to your list as you find you're able to embrace them.

Make a point of being around or spending some time with and observing people who are ESFJs and ESTJs, especially pastors. Again, this is following a model, as Paul encourages in the New Testament. It's good to have knowledge about leaders with these re-envisioning temperaments, but you'll learn much more by observing the life of such a leader.

Extroverts

Strengths	Weaknesses
___Remember names and faces	___Impatient with processes
___Greet people well	___Talk too much
___Like variety and action	___Say what's on mind
___Handle interruptions well	___Impulsive
___Easy to get to know	

Introverts

Strengths	Weaknesses
___Use quiet for concentration	___Don't remember names and faces
___Lengthy focus on a single project	___Don't greet people well
___Good with ideas	___Not team players
___Observant	___Private and slow to act

Judgment

Strengths	Weaknesses
___Good at planning and following plans	___Make decisions too quickly
___Deliberate	___Don't handle interruptions well
___Manage time well	___Need to feel in control
___Orderly	___Little down time
___Focused	___Inflexible

Perception

Strengths	Weaknesses
___Spontaneous	___Postpone unpleasant tasks
___Adapt well to change	___Not good at planning and follow-through
___Able to relax and play	___Not finishers
___Flexible	___Too many projects
___Right brain	___Slow decision makers

Phase 3: The Pastoral Leadership Audit (PLA)

PHASE 3: THE PASTORAL LEADERSHIP AUDIT (PLA)
Step 1: Observe the Results of the PLA
Step 2: Compare Your Characteristics
Step 3: Attempt to Validate Your Results
Step 4: Attempt to Understand Your Results
Step 5: Apply the Results to Your Life and Leadership

The Pastoral Survey we used in our exploration was made up of three parts: information about the pastor's ministry, the Personal Profile (DISC) and the Myers Briggs (MBTI), and the Pastoral Leadership Audit (PLA). In this final phase, we'll observe the results of the Pastoral Leadership Audit to see if they provide any help in your becoming a re-envisioning pastor.

Step 1: Observe the Results of the PLA

Discovery 2 surfaced a number of identifiable characteristics of turnaround or re-envisioning pastors who took the PLA. Following is a list of what we discovered:

More a leader than a manager
Has a clear, compelling vision
More innovative than traditional
Outgoing
Above average people skills
Very energetic
Young in ministry, regardless of age
Team player
Delegator
An inspiring preacher and communicator

Exerts a strong influence in the church
Embraces change and innovation
A conflict resolver
A problem resolver
A visionary preacher
More directive than passive
Passionate vision communicator
Developer of new leaders
Empowers people to use their gifts
Is a self-starter
Has or has had a mentor or coach
Effective at leading various generations through change
Prepared to pay the price to lead change
Has led a church through a turnaround

All the pastors in our sample of re-envisioning pastors didn't reflect all these characteristics, nor did they have to. But the more of these characteristics they had, the better. (One pastor did reflect all but one of them.) Also non–re-envisioning pastors did reflect some but not many of the characteristics.

Step 2: Compare Your Characteristics

Look down the list of characteristics and mark those that you believe might be true of you and those that might not, based on what people say about you and what you've observed about yourself.

Step 3: Attempt to Validate Your Results

Since step 2 is fairly subjective, attempt to validate as best you can your results. The best way to validate your perceived results is to ask someone who knows you well, such as a spouse, lay leader, staff person, best friend, mentor, or coach, if they agree with your findings. If not, ask why they disagree. What would they change or correct?

Step 4: Attempt to Understand Your Results

The characteristics listed above are rather brief and self-explanatory. Thus this should not be a difficult step for you to pursue. If this is a problem, then go back to chapter 7 and review the twenty-four discoveries that we list there.

Step 5: Apply the Results to Your Life and Leadership

Now you need to apply the results to your life and leadership. What can you learn from the characteristics that will help you re-envision churches? Following are several applications.

Look back at the characteristics in the list that you checked, believing they are true or not true of you. Prioritize those which are not true of you in terms of importance. Then study them and be sure you understand what they mean.

Then note that these characteristics are skills and therefore learnable behaviors. The goal is to embrace as much as possible over time the characteristics that you do not share with re-envisioning pastors. The way to begin this process is to note those characteristics that you think will be fairly easy to absorb. Put at the top of your list those that may not require a lot of effort on you part. For example, it won't take too big an effort on your part to find a mentor or coach. This won't involve your changing or embracing some behavior, which can be more difficult than finding the right person for a mentor.

Finally, don't attempt to implement all of the unshared characteristics at once. Instead, start with a few—the ones you noted above as high priority—and focus on them. Which one, two, or three would result in the biggest gains for you in being or becoming a re-envisioning pastor? Make them a part of your personal leadership development plan, and discipline yourself to apply them in your life and ministry. Add others to your list as you find you're able to embrace them.

Questions for Reflection, Discussion, and Application

1. Do you believe that your temperament or type has changed over time since you took one or both of the tools? Why or why not? Do you agree with the authors' view that temperament doesn't change but as you get to know yourself better, your perception of your temperament changes? Why or why not? How well do you think you know yourself? If not well, how would you explain this?
2. Would you agree with the authors that it's important to validate your scores on the Personal Profile or Myers-Briggs? Why or why not? Has asking someone who knows you well about the results proved helpful

and reasonably accurate? Why or why not? Who has proved to be the most accurate source? Why? Who has proved least accurate? Why?

3. After reading the section on understanding one's results on the DISC and MBTI, do you feel that you understand them sufficiently to be of help to you? Why or why not? Do you believe that you need more explanation? If so, where would you get this information?
4. In this chapter, the authors address the topic of one's ability to change and become a re-envisioning pastor. They conclude that while this is possible, it depends on the leader. Do you agree or disagree with them? Why? Having read the chapter, do you believe that you could make some changes in your life and become a re-envisioning pastor or at least adopt some of their characteristics? Why or why not?
5. Do you believe at this point that you have a reasonably clear direction or plan in terms of becoming a re-envisioning pastor or more like one? Why or why not? If not, what do you believe might be missing? Note that each tool included a section on application. Did it help you to come up with a plan to absorb and implement the characteristics of a turnaround pastor? Do you need to go back and review those sections?
6. Are you a re-envisioning pastor? If so, have you found the information in this chapter helpful? How so? Has it confirmed your identity? Has it helped you focus on and hone some of your abilities?

10

How to Create and Cast a Compelling Vision

Haddon Robinson, the Harold John Ockenga Distinguished Professor of Preaching at Gordon-Conwell Theological Seminary, writes: "As Christian leaders we have something in common with Walt Disney. Soon after the completion of Disney World someone said, 'Isn't it too bad that Walt Disney didn't live to see this!' Mike Vance, creative director of Disney Studios, replied, 'He did see it—that's why it's here.'"[1]

But what is the *it*? The answer is a vision. First, Walt Disney had a vision of what Disney World would look like. Then once he had the vision, there was no stopping him, and Disney World was born.

One of the primary, leading characteristics of re-envisioning pastors is vision, as indicated by the terms *envision* and *re-envision*. Whereas the majority of pastors and churches have lost their vision along the way, re-envisioning pastors have a clear, exciting vision that prompts much of what they do in ministry and explains their growth. Of the twenty-five characteristics of re-envisioning pastors on the Pastoral Leadership Audit, three relate to vision.

Because vision is essential to the leadership of re-envisioning pastors and their churches and seems to be missing in non–re-envisioning pastors and their churches, we must include a chapter on vision if we're to equip non–re-envisioning pastors well and blow off any cobwebs for re-envisioning pastors who want to hone their skills. In this chapter we will address why a vision is so important to growing, maturing churches; we'll define *vision*; we'll identify the vision personnel or those who develop the church's vision; we'll learn the vision process or how to develop a vision; and finally, we will discuss how leaders cast vision.

The Importance of a Vision

THE IMPORTANCE OF A VISION
Vision Clarifies Direction
Vision Impacts Leadership
Vision Motivates People
Vision Prompts Giving
Vision Creates Energy
Vision Fosters Risk Taking
Vision Sustains Ministry

Vision is essential to any ministry whether church or parachurch. Ministry without a clear, God-inspired vision is futile, because it fails to articulate what God has called it to do. Thus it is crucial to the ministry of re-envisioning churches and their pastors. To attempt a revitalization of a church without a clear, compelling vision from God is like asking a surgeon to operate without a scalpel or a carpenter to build without a hammer. It simply won't happen. Following are seven reasons a vision is so important.

Vision Clarifies Direction

Two tools that should be in the pastor's tool kit are mission and vision. Both are critical because they address the church's direction. They answer in their own way the question, Where are we going? A church without some direction is much like a freighter out on the ocean going wherever the tides and currents take it. As someone has said, "If you aim at nothing, you'll hit it every time." This certainly applies to vision.

Leaders in the Bible demonstrated a clear, compelling vision from God that provided direction for them and their followers. For example, Moses' mission from God is found in Exodus 3:10, "So now, go. I am sending you to Pharaoh to bring my people the Israelites out of Egypt." His mission was clear: Lead God's people Israel out of Egypt. However, he needed a vision to help accomplish this mission. In Deuteronomy 8:7–9 he casts the vision:

> For the Lord your God is bringing you into a good land—a land with brooks, streams, and deep springs gushing into the valleys and hills; a land with wheat and barley, vines and fig trees, pomegranates, olive oil and honey; a land where bread will not be scarce and you will lack nothing; a land where the rocks are iron and you can dig copper out of the hills.

Congregants need to know where their pastors are leading them. The all-important question is, Where are we going, and what will it look like when we get there? It's important that the congregants know where they are headed in case they have some other direction in mind. The same is true for staff. Both the congregation and the staff must align with the church's direction or disaster will be the result. People will be moving in multiple directions and not the right direction and this normally leads to a church split.

When pastors cast a clear, compelling vision, not only do people know where they're going but where they're not going as well. Usually there are people in churches who have their own agendas for the church. One example is the Bible church movement. These people value good Bible teaching, and who could argue with that? The problem is that this is their vision for the church—simply teach the Bible. And as we'll see later, there must be more to the church's vision than good Bible teaching, as important as this is.

Vision Impacts Leadership

A question that many of us are asking in these days of church decline is, Where have all the leaders gone, especially leaders in our churches? As stated earlier in this book, 80–85 percent of our churches are plateaued or declining in attendance. While this is a bad omen for the future, what is it saying about our church leaders? We believe that 80–85 percent of these leaders are struggling because of the decline of their churches. They blame themselves as well as others in the church. And again we can point the finger at vision. Leaders are by definition visionaries. Our short definition of a leader is *a godly servant who knows where he or she is going and has followers*.

A leader is *a godly servant*; this focuses on his or her character. Jesus set the example in Matthew 20:28 when he said that he came not to be served but to serve. And he used the giving of his life as the illustration of his servanthood. For leaders, it's all about servanthood. And they are to be godly servant leaders. Godly character and servanthood walk hand in hand in the leader's life. The character qualifications that Paul provides for first-century house church pastors still apply today. They are found in 1 Timothy 3:1–7 and Titus 1:6–9.

Because our definition includes the requirement of *followers*, it gets to the heart of leadership. Leaders have followers. When they pause to look behind them, they see people. And the best way to summarize this is influence. If you want a one-word definition of leadership, it would be *influence*.

In the middle of the definition we see *direction*—a leader knows where he or she is going. Direction includes the leader's mission and vision, which are twofold. First, the leader's mission and vision should be the church's mission and vision. (And the congregation must have the same mission and vision.) Second, leaders should have a personal mission and vision that address the direction of their lives. This is God's will for their lives. It could be the pastorate or some other form of Christian ministry.

Without a vision, one's leadership would be seriously impaired. Without vision, the re-envisioning pastor is shortsighted. Rather than 20–20 vision, it will be off the charts in a negative direction. A pastor without vision will not be able to paint a picture of where he is going, much less where the church is going.

Vision Motivates People

As we said above, a leader's direction consists of both his or her mission and vision. But what's the difference between the leader's mission and vision in terms of function? First, mission defines where the church and ultimately its leaders—especially the pastor—are going. Jesus has given his church its mission in Matthew 28:19 and a number of other texts. The church's mission is to make disciples. This includes evangelism, winning people to Christ, and edification, growing people up or maturing them in Christ.

While this mission to some degree may motivate the congregation, it is the vision that must be the motivator. Congregants respond in various ways to the church's mission. Some will be motivated and some will not. Just because a church has a mission doesn't mean that everyone will be excited about it. That's the job of the vision and the vision caster. The vision paints a picture of what the church will look like when it arrives at or accomplishes its mission. The painter of the picture is the vision caster. The mission clarifies the church's future, while the vision inspires people to want to go there. The vision should get people excited, rallying them to go where the mission directs.

Vision Prompts Giving

A church's vision not only motivates people to want to accomplish the mission, it motivates people to give their finances in response to and in support of the mission. Vision is the key to giving. Those of us involved in Christian education discovered this early. People didn't respond well to requests for funds to pay the light bill or faculty salaries. Certainly some would respond to these appeals, but only so often. People do not want to give regularly to bail out a ministry that's constantly in the red. Let's face it, who wants to support any organization that is adrift in debt? But people do respond to appeals in the context of vision. At Dallas Seminary, we raise funds that provide scholarships for international students. We've found that's not difficult. Many of our international students are leaders in churches and even the government in the countries they are from. We make our constituency aware of this with the result that they want to be a part of this ministry.

People are motivated to give to churches and organizations that project a clear, compelling vision of what they believe is God's future for them. The vision announces loudly that the church isn't static but dynamic. It's not stuck somewhere in the past but going somewhere in the future. Vision announces not only that God is doing something now, but that the best is yet to come. People are willing to invest their finances when they know the investment will reap a rich return.

An exciting response to the vision is that it motivates people to give not only their finances but their time and talent as well. Both are vital to any ministry's future. Most ministries, churches in particular, depend heavily on volunteers, and it is vision that contributes the most to people offering their time and talents to ministry.

Vision Creates Energy

One lesson that I (Gordon) learned in studying re-visioning leaders is that they need large doses of energy to accomplish the vision. It takes energy to accomplish ministry, especially when leading a church through a turnaround. You often encounter opposition and other obstacles that tend to wear you down and deplete your energy.

Unfortunately not much happens without a clear, inspiring vision of the ministry's future. This was true in Nehemiah's day. The Israelites had no vision. Jerusalem lay in ruins with the result that the people had become lethargic. They needed a hot, steaming cup of vision to wake them up, to energize them, and get them moving. Then along came an energetic Nehemiah with a mission and vision from God that involved rebuilding the gates and walls of Jerusalem. And it happened.

A good, well-articulated vision not only excites but energizes people. It supplies the fuel that lights the fire under a congregation; it enables leaders to stop putting out fires and start igniting fires. And it has the potential to turn a maintenance mentality into a badly needed ministry mentality.

But how do visions generate energy? One way is that they inspire people. The vision of people coming to faith and developing spiritually touches leaders and moves them to action. This is what's supposed to happen, and when it does, it's energizing. Another way is that a vision challenges people. On the one hand, far too many Christians have languished in ministry because no one has challenged them, including their pastors, to charge the enemy's fortresses. On the other hand, it's energizing to think of the number of outstanding pastors today who are leading spiritually mature churches because someone took the time to challenge and energize them early in their spiritual development.

Vision Fosters Risk Taking

Two words that rarely go together are risk and church ministry. We find it so difficult to step out in faith and trust God because it involves some element of risk and we tend to be risk aversive. However, a shared compelling vision fosters congregational risk taking, making ministry in the name of Christ an exciting venture of faith into the mystery of God's unknown plan and will for the life of our churches.

Unlike Gideon, though, we must not ask for any kind of guarantee from God. He doesn't work that way. Instead, we move forward by faith, knowing the risks at times can be great. This is especially true when God directs us to plant a church. I (Aubrey) believe that God would have all of our churches plant churches some time during their life and this will entail some kind of risk. It was how the early church accomplished the Great Commission. I'm also convinced that God would have us re-envision struggling churches that have lost their vision. Churches don't have to struggle, and when they do, there are clear reasons why. One of these reasons is lack of vision. So let's address these clear reasons and get on with church planting and revitalization. Church planting and revitalization are faith ventures that invite us to take risks—often big risks—for God. And it's a clear, compelling vision from God that will walk us through whatever risks we have to take.

Vision Sustains Ministry

While it may come as a surprise to parishioners, those who pastor and lead churches agree that ministry can be very difficult, even painful at times. Some seminarians go into pastoral ministry thinking that all it entails is teaching the Bible and loving everybody. They are so naïve, and in my (Aubrey's) job, I have to address this. Pastoral ministry in general and re-envisioning churches in particular can be very hard work. Often discouragement and disappointment lurk in the church's hallways and boardrooms, especially in struggling ministries that are on the downside of the organizational growth curve. Add to this the fact that our Enemy incites persecution against Christ's church and its pastors (Acts 8:1). Also spiritual warfare comes with the ministry territory, though we're seldom aware of it (see Eph. 6:10–18 for how we are to arm ourselves against spiritual warfare).

Along with accounts of persecution in the Bible, a study of church history reveals a long list of martyrs for the faith; see the book of Acts, for example. Christians began dying for their faith in biblical times and still do today. Hardly a week goes by that we don't hear of some form of persecution of Christ's church, including acts of martyrdom. We must ask, What has sustained believers from the early church up to the present? What has kept people like Peter, Paul, James, Calvin, Luther, Billy Graham, Chuck Swindoll, and others on the ministry track? The answer, as you expected by now, is vision. It challenges believers to look beyond the pain and the mundane. It constantly holds out a picture of what could be. When we focus on Christ and his vision for us—his church—we find that we're able to rise above the ministry pain and mundane. Christ's vision holds out a wonderful picture of hope and invites us to hang in there spiritually. It's a wonderful story with a happy ending, and we must never forget that, especially when ministry seems impossible.

The Definition of *Vision*

THE DEFINITION OF *VISION*
What a Vision Is Not
What a Vision Is
The Vision Audit

I (Aubrey) enjoy going to a good church conference or a seminar led by some of our outstanding Christian leaders, but I bring to these meetings a pet gripe. It's not unusual for these leaders to articulate terms without defining them, terms such as *vision, culture, leaders* and *leadership, mission, the missional church, systems*, and *kingdom,* to name a few. My fear is that though we all use these terms, we may all mean something different by them. The danger is that we're not talking about the same thing and, even worse, we aren't aware of it. This calls for communication clarity. We need to take time in our seminars and writings to define or explain precisely what we're talking about. We need to articulate the definitions for these terms. So we want here to define what we mean by the term *vision*. It may help if we first clarify what a vision isn't and then define what a vision is, and include what we refer to as the vision audit.

What a Vision Is Not

Often we hear people confusing *vision* with a dream, goals and objectives, or the purpose and the mission of the church.

A vision is not the same as a dream. The problem is that Dr. Martin Luther King Jr. used the term *dream* for *vision* in his famous "I Have a Dream" speech. Thus when people hear the word *vision*, they may think of a dream. From time to time I (Aubrey) too find myself using *dream* as a synonym for *vision*.

So am I "nitpicking" here or are there some real differences between a vision and a dream as we use it? First, I believe that dreams are bigger than or more encompassing than visions. We may begin our envisioning process with a dream. For example, we may find it helpful to ask, What do you dream about when you think of the future of this ministry? But we must not stop there. We take the dream that is broader, more expansive than a dream, and fashion it into a vision. Thus our dreams initiate or fuel our visions but aren't the same. Visions are the product of people who dream great dreams for God.

A vision is not goals and objectives. One distinction between the terms is emotional. *Goals* and *objectives* are emotionally cold terms. On the one hand, these terms do not warm the heart, which is important to a vision. On the other hand, *vision* should serve to melt the coldest heart. It has a positive emotional impact on people. Another distinction is that, just as a dream precedes vision, so vision precedes goals and objectives. You develop the vision first and then follow it up with goals and objectives that serve to ultimately implement the vision. Hence there is a single vision with multiple goals and objectives.

A vision is not the same as a purpose. It is very common in the corporate or business world to confuse the vision and especially the mission with the organization's purpose. While this may be a practice in the business world, it should not be done in the church. The purpose of the church is broader than the vision and the mission. The purpose is why the church exists. It gets at the church's raison d'être. I believe that the Bible teaches that the purpose of the church is to glorify God (Rom. 15:6; 1 Cor. 6:20), whereas the mission and vision concern the Great Commission.

A vision is not the same as the ministry's mission. The ministry's mission is a clear statement of where the organization is going. The vision is a snapshot of what it will look like when the church gets there. The function of the mission is planning; the function of the vision is communicating that plan. The length of the mission is short—it should be stated in a few words that can easily fit on a business card; the vision statement may be as short as the mission or several pages long. The purpose of the mission is to inform; the vision's purpose is to inspire. The source of the mission is the head, but that of the vision is the heart. Finally, we develop mission and vision differently. Developing a mission is a science in the sense that it can be objectively taught. The vision is an art in that it comes from the heart and is more caught than taught.

Summary of Differences between a Mission and a Vision

	Mission	Vision
Definition	statement	snapshot
Function	planning	communication
Length	short	short or long
Purpose	informs	inspires
Source	head	heart
Development	taught	caught

What a Vision Is

WHAT A VISION IS
A vision is clear.
A vision is exciting.
A vision is a picture.
A vision is God's vision.
A vision is future focused.
A vision can be.
A vision must be.

Now that we have eliminated a number of terms or concepts that are often confused with vision, we are ready for a definition. *Vision is a clear, exciting picture of God's future for your ministry as you believe it can and must be.* This definition consists of six key concepts.

First, *a vision is clear*. I refer to this as vision clarity. The church's mission statement is not clear because it is short. While you want to keep it short so that the congregation will remember it, this works against clarity. You walk away from the mission statement wanting more information. The fact that the vision is longer encourages clarity. You can say more in the vision statement, which can sharpen and focus its message.

A vision is exciting. When you hear the vision cast, it should excite you to want to be a part of it, to want the church's future to be your future. It makes you feel good about the church's direction because it captivates and moves you. It's like caffeine for the soul— it has the potential to keep you up at night.

A vision is a picture. It's a portrait of the church's future. You see what it will look like when the church arrives at the vision. It's also how you will know that you've reached the vision—you can see it. This takes us back to the beginning of this chapter to Mike Vance's response to the person who was lamenting Walt Disney's death before the completion of Disney World. The individual states, "Isn't it too bad that Walt Disney didn't live to see this?" To which Vance responds, "He did see it—that's why it's here."

In my (Aubrey's) book on vision, I have a cartoon with two Eskimos standing out in a searing hot desert. One says to the other, "We'll build the igloo here!" When discussing the seeing aspect of vision, I like to use the cartoon with my audience and ask them what they see in it? Their answer is "Two Eskimos, cacti, desert, the sun," and so forth. Then I tell them, "The vision question isn't what do you see; the vision question is what do the Eskimos see?" Of course the answer is an igloo. That's vision!

A vision is God's vision for your church. Our vision must be God's vision for our future. How do we know what God's vision is? One way is to ask, Does our vision align with Scripture? If not, it can't be God's vision. To be God's vision, it must be too big for us to pull off on our own—it has to be of God or it doesn't happen. If it's God's vision, you will be passionate about it. If you feel strongly and care deeply about the vision, then likely it is God's vision and captures your heart.

A vision is future focused. Every church has a past, a present, and a future. Most churches, 80–85 percent, are living in the past. This can be described as attempting to drive forward by looking in the rearview mirror. That's difficult if not impossible. Some churches are living in the present, but the church's vision is a picture of its future. It's a clear statement of the church's future. No matter where it has been or where it is now, the vision is where it's going and what it will be when it gets there.

You believe that the vision can be a reality. For you the vision drips with potential. You believe it can be, that it can happen, so you have no plan B. Perhaps this is best summed up by Robert Kennedy who said, "Some people see things the way they are and ask why; I see things the way they could be and ask why not."

Finally, *you not only believe that the vision can be, you believe that it must be*. This is the passion part. Since passion is what you care deeply about, what you feel strongly about, it's the emotional element of the vision, touching your very soul! Your passion will see that the vision comes to fruition or is implemented.

The Vision Audit

By checking our vision against the elements of the vision definition, we can determine if our final vision meets the criteria of a good vision statement. Answer the following questions about your vision.

Is the vision clear? Do people understand it?
Is it exciting? Do people get excited when they hear it?
Is it a picture of the future? Can people see it?
Is it God's vision for the church?
Is it future focused?
Do people believe that it can be? Is it feasible?
Are you convinced that it must be? Are you passionate about it?

The Vision Personnel

When working with a church, I (Aubrey) task the lead pastor, staff, and a lay team with developing the ministry's vision. By lay team I mean some kind of implementation team (we say more about this in steps 3 and 4 in chapter 11). I believe that the lead pastor should take primary responsibility for both developing and implementing the vision. I like to refer to him as the "keeper of the vision." Visions need "keepers" or they will get lost along the way. When the pastor takes this role, it sends the message that he is fully supportive of the vision concept.

Vision personnel, including the pastor, will score as sensing or intuitive types on the Myers-Briggs. Sensing type people are the practical, hands-on realists. They have a vision but arrive at it in a different way. They are "vision catchers." They outnumbered the intuitive types in our exploration. While the intuitive types see the vision naturally in their heads as "vision creators," sensing types have to see it literally with their eyes—they perceive it through their five senses. Thus they "catch" a vision by actually, physically visiting a church where they can see, smell, taste, and touch the vision. They are able to form their vision as they walk the church's corridors and experience its ministries. The intuitive types (Ns) are the abstract, imaginative, natural visionaries. For them vision is a sixth sense. They create or "catch" a vision and carry it around in their heads. Both can be vision personnel, only they arrive at it differently. So which are you? Use the assessment in appendix H to find out.

The problem the intuitive types face is that they tend to be dreamers who spend much of their time dreaming about the vision and they never get around to implementing the vision. The advantage the sensing types have is that they get to work on the vision. They get it done.

The Envisioning Process

THE ENVISIONING PROCESS
Step 1: Pray Envisioning Prayers
Step 2: Think *Big*!
Step 3: Connect Emotionally with the Vision
Step 4: Decide on the Vision's Contents
Step 5: Determine the Vision's Length
Step 6: Answer the Vision Question

At this point you should be convinced that a vision is important, that it's crucial to any ministry in general and the church in particular. You also know what a vision is. Now you are ready to address the envisioning process—developing a vision for your church, which desperately needs a large dose of vision. The answer is the following six-step process.

Step 1: Pray Envisioning Prayers

We begin where everything Christian begins—with prayer. We must bathe the entire process in constant prayer. In the case of vision development, it is envisioning prayer. It is the place where Nehemiah began when he discovered the state of the Jewish remnant that survived the exile and the state of Jerusalem (Neh. 1:1–11). It's primarily a prayer for God to give him favor with the reigning pagan king Artaxerxes as Nehemiah went to him to seek permission to pursue his vision—to return to and rebuild the city of Jerusalem (2:11, 5). In the same manner, it is biblically acceptable for us as well to pray for God's favor as we seek to convince our people of his vision for their future. It's imperative that God intervene if the vision is to catch and become a reality.

Step 2: Think Big!

The next step of vision development is to think *big*! I suspect that some may view this as presumption on our part. However, small churches tend not to motivate their people to ministry—that is why they remain small. Paul challenges his Christian community to pray and think big in Ephesians 3:20 when he writes, "Now to Him who is able to do far more abundantly beyond all that we ask or think, according to the power that works within us." Paul seems to be saying that we're not thinking big enough when it comes to what God can do in and through our churches. Should I (Aubrey) plant another church, I would need to think bigger than I have in the past. For example, I would envision reaching Dallas rather than a few people in some part of Dallas. God could reach Dallas through me and a team by our planting church-planting churches. These are churches that would, once they're started, plant other churches all over Dallas—its inner city, suburbs, and rural parts.

J. B. Phillips, who was an English Bible scholar, author, translator, and pastor, wrote the book *Your God Is Too Small*. Is that true of our God? I suspect that the way to find out would be to listen to our prayers. Are we praying to a big God or a small God? Someone once said, "Make no small plans, for they have not the power to stir the souls of men." So what might our plans say about us? Do they have the power to stir the souls of our people?

Step 3: Connect Emotionally with the Vision

Does your vision language connect with your people at an emotional level? Does it engage the heart and touch the emotions? Is the language "image-laden"—does it use similes and metaphors that create mental pictures? A biblical example is God's vision, found in Deuteronomy 8:7–9, which was given to Moses and ultimately Israel found in the Promised Land. We examined it earlier in this chapter as a biblical example of a vision statement. Here note the language and terms Moses uses to convey the vision statement: *brooks, streams, deep springs gushing into the valleys*, and so forth.

> For the Lord your God is bringing you into a good land—a land with brooks, streams, and deep springs gushing into the valleys and hills; a land with wheat and barley, vines and fig trees, pomegranates, olive oil and honey; a land where bread will not be scarce and you will lack nothing.

When working with a strategic planning group, after reading this I like to ask, "Can anyone not visualize this? Can you not see it?" Another descriptive phrase for the Promised Land is "a land flowing with milk and honey." Moses' vision is more literal, while these words are more symbolic. He's telling the people that this will be a wonderful place, and they will enjoy it just like they enjoy their favorite dessert—milk mixed with honey.

Another great example is Dr. Martin Luther King's "I Have a Dream" speech. In it he connects emotionally by using such terms and figures as "the sons of former slaves and the sons of former slave owners." White and black people will both connect with this as it reflects a former way of life that was often brutal and repressive for black people. Then in his speech King has them sitting down together at a table—it's not a literal table but the table of brotherhood. Finally, he describes Mississippi as "a desert state sweltering with the heat of injustice and oppression," and says it will be "transformed into an oasis of freedom and justice." Not only do you see it in your head but you feel and connect with it emotionally.

When you write your vision, be creative. Let your creative juices flow. Of all the steps for developing your vision, this likely will be the most difficult for you—especially if you tend not to be a good writer. Because of this, you would be wise to have at least one good writer on the vision development team.

Step 4: Decide on the Vision's Contents

This step asks, What will go into your vision statement? What will you include in it? There are a number of possibilities that would convey the vision you see. Following are some: the church's desire to reach its community, its vision for making disciples, its dream for mobilizing the congregation, its vision for staffing, its vision for its future location and facilities, its vision for stewardship. What will these look like in the future? What do you see when you contemplate each one? Some more possibilities are your mission statement, core values, size, creativity/innovation, prayer, technology, multicultural goals, social issues, treatment of outsiders, church planting, multisite ministry, missions, various types of ministries, areas of passion, and so forth.

Step 5: Determine the Vision's Length

You need to decide if the statement of your vision will be short or long. If short, how short? If long, how long? This will be determined by all that you wish to include in the statement. When churches write a mission statement, we recommend that they make it short—short enough to fit on a business card. This encourages people to remember the church's mission, and that is what you want.

The same could hold true for the vision statement. Research in both the business and church worlds reveals that a number have opted for the shorter vision statement—one or two sentences. Others, however, have opted to include more details in their statement, making it one to two pages.

The chart on page 160 lists the advantages, the disadvantages, and an advocate of each.

Who will make this decision regarding the length of the vision? We believe the decision rests with the pastor. This does not exclude much input from his elders, deacons, or vision development team. Yet as the chief vision caster, he needs to be comfortable with as well as excited about the final vision. According to our current culture, people will look to him for the vision, even though others will be involved in articulating it.

The Longer Vision	The Shorter Vision
The advantage of the longer vision is *clarity*. Saying more should lead to clarity, though this is not always the case if the writer gets too wordy.	The advantage of a shorter vision is that *people will remember it*.
A disadvantage of the longer vision is that it's *not as easy to remember*. No one is going to commit a one- to two-page vision statement to memory. They may memorize some of it but not all of it.	A disadvantage of the shorter vision statement is its *lack of clarity*. A one- or two-sentence statement doesn't give you a lot to go on and it *may be confused with the mission statement*.
Rick Warren's initial vision statement (found in his book *The Purpose Driven Church*) for Saddleback Church is around one page and is a great example of a longer vision statement.	*Andy Stanley*'s vision statement is one sentence—"To create a church that unchurched people love to attend." His mission statement is quite different—"To lead people into a growing relationship with Christ."

Step 6: Answer the Vision Question

The vision question is this: Will you be a church simply with a vision statement or a truly visionary church? In other words, if someone inquires about the vision of your church, will you need to go to the church office and look in the filing cabinet under *V*? Or will you be able to articulate it clearly from memory and with excitement?

Following are five characteristics of a visionary church.

CHARACTERISTICS OF A VISIONARY CHURCH
People are excited about the vision.
People want to be a part of the vision.
People speak favorably about the vision.
The vision impacts all the church's major decisions.
Some people leave the church.

1. People are excited about the vision. The mission announces where the church is going; the vision gets them excited about going there.
2. People want to be a part of the vision. They like what they see and want to invest their lives in being a part of it.
3. People are talking favorably about the vision. If you listen carefully, you can hear it being discussed in the church's hallways, parking lot, and the kitchen.
4. The vision, along with the mission, truly impacts all the church's major decisions. In making any decision, the questions are asked: How will this affect our mission and vision? And how do they speak to or into this decision?
5. Some people will leave the church. No matter what your vision says, some will be unhappy with it. In fact, if everybody is happy with the

vision, then something may be wrong with it. Visions are like that. They can divide a congregation as well as unite one. Some people don't want to reach out to the lost, especially if they're from the other side of the tracks. Some people don't want any change, no matter what that may be. Their motto is, "Come weal or come woe, our status is quo."

Communicating the Vision

VISION CASTING
The Leader's Life
Visual Images
Ministries
Sermons
Vision Statement
Annual Staff Evaluations
Language and Metaphor
Newcomers Class
Brochure

If you aren't able to articulate the vision, then no one will be able to act on it. You might as well not have one. You must cast the vision if people are going to catch it, and you must cast it regularly and repeatedly. Most vision casters agree that it takes only about a month for people to forget the vision. The general rule is to repeat it over and over every day in a different way. This will be a primary responsibility of the pastor. If he's a re-envisioning pastor, he will do this well. If he isn't, then he'll need to work hard at learning how to vision cast. There is hope here. We believe that a non–re-envisioning pastor can become a re-envisioning pastor. Following are a number of practical ways to cast the vision.

The Leader's Life

The leader's life communicates the ministry's vision. He must live the vision. He must personify the dream. This happens when he models the vision. To accomplish this, he must own the vision himself. This is the reason it is so important that not only should he be involved in developing the vision (its length and wording) but he must have a big say in what it is and how it is communicated. The vision should so motivate him that he finds himself constantly dreaming, thinking, and talking about it. When the leader personifies the vision, several things happen. He models visionary behavior for the ministry team, whether it is a strategic planning team, a vision development team, the staff, or a board. They will be watching him to see if he really practices what he preaches when it comes to living the vision. Also his visionary lifestyle brings credibility to him and the vision. The congregation and others will constantly observe his life for evidence of vision credibility.

Visual Images

Visual images are a most effective means for casting the vision. They function not to communicate the vision by itself but to call attention to a dream that already has and is being communicated. Often they serve to touch the senses as well as the intellect. Different images affect people in different ways. Some impact younger people more than older people, and vice versa, so a variety of images is needed.

Video Presentation

The video presentation communicates effectively with both a younger and an older audience. Problems with the slide-tape presentation is it takes a lot of time and work to produce and it is being left behind by the newest technology. So be aware of this should you choose to use it.

Well-Designed Logo

The power of a good logo to communicate is found in the following quote from an article in the newspaper: "The McDonalds's logo—an arched M—and the shell used by an international petroleum company ranked higher in recognizability than the Christian cross according to a survey of 7,000 people in six countries [including the United States]."[2] Logos are easy and inexpensive to create and reproduce. The idea is that a logo should be so memorable that every time people see it, whether in a bulletin, a video presentation, a newsletter, or your website, they remember what it refers to—your vision.

Website and Social Media

Young people and some older people would expect to see the vision on the church's website. You could also communicate it via social media—Twitter, Facebook, and so on. You would be wise not to disappoint them.

Ministries

A church's ministries communicate its vision. So if a church's vision includes evangelism, it will have several evangelistic ministries. If it's discipleship, it will have a number of discipleship ministries. What it does speaks louder than what it says. Consequently, a church must be careful to back up its vision with its ministries. If evangelism is part of its vision yet there is no evangelism ministry, people will write off the vision as an exercise in futility.

Sermons

The sermon is an excellent medium for casting the church's vision. This almost goes without saying. And every sermon has the potential to communicate the vision either directly or indirectly. The pastor can preach a sermon that focuses directly on the vision or he may allude to it in some way. An example of the latter is to make heroes out of those congregants who live out the vision. If the vision includes disciple making, then he would hold up the church's disciple makers as heroes of the faith.

The pastor could also use a vision sermon in the context of a vision night or a vision Sunday when the focus is strictly on the vision. The pastor would use this opportunity to cast the vision and let people know how well the church is doing in implementing the vision.

Vision Statement

We encourage you in the development of your vision to write it down initially as a vision statement. It should be no longer than a page, or at the most two pages. Then you can place it on your website, in a brochure, and so forth. However, keep in mind that it is more effective when you verbally articulate or preach it than when people read it.

Annual Staff Evaluations

You should expect your ministry staff not only to align with the vision but to communicate it as well. And you can use your staff evaluations to encourage them to do so, reminding them that casting the church's vision is part of their job description. And whenever you hold your staff reviews or evaluations, one of your questions should be, How and how often have you communicated the vision over the last year?

Language and Metaphor

We were surprised when we first learned that Disney World hires no employees. We wondered how they could carry on their entertainment business. Then we were told they don't hire employees, they hire a cast. They consider all of their employees part of their cast. Whether Snow White or the person who empties the trash, they are viewed as an important part of the show and are referred to as *cast*. That is part of Disney's vision.

The same could be true of the church. For example, you might refer to your people as missionaries rather than members. Thus they will self-identify as evangelists who are critical to realizing the evangelistic aspects of the vision.

Newcomers Class

A number of churches conduct a newcomers class. Typically it introduces new people to the church—its beliefs and practices. It catches them at a time when they are interested in the church and says, "Come and check us out!" It also affords the church the opportunity to communicate to them its vision and the importance of it. People can listen intently to and ask questions about the vision and they can do so before they have made a commitment to be members.

Brochure

We commented on this above when discussing writing down and verbalizing the church's vision statement. A well-designed, attractive brochure can be an effective means of casting the church's vision—especially when it is a page or less in length. Having a professionally produced brochure is important in our age of information when the public demands to know something about the church, often even before they attend. Having a brochure allows you to put the vision in their hands.

Questions for Reflection, Discussion, and Application

1. At the beginning of this chapter, the authors make their case for the importance of a vision. Did they convince you? Why or why not? Can you think of some other reasons why a vision is important to you and your church? If so, what are they?
2. The authors define the vision as a clear, exciting picture of God's future for your ministry as you believe it can and must be. Was the authors' clarification of what isn't a vision helpful in determining what is? Why or why not? Do you think this definition is accurate? Why or why not? If not, what would your definition be? What would you change and why?
3. Were the authors' six steps in developing a vision helpful? Why or why not? Did you disagree with any of them? If so, explain your disagreement. Did you find any extremely helpful? If so, which ones? Do you agree with the authors' interpretation of Ephesians 3:20? Why or why not? Do you believe that it's presumptive on our part to cast a large vision? Do you

believe that the size of your vision is indicative of the size of your God? Why or why not?

4. Are you a good writer? Are people attracted to your style? How might this affect the wording of your vision? Do you agree with the authors that in general this step could be the most difficult? Why or why not?
5. While you may not yet have started developing your vision, what do you think will be some of the important contents that will go into your vision? Did you find the authors' list helpful? Why or why not? What might you add to the list?
6. Which do you think is best, a long or short vision statement? Why? In your opinion, what are the advantages and disadvantages of both? Who should make the decision about the length of the vision statement? Why?
7. How would you answer the vision question? How would your church answer the question? How do you hope they will answer it? How do you really feel about people becoming upset and leaving the church over the vision? Why? Non–re-envisioning pastors struggle with this. What does your response say about you?
8. The authors mention several practical ways to cast vision. Which did you find most helpful? Why? Which were not very helpful? Why? Would you add any that the authors didn't mention?

11

Creating a Culture for Change

In this chapter we discuss the church culture. As you've seen, we want to be clear about our terms, so we will define what we mean by *culture*. Before we do that, though, we will make a case for the importance of culture in the life of the church—especially if it is to change for the better. In this chapter we will also address the kind of envisioning leader who can lead the church through change. Finally, we will discuss how non–re-envisioning pastors, as well as re-envisioning pastors, can lead a church through the process of change and thus create a culture for change.

The Importance of Culture

THE IMPORTANCE OF CULTURE
Culture Affects Everyone
Culture Is Vital to Effective Ministry
Culture Affects the Way We Do Church
Culture Recognizes Ethnic Diversity
Culture Cannibalizes Strategy
Culture Impacts Churches Differently
Culture Adapts to Change

Most of us sense intuitively that culture is important but do we know why and can we articulate it? Following are some reasons why it is imperative that we understand and acknowledge the importance culture has in relation to change in our ministries.

Culture Affects Everyone

We all live in and thus have a culture, and none of us can separate ourselves from our culture. We are a part of it, and it is a part of us. However, most people are not aware of the profound and subtle effect it has on us. We use it to bring order to our lives, to interpret our daily experiences, to validate what we believe, and to evaluate behavior—both our own and that of others. And most of this takes place at an unconscious level—we're hardly aware of it.

Culture Is Vital to Effective Ministry

We must understand culture in general if we are to minister effectively to people. When there is a group of people with a different culture who live near us, we need to gain specific understanding of that culture if we are to reach them with the gospel. This will happen more easily when we are not only aware of their culture but when we learn how it is similar to or strikingly different from our own.

Language is a vital element of culture. If we speak English in a neighborhood that speaks only Spanish, we will not connect. This is what has happened to many of our neighborhoods in America in general and some of the states bordering Mexico in particular (Texas, New Mexico, and Arizona). A number of churches were planted by Anglos in Anglo communities to reach Anglos, but in time the Anglos moved out of the community and were replaced by Spanish-speaking people. The churches that failed to adjust to the new culture have died or are in the process of dying. The solution is to read and then adjust to the culture, or there won't be any ministry. This is Paul's challenge in 1 Corinthians 9:19–23. An example from the mission field is a tribe of Indians in Papua, New Guinea, who pride themselves in betrayal. In their culture it's okay. Therefore, when they read about Judas's betrayal of Jesus, they virtually cheer for Judas.

Culture Affects the Way We Do Church

Our own unique culture—both past and present—has shaped much of our practice of the faith or how we do church. (I suspect that it may affect what we believe or hold as biblical doctrine as well.) For example, most of our older, traditional churches across North America were "made in Europe" and thus were modeled after a European church culture. Many of these people prefer a church building that "looks like a church." Being translated, this means that the building has arches and columns with a steeple and a cross on top. Their organization is hierarchical, and their clergy is likely well-educated. Their dress is probably rather formal for the services, women in skirts and men in coats and ties. And all this is just how they did church in Europe. Is this wrong? Not at all. It is cultural.

We should be concerned, though, if churches believe that they're doing church as it was done in the first century, and everyone else should do the same. This is wrong, according to 1 Corinthians 9:19–23. Such churches fail to change in ways that will help them reach those who are part of a different culture.

The same can be said about our churches that are "made in America." They have been influenced by an American church culture. For example, their organization is more horizontal, they dress less formally, and the pastors may or may not be well-educated. These practices are not wrong—they are cultural—but they can prevent churches from reaching people for Christ.

Culture Recognizes Ethnic Diversity

America has become a global, multicultural nation. In the past, corporate America conducted business mostly on American soil. Now they do so globally and this practice is expanding rapidly all over the world. At the same time, the nation is no longer a melting pot, it is a salad bowl made up of all kinds of vegetables. It is important for the church to make ourselves aware and accepting of differences due to ethnic diversity. We must be careful about our terminology, be willing to accept people who are not like us, and work at understanding and even cherishing what they bring to the body. For the church, it is imperative that it asks the important question, What are our plans to minister effectively to all these people in the name of Christ?

Culture Cannibalizes Strategy

It is essential that churches do strategic planning. We hear some voices out there that argue that churches no longer need to plan strategically. What they should be saying is that churches should no longer attempt to do and rely on long-term planning. Our world is changing too quickly for long-term planning to be effective. Strategic planning that involves thinking and acting strategically will always be useful. Just as Paul planned and operated strategically in his missionary journeys of the first century, so today's churches must follow suit.

As important as strategic planning is to the impact of the church (the past, present, or future), culture "eats strategy for lunch." You can have the world's best strategic plan in place but if you don't have a healthy culture—one consisting of biblical values and beliefs—it won't make a difference. This is because culture feeds on strategy. It controls and dictates a ministry's strategy. A good culture results in a good strategy; a bad culture results in a bad strategy. A culture supplies the beliefs and values that direct a strategy. Yes, culture is that important.

Culture Impacts Churches Differently

The pastor or church revitalizer who is called to an existing church will experience culture differently than the church planter. The pastor whose vision is to revitalize a church is joining a church that already has a culture in place. What that means is that he will need to read that preexisting culture to understand it and impact it. We call it exegeting the culture. Just as we exegete the Scriptures to understand what they mean, so we must exegete the church to understand its culture and ultimately lead it to change and re-envision itself. In this situation pastors function not as cultural custodians but as culture sculptors. They aren't there to simply maintain the preexisting culture but to shape and change it for the better.

Church planters are culture creators or architects. Rather than adopt a preexisting situation, they create their own. Unlike the culture sculptor, they are there first. Other people are joining them, not vice versa. This means that the church planter has a lot of say about the church's culture. And often that culture will look like the culture of a church that has highly influenced the planter or the architect. He may have come to faith in that church or it may have had a profound impact on his life. It was under its ministry that he committed his life to Christ. And if it worked for him in that church, he believes it should work for him in the new church.

Culture Adapts to Change

The external environment that the Bible sometimes refers to as the *world* bears down on churches and can pose a threat to their very existence. Thus it is critical to the church that it learn how to cope with that constantly changing external environment. The culture that works hard at reading and adapting to these changes is more likely to survive them. If it can't or does not know how to change, it will not survive. But the church that reads and adjusts to the culture will not only survive but thrive spiritually. And it is the job of the rest of this book to help you thrive.

The Definition of Culture

Before you read our definition of *culture*, humor us by doing a little exercise. Take a short break from reading and write out your definition of *culture*. What did you come up with? Did you find this difficult, if not frustrating? What picture forms in your mind when you see or hear the word? The answer most likely is nothing. No, we are not playing mind games. It is an abstract term that is hard to wrap your mind around. Don't feel dumb should you not be able to come up with a definition, even though you probably hear the term every day. You are not alone. A colleague believes that there are more than two hundred different definitions of *culture*.

So what are we talking about when we use the term *culture*? In this book we are defining what we refer to as congregational or organizational culture. We believe that our definition applies to culture in general but we don't want to take the time to develop this idea in this chapter. We will take the same approach to defining culture as we did with vision. First, we'll identify what it isn't, then what it is.

What Culture Is Not

We are aware of a number of misconceptions that some well-meaning Christians have of the culture concept that have led to wrong thinking and unfair criticism of certain church models of ministry.

WHAT CULTURE IS NOT
Culture is not inherently evil
Culture is not a product of the fall
Culture is not independent of the Godhead
Culture is not temporal
Culture is not always good
Culture is not an end in itself

Culture Is Not Inherently Evil

Perhaps the most common misperception is that culture is inherently evil. Hardly a day goes by that some well-meaning but naïve Bible teacher or pastor confuses it with Satan's world system. This represents a total misunderstanding of what Scripture teaches about Satan's world system and culture. The Scriptures teach that there is a system at work in our world. We refer to it as the *world* or *worldliness*. You'll find mention of it in Matthew 16:26; John 15:19; 18:36; 1 Cor. 3:19; and elsewhere. However, we are the ones who attempt to connect it to culture. The Bible doesn't make this connection. And this same confusion prevails when we talk about cultural relevance. Some interpret this as saying that we need to be like the world, which is hardly the case. We will say more about this later in this chapter.

Culture Is Not a Product of the Fall

Culture was not the result of the fall but an intrinsic part of the everyday lives of Adam and Eve. You can find the culture apple in the Garden (and it's not the forbidden fruit mentioned in Gen. 3:2–3). God embedded in Adam a number of beliefs and values as found in Genesis 2. One belief is that a man should not be alone but needs a helper (wife) to complete him (v. 18). When God created Eve (a man's wife), he taught Adam that her role was to be man's helper (vv. 20–22). And as Adam acted on these two core beliefs, they became values that manifest themselves outwardly as part of culture.

Culture Is Not Independent of the Godhead

The Godhead operated in a cultural context just as Adam and Eve did. In Genesis 1–2 it was the Godhead or Triune God whose creative acts established various beliefs that when acted on became values that resulted from their creative thought and planning (see Acts 4:24). Therefore we see that the Godhead related to and operated in a cultural context.

Culture Is Not Temporal

The biblical evidence indicates that culture will be an intrinsic part of our future in heaven. For example, Revelation 7:9–10 clearly reveals that people's cultural distinctives, which are unique expressions of their beliefs and values, such as ethnicity and language, will be present in heaven (also see Revelation 20–22, specifically Rev. 21:26).

Culture Is Not Always Good

We are not attempting to argue here that culture is always good in every context. It can be good or bad. For example, the fall had a devastating effect on culture. Sin pervaded everything, including culture (Gen. 3:14–19; 6:5). The result was that it wreaked havoc on people's beliefs that, in turn, impacted their values.

Culture Is Not an End in Itself

Culture itself is not an end but a means to an end. Paul indicates this in Romans 14:14 where he refers to food, a vital aspect of culture, as not unclean in itself. But if a person believes that a certain food is unclean, then to that person it is. Thus it can be used for good or bad, depending on the individual. In James 3:9–12, James distinguishes between the good use of the tongue or language that is a vital part of culture and its bad use. A hunter can use a gun to provide food for his family while a criminal may use the same gun to rob that family. So language, like a gun, is not bad in itself; it depends on how it is used. Regardless, it's a means to a good end whatever that may be—the good use of language or the provision of food for one's family.

What Culture Is

HOW CULTURE IS LIKE AN APPLE
Layer 1: The apple's skin—the church's outward behavior
Layer 2: The apple's flesh—the church's core values
Layer 3: The apple's core—the church's core beliefs

With the above distinctions in mind, we are ready to identify what culture is. We have both a short and a long definition. Our long definition is: *a church's congregational culture is its unique expression of the interaction of its shared beliefs and values, which explain its behavior in general and display its unique expression of its shared values and beliefs.* If you read this out loud, you may have to pause and catch your breath. It's a mouthful. Our short definition is: *a church's organizational culture is its unique outward expression of its shared beliefs and values.* We like this definition because we believe that more often than not, less is more.

So what does it mean? We use several terms in our definition that demand defining. We like to use an apple to help explain our short definition, because it brings some concreteness or objectivity to such a subjective, abstract concept. Now, when you hear the word *culture*, do not go blank, picture an apple. We will refer to it as a culture apple. Reading a congregation's culture is like peeling back and examining the layers of an apple. Our culture apple consists of three layers.

Layer 1: The Apple's Skin—The Church's Outward Behavior

We suspect that there isn't a person who reads this book who hasn't peeled or attempted to peel an apple, so we are on safe ground when we use it as an illustration of our definition. The skin of an apple is a unique, outward expression of that apple. It is an outward expression in that you can literally see it. It is unique because no apple though similar is precisely identical with another. An apple may be green or red, but beyond that you can see distinctions in its shape and smoothness and so forth.

In the same way the church's first layer— its outward appearance and behavior—is its unique outward expression of its values and beliefs. Churches are behavior-expressed. They express themselves through their behavior or outward appearance. This is what you experience through your senses—what you see and hear when you visit a church—its skin or outward expression of itself. This outward expression consists of the church's physical presence: its facilities, parking lot, grounds, and so forth. It also includes such things as the language or languages you hear spoken (English, Spanish, or Asian), clothing (formal or casual), symbols (the cross), rituals (the public reading of Scripture), ordinances (baptism or the taking of communion), music (traditional or contemporary), even technology (high- or low-tech). And these are also the very things that make the church unique. While the church may, like other churches, conduct traditional or contemporary worship, its worship will not be the same as that of other churches. What is unique about your church's outward expression?

Layer 2: The Apple's Flesh—The Church's Core Values

If you peel the apple and stop there, you will not partake of what may be its best part—its flesh or meat. Most of us don't like the skin anyway and prefer the apple without it. So if you stop with the skin, you have not gone far enough and you will have experienced only one part or layer of the apple.

Much the same applies to our culture apple. Congregational culture has an important second layer, which consists of the church's core values. Churches are behavior-expressed but values-driven. The values explain the behavior that can be seen. While visiting a church, you may observe a contemporary band playing contemporary Christian music. This outward expression announces that the church values contemporary Christian music and worship. You will discover also what the church does not value. If there is no gospel presentation in the service or you observe no one sharing his or her faith, chances are good that evangelism may not be a value of the church.

Layer 3: The Apple's Core—The Church's Core Beliefs

We will use the terms *convictions* and *assumptions* to describe the church's beliefs. At this point you have observed and promptly peeled the apple's skin and most likely have thrown it away. You have eaten and enjoyed its flesh—that is why you bought it to begin with. Now you will be tempted to go no further. But there is more to an apple than its flesh. It has a core. And while you would not want to eat the core, you must realize that there would be no flesh without the core. *The core comes first and produces the flesh.* Also the core contains seeds that can ensure, if they are healthy, that there will be a good supply of apples for the future.

As you arrive at the church's cultural core, you will encounter the beliefs or convictions on which the culture is based. Churches are behavior-expressed, values-driven, and beliefs-based. When you hear the term *beliefs* in the context of a church, what first comes to mind? Most think of the doctrines of the Christian faith that could also be found in a church's doctrinal statement or a creed. And the church's culture certainly includes these beliefs, but it is more than this. The culture may include how the church views time (is the church living in the past, the present, or the future?); its beliefs about technology (is it high-tech or low-tech?); the church's beliefs about communication and the use of social media; and the churches beliefs about change that contribute to a culture of change.

An important question here is, How do these three layers work together? Let's work from the inside of the apple, the core, out to the peel. A belief that almost all Christian churches share is evangelism. However, if it doesn't do evangelism, then it remains a belief and not a value and does not show up at the skin or outside layer. If, on the other hand, it believes in and actually does evangelism, evangelism is a value of the church that will express itself at the outside layer. At this church you will see or hear about people sharing their faith with the lost.

The Change Personnel

THE CHANGE PERSONNEL
Character Qualifications
Spiritual Qualifications
Divine Design

Now that you have an understanding of culture and its importance, we can address the kind of envisioning or re-envisioning leader who can lead the church through change. We will refer to him as a re-envisioning pastor or as a culture sculptor. One descriptor refers to his vision, while the other to how he impacts his culture. Our question is, How does a culture sculptor lead an established church to change its culture? Our answer is threefold and will examine his character qualifications, his spiritual qualifications, and his divine design, based on our exploration.

Character Qualifications

Personal character qualifications are essential to the re-envisioning pastor's ministry. This was true in the first century and it is true in the twenty-first century. In 1 Timothy 3:1–7 and Titus 1:5–9 Paul spells out the specific character qualifications for first-century house church pastors who were called elders. The early church existed at two levels. One was the house church. A number of first-century congregations met in houses (Acts 8:3; Rom. 16:5; 1 Cor. 16:19;

Col. 4:15). The other level was the citywide church that was made up of the various house churches in a particular city—an example of which was the city church of Corinth (1 Cor. 1:2; 2 Cor. 1:1).

We have listed these qualifications in appendix I, Character Assessment for Leadership. The list identifies and explains twenty-two character qualifications in an assessment format that you can use to evaluate your qualifications for leadership.

The envisioning leader who desires to lead his church in creating and shaping a culture for change must be sure to meet these qualifications and characteristics. While none of us is perfect, we must be comfortable with where we are. This does not mean that we do not need to work on some of them. That will always be the case. When we recognize what is lacking, we must be sure to work on improvement.

Spiritual Qualifications

In addition to the character qualifications to lead a church, there are some spiritual qualifications. Paul indicates this in Galatians 5, where he says that a spiritual person is one who keeps in step with the Spirit (v. 25). In verses 22–23, he provides us with a list that characterizes those who keep in step with the Spirit. He says they possess the following: love, joy, peace, patience, kindness, goodness, faithfulness, gentleness, and self-control.

I believe that Paul is referring to the fruit of the Spirit in Galatians 4:19 where he tells the Galatian Christians that Christ needs to be formed in them. What does this mean? Jesus had the presence of the Spirit in his life just as we do today (Mark 1:10–12). And the Spirit produced in Jesus the fruit of the Spirit described in Galatians 5:22–23. When people observed the Savior, they saw the fruit of the Spirit. The same is true of us today. So, in essence, when people look at us, they should see the fruit of the Spirit or Christ. The obvious question for the culture sculptor is, Do people see the fruit of the Spirit in me? When they watch me, do they see Jesus? Whether intentional or not, people observe pastors to see if they are spiritual people who meet the spiritual qualifications for the job.

Divine Design

God has blessed all his children—pastors and congregants—with what I (Aubrey) have referred to for years as the believer's divine design. It consists of one's natural and spiritual gifts, passion, and temperament. The question we want to address in the following is, What is the re-envisioning pastor's divine design? Is the re-envisioning pastor wired differently than non–re-envisioning pastors?

Natural and Spiritual Gifts

Because culture sculptors are believers, they have both natural and spiritual gifts. But do they have gifts that non–re-envisioning pastors don't have? In my exploration of turnaround pastors, I (Gordon) discovered that the leader's spiritual gifts were not a deciding factor in leading a church to re-envision itself. We believe there are gifts that can be helpful but are not essential, such as leadership, teaching, faith, exhortation, preaching, and evangelism.

Passion

Though not necessarily supported by our exploration, we believe that passion can make some difference in a turnaround. We define passion as what one cares deeply or feels strongly about. We believe, as does church consultant Lyle Schaller, that passion is critical to any pastor's ministry. Schaller writes, "I think passion is the critical variable. It has taken me a long time to come around to that, but if a pastor does not have a passion for the mission, you can forget the rest. I would insist that the number one quality for a leader is passion."[1]

What touches the culture sculptor's passion? Often re-envisioning pastors display a passion for Christ's church in general and plateaued or dying churches in particular. Then passion serves to focus their gifts and talents on these churches. They are convinced that they can make a difference in difficult situations that require a turnaround.

Temperament

As we discovered earlier in chapter 7, re-envisioning pastors do pattern a certain way behaviorally. Though we have not mentioned it earlier in this book, Pastor Robert Thomas used the Biblical Personal Profile in his groundbreaking doctor of ministry project to attempt to determine whether effective revitalization pastors have specific personality characteristics. Thomas discovered that effective turnaround pastors he worked with were high Is in combination with a secondary D.

We conducted a similar but much broader study, using the Personal Profile (DISC) and the Myers-Briggs Type Indicator (MBTI). We presented the results in chapter 7, where we note that those pastors who could effectively re-envision churches scored as DIs, IDs, Ds, or Is on the DISC and they scored as ESTJ,

ENFP, ESFJ, or ISTJ on the MBTI. We believe that ENTJs, by nature of their strong intuitive abilities, could have the same results.

The Change Process

THE CHANGE PROCESS
Step 1: Read the culture
Step 2: Thaw the culture
Step 3: Transition the culture to a new level
Step 4: Reform the new culture at the new level

Once you have the proper change personnel in place, you are ready to create a culture for change. I (Aubrey) have been influenced by the work of the German-American psychologist Kurt Lewin, who back in the 1950s proposed a three-step model for change. He compares culture to a block of ice, and his process consists of unfreezing a culture, changing the culture, and then refreezing the culture at the new level. While I like his model, I have problems with his refreezing the culture as the third step. Would not this mean that we would be frozen at the new status quo where our problems would start all over again? My model addresses this issue and adds a step. It consists of the following four-step process.

Step 1: Read the Current Culture

The first step you must take is to read the current culture of which you are a part. To understand this, we need to return to our culture apple. To read the culture is to start outside the apple with its peel and work your way to the core. You accomplish this by exegeting your culture, which involves observation, interpretation, and application.

Observation

We begin with observation, looking at the skin of our culture apple. What do you see? As the pastor or the prospective pastor of the church, what would you see if you visited the church? Do people carry their Bibles? Do they laugh and seem to enjoy one another's company? Do they pray and worship together? The temptation at this point is to attempt to interpret what this means. Resist that temptation for now. Your job is to gather as much information as possible by simply observing the culture.

Interpretation

Next we move to interpretation. We work our way from the skin of the apple to its flesh and core. Here we ask, What does what we see mean? How are we to interpret our observations? The answer is found in uncovering both the church's core values and core beliefs that make up the flesh and core of the church. The church's core values and beliefs will influence what is seen on the outside.

Application

Finally, we are ready to make application. We ask, What difference does this make? The answer lies in discovering the culture's commonalties and uniqueness, its strengths and weaknesses, whether it is mature or immature, and whether you as a leader or pastor in this context will be effective or ineffective. These flow from the values and core beliefs. For example, Ed Young is the pastor at Fellowship Bible Church in Grapevine, Texas. His ministry is renowned for its creativity. What they do on Sunday morning is very creative. That is a reflection of the application of his values (in this case, creativity).

Step 2: Thaw Out the Current Culture

Having taken the first step and discovered the church's culture, you are aware of how the church is doing. Most churches in North America, 80 to 85 percent, are not doing well. And we suspect that this might be true of the situation where you are. At the heart of the problem is the status quo, which is Latin for the "mess we are in." So where do we go from here? While an accurate awareness of the problem is an important start, what are we to do to move churches toward change and renewal? Let's return to our block of ice metaphor. Now that we have identified the ice, what do we have to do to melt it? We have three suggestions.

Inflict Pain

One way to initiate change is to inflict emotional pain. Often medical doctors have to hurt people to heal them. The same goes for our churches. You have to get their attention, and a good way is to cause them pain or discomfort. You see, they have become too comfortable while immersed in the status quo. Consultant Lyle Schaller calls it rubbing raw the wounds of discontent. Bill Hybels says much the same when he writes, "Leaders move people from here to there. . . . The first play is not to make 'there' sound wonderful. The first play is to make 'here' sound awful."[2] If you make "there" look good and don't make "now" seem awful, "now" will hang around and compete constantly with "there" for people's allegiance.

So how do you "rub raw the wounds of discontent"? How do you make "here" seem awful? The answer is to tell the people the truth. Most churches are in steep decline, sliding quickly toward an early funeral; your job is to constantly remind the people of this. Many of these churches tend to act like the proverbial ostrich and at the sign of trouble simply bury their heads in the sand, believing that "out of sight is out of mind." Your job is to pull their heads out of the sand, invite them to look around, and ask, "What do you see?"

We at the Malphurs Group do this; we refer to it as checking the church's vital signs: worship attendance, congregational giving, and strengths and weaknesses. We point out where the church is on the organizational growth cycle, and ask, "If the church continues to decline at this rate, when will you have to close the doors?" Because we have computed the rate of decline, we can actually give them the year in which this will happen if they do not do something. Our experience is that this hurts and we get their attention. We do the same with the giving and ask, "When can you not afford to keep the doors open?" And finally, we address their strengths and weaknesses, which are numerous. We may conclude by asking what they want their legacy to be. Do they want to be remembered as the generation who let the church die? Do they want people to point at them and say, "It happened on their watch"?

Having heard this, you may be thinking that there are some churches that still would not respond. Should this be the case, we would suggest that you let them die. In these situations, most are too far gone to recover.

Ask Sixteen Questions

Occasionally we at the Malphurs Group work with a church that has been growing but is dangerously close to a plateau. The problem is with their mindset: if it ain't broke, don't fix it. The problem is that it *is* "broke" but either they cannot or will not see it. They are not there yet, because the church is still growing. In these situations, we use a tool we call Sixteen Make-or-Break Questions. You will find a copy of it in appendix J. Turn to it and give it a quick read to see how it works. So far, we have not had a church that is not silenced by this tool. It is articulated in such a way that most churches realize that while they have made a lot of progress, they have some more work to do.

Develop Opportunity Eyes

A third way to unfreeze your culture is to develop opportunity eyes. There are times in the life cycle of every church when God intervenes in the status quo and opens a window for potential change. We refer to these as "divine interruptions." The alert culture shaper must look for these and not let them slip by without taking advantage of them to thaw out the culture and move the church toward a turnaround.

We will give you five possible "divine interruptions" that you can use to thaw out the church culture.

1. *A crisis* such as a fire or the untimely death of the pastor or some other prominent person in the church.
2. *A change of pastors.* A new pastor has the opportunity to cast a new and exciting vision for the future.
3. *A renewal of the pastor.* Something happens in your life that motivates you to seek God anew and pursue his vision for the church.
4. *A renewal of the lay leadership.* One pastor in Dallas took his lay leaders to one of Rick Warren's conferences at Saddleback. When they returned, the men were challenged and ready to attempt great things for God.
5. *The expertise of a church consultant or mentor.* These people can come into the pastor's life and give him needed wisdom and advice—especially if he is facing a crossroads in his ministry.

Step 3: Transition the Culture to a New Level

When you reach step 3, you may find yourself tempted to stop for a while and catch your breath. This would be a mistake. To pause now could be disastrous. The reason is that there are always forces in every church that will attempt to keep things where they are—to preserve the status quo. They are like barnacles on the side of a boat; they serve no purpose but to slow things down.

At this point you need to pursue three things.

1. *Determine the new culture.* The exegetical shaping question here is not what do you see, but what *should* you see? What does a spiritually mature church look like?
2. *What should it mean?* What are your actual biblical core values that arise from good beliefs? There should be at least five: worship, fellowship, biblical instruction, service, and evangelism.
3. *What difference should it make?* The answer is all the difference in the world as you take the gospel to the world.

Once you have determined your new culture, you will need to implement it. You accomplish this by recruiting a strategic implementation team, consisting of no more than nine key leaders in the church. Next, use this team to discover your core values and develop your mission and vision statements (to make disciples and what that looks like), along with a strategy to implement them in the church. The strategy will address the following:

- Community outreach
- Disciple making
- Congregational mobilization
- Staffing
- Raising the finances necessary to support the ministry and pay the bills. My book *Advanced Strategic Planning*[3] would prove immensely helpful in accomplishing this.

Step 4: Reform the New Culture at the New Level

As we said earlier, Lewin describes this step as refreezing the new culture at the new level. He refreezes the ice block to preserve the gains that have been made. We don't think he makes his point. Once you refreeze at the new level, what is to keep you from getting stuck at the new level? Then you have to repeat the process all over again.

Instead, we change his block-of-ice metaphor to a slushy or milkshake. You would accomplish this with the strategic implementation team mentioned above in step 3 or you could draft a select group known as a special culture implementation team. The team would take responsibility for seeing that the church follows through with culture development. The team would draft a leader who would report directly to the pastor, and the pastor would report to any governance board (elders or deacons), should the church have such a board. This is for accountability. The team would consist of no more than nine people who would embrace and share the implementation of the goals and objectives of the group. Each person on the team would adopt and be working on several of these goals with one or two others. The job of the team leader is to coordinate the work of the team, check with the team members, troubleshoot, and make sure the goals are being accomplished.

Another option is that your strategic implementation team might consist of several teams with different objectives and goals. Each would have a leader who would report to the pastor. One team would work on forming the mission, vision, and strategy mentioned in step 3. Another would be the special culture implementation team mentioned above. A third team could be a creativity and innovation team with the primary objective of helping the church recognize and adapt quickly to cultural change. Here are some optional goals of such a team:

- Determine if the church keeps up with and relates well to the culture in its community.
- Interview people within and outside the congregation and ask what the church is doing that's become outdated and irrelevant. (What's not changed in the last five years?)
- Develop and apply a biblical theology of change.
- Constantly challenge the church's views and assumptions about what is true about your community, your congregation, your ministries, your leaders, and the way you do things inside your organization. Take nothing for granted.
- Develop a process for generating hundreds of new, strategic ministry ideas each year (team and staff brainstorming sessions, for example).
- Gain congregational permission to experiment with new things. (This means they and you will have to become comfortable with failure. It's far better to have tried and failed than not to have tried at all.)
- Consider and evaluate creative and innovative ideas from the congregation and others.
- Identify innovative and creative churches in America and discover what they are doing and how that may help you in your ministry.
- Allocate funds in the budget to fund new ideas (recommend 1–5 percent of the ministries budget).
- Read books and articles on creativity and innovation (for example, check out the magazine *Fast Company*) and on innovative, creative churches.
- Invite new staff and new members and even outsiders to tell you what they think you need to change to be more effective as a church.

A Warning

As they work through this chapter's cultural change process, change architects or re-envisioning pastors must be aware that there will always be a group of people in the church who will want to return the church to its "good ole days," better known as the status quo. Hopefully they will be only a small group. Some of these people are late adopters who will come around eventually. You will have to give them some time. Others are never adopters who refuse to change and who will complain and whine. Their attitude will be "my way or the highway!"

You don't have to tolerate these people and you may want to encourage them to find a church frozen in the status quo where perhaps they can be happy.

In this situation, you may want to try a grievance process through which these people can air their disagreements. Such a process asks people not to meet together and complain to one another about the changes but to go to the person in charge of or responsible for a particular area of change. This would be the biblical approach (Phil. 2:14–15). Regardless, you must not tolerate gossip or malicious rumors. People need to know that such behavior is not Christian and is "out of bounds."

Mini-Bio: What Does It Mean to Be a Re-Envisioning Pastor?

Good News Community Church in Broomfield, Colorado, had twelve years of consistent decline in numbers of people (down to ninety in worship), spiritual growth, salvations, baptisms, finances, and finally, hope. At the completion of an assessment of the church, the current pastor realized he could not lead the church through the transition. Wisely, he resigned.

Matthew Fite, on staff at a church in Nevada, had no senior pastor experience. He received a call to see if he would consider becoming the next pastor of Good News Church. After reading the assessment report and seeing the situation, he hesitated to take the reins. The church continued its freefall; the finances were shaky and the people shell-shocked. Nevertheless, Christ directed Fite's steps to Broomfield.

Matthew faced a dilemma that every first-time pastor faces. In his words, "When I became a pastor, I had to decide if I was going to be a chaplain or push back the gates of Hades. I chose to push back the gates!"

That meant he and the church had to make gut-wrenching choices. They didn't have enough money or people power to continue with the status quo. Matthew writes, "We stopped AWANA (that had turned into a midweek kidcare for families who attended other churches), Men's Ministries (that was just for us, using up people's time and prevented them from serving the community), Women's Ministries (that was just for us, using up people's time and prevented them from serving the community), potlucks (that was just for us), the dinner ministry (that just gave meals to families inside of the church), and the list goes on. These were all things that were eating up our limited time, energy, resources, and attention, and everything was focused inwards. They were good things, but they were keeping us from the great thing, the Great Commission, rescuing people from the dominion of darkness.

"We figured we can really only do three things, and should focus only on those three things:

- Love God (Worship gatherings—bragging on God and pointing people to him).
- Love others (small groups for congregational care and community).
- Serve the world (intentionally serving someone else in Jesus' name)."

Their vision statement reads: "Good News Community Church exists to be and to make disciples of Jesus Christ who love God, love others, and serve the world."

Matthew adds, "What's the outcome? We currently have 4 worship gatherings each Sunday (on two campuses) and are averaging 400. Last Easter we added 2 extra worship gatherings for that day and had 738 people across the 6 services. None of this happened overnight. I have been at Good News now for 5 years. We just keep plodding along, slowly moving forward.

"You know me; I'm not a superstar or anything. God has been very gracious to us. I am convinced that the catalyst that God used to turn this church around was the assessment, which happened before I arrived, but it gave me the leverage we needed to turn things around. When the church was told that they were disobedient to the Great Commission, it hurt, but the people owned it, repented, and God poured out his grace. God used the assessment to create a spiritual turnaround, which led to total turnaround for the entire church. The assessment also pointed out the very ineffective governance model we had and asked that we change that model. This freed me up *to lead the church*, not just manage it, and keep everyone focused on the Great Commission; pushing back the gates of hell" (emphasis the authors').

The question: "Am I a re-envisioning pastor?" Matthew's answer: "We're pushing back the gates of hell!"

What are you pushing?

Questions for Reflection, Discussion, and Application

1. The authors believe that culture is very important to the church. Do you agree or disagree? Do they make their point? Why or why not? What do you believe is their strongest argument for the importance of culture? What is their weakest argument?
2. Do you agree or disagree with the authors' gripe about people not defining what they mean when they use certain terms, such as *kingdom,*

missional, mission, vision, and *culture*? Why or why not? Does this affect clarity? Do you think that maybe they just had a bad day?

3. Do you agree with the authors' definition of organizational (or better in this context, congregational) culture? Why or why not? How would you define it? Does their use of the culture apple image help to clarify their definition? Why or why not?
4. Did you find the authors' emphasis on exegeting the culture helpful? If so, how? If not, why not? What are the three steps involved in exegeting the church's culture? Do you agree with them? Why or why not?
5. In defining culture, the authors identify what it is not as well as what it is for the purpose of greater clarity. Did you find this approach helpful? Why or why not? Did you agree or disagree with what they believe is not true of culture? Why?
6. Have you taken the "Character Assessment for Leadership" in appendix I? Why or why not? If you have, did you meet the character qualifications? If not, where do you struggle? What will you do about this?
7. Do you meet the spiritual qualifications to lead a church that are found in Galatians 5:22–23? Do people see the fruit of the Spirit or Jesus in your life? Why or why not? Where are you strong? Where do you fall short? What will you do about the areas where you fall short?
8. What are your spiritual gifts? In spite of what the authors say, do you believe that a pastor's spiritual gifts make a difference in leading a church to change? If so, how so? Have your spiritual gifts helped you lead a church to change?
9. What are your scores on the Personal Profile (DISC) and the Myers-Briggs Type Indicator (MBTI)? Did your scores align with those who are good at leading churches to re-envision themselves?
10. Did you agree with the authors' four steps for creating and cultivating a change culture in the church? Why or why not? Do you think they will work for you in your church? While most metaphors fail at some point, did the block-of-ice metaphor help you understand the purpose of each step? Why or why not? Did you agree with the authors' concern over refreezing the block of ice at the new level as suggested by Kurt Lewin? What were the authors illustrating by suggesting a slushy or a milkshake rather than a refrozen block of ice?
11. How will you handle those who likely will never agree with the changes to your church's culture and constantly complain about them? In these situations, does the authors' grievance process make sense? Why or why not?

12

Recruiting a Mentor or Coach

The story is told of a young banker who approached an older banker and asked, "How is it that you're so successful?" The banker responded, "I can tell you in two words—good decisions." Not satisfied with that terse answer, the young man inquired further, "How did you learn to make good decisions?" Without batting an eye, the banker said, "I can tell you in two words—bad decisions."

This story illustrates the minefields that we all face in life, regardless of the venture. In ministry there are two different ways we can learn how to navigate uncharted waters. We can learn through bad decisions or we can learn from someone who has been there and done that. We call these people mentors or coaches. In this chapter we want to challenge you to examine the following topics related to the subject of mentoring and coaching.

- The definition of a mentor, a coach, and a protégé.
- Why having a coach or mentor is so important to re-envisioning ministry.
- What we learned about mentoring or coaching from our pastor surveys.
- The attitudes essential to mentoring and coaching success.
- What to expect from a good mentor or coach, and what a mentor or coach should expect from a protégé.
- The specialized areas of mentoring and coaching available through internships and apprenticeships.

- Some approaches for recruiting a mentor or coach for your ministry and approaches to recruiting a protégé.
- A leadership challenge to re-envisioning pastors to encourage them to proactively seek to become mentors or coaches.

What Is a Mentor or Coach?

MENTORS AND COACHES
What is a mentor or coach?
Why are mentors and coaches important?
What is the value of mentors and coaches?
What are the essential characteristics of mentors/coaches and protégés?
What are the expectations of a mentor/coach and a protégé?
What are some specialized areas of coaching and mentoring?
How should you recruit a mentor/coach or protégé?
Why should you become a mentor or coach?

As we mentioned in the introduction to mentoring in chapter 3, the word *mentor* is not found in the biblical text. However, the concept of mentoring surfaces with great regularity as one examines leaders who pass the baton to next-generation leaders. We turn our thoughts more fully to mentoring and coaching in this chapter.

As we begin this section, we must realize that the mentoring and coaching disciplines are changing with regularity. In many cases the terms *mentor* and *coach* are interchangeable. And often when we use the term *protégé*, people stare in bewilderment. So we begin this section by defining these terms.

Defining Mentor *and* Coach

In the classic work, *As Iron Sharpens Iron*, Howard Hendricks, noted teacher and mentoring expert, and Bill Hendricks, president of the Hendricks Group, raised the banner of mentoring before the Christian community. Their remarks trace the root of the term *mentor* and assess the current need for mentoring in our culture.

> Wherever you turn today, you will find men looking for a guide, a coach, a model, an advisor. They are looking for someone who knows about life.
>
> In essence, they are looking for a mentor. When the Greek warrior Odysseus went off to fight in the Trojan War, he left his young son, Telemachus, in the care of a trusted guardian named Mentor. The siege of Troy lasted ten years, and it took Odysseus another ten years to make his way home. When he arrived, he found that the boy Telemachus had grown into a man—thanks to Mentor's wise tutelage.
>
> Based on this story, we now speak of a mentor as someone who functions to some extent as a father figure (in the best sense of the term), a man who

> fundamentally affects and influences the development of another, usually younger man.[1]

They continue: "Mentoring is defined by the relationship. That being the case, we have to define a mentor not in terms of any formal roles that he carries out, but in terms of *the character of his relationship* with the other person, and the *functions* that that relationship serves."[2] According to the authors, a mentor is an older, more experienced person who is a guide, model, or advisor. This is the classic view of a mentor.

Since this book was written nearly twenty years ago, mentoring, like so many other areas of our society, has undergone a great deal of refinement. Now *mentoring* is not the only term used. *Coaching* is now a part of personal and professional development. The concepts of mentors and coaches have taken on their own special meaning in ministry and business circles. So our objective is to provide workable definitions of *coach* and *mentor* as they apply to ministry. We will begin with a discussion as to how these terms are used in business and ministry circles today.

Don Hahn, president of Hahn Training, defines coaching and mentoring in the following way:

> Coaching and mentoring are the 2 highest levels of professional development available in today's workplace. . . . It is easy to become confused about the differences between coaching and mentoring. Often times the two terms are used interchangeably when in fact there are some very specific distinctions. In mentoring, the course of action is usually provided by the mentor, whereas in a true coaching engagement, it is the coachee who creates the action plan.[3]

In Hahn's definition, a mentor provides a course of action for a protégé (this term is defined below), whereas a coach has the protégé develop his own course of action.

Many other voices join the chorus to agree with this distinction. These include Management Mentors[4] and the English coaching and mentoring Brefi Group. The Brefi Group provides a sharp distinction as they describe mentoring and coaching.

> Coaching: helping another person to improve awareness, to set and achieve goals in order to improve a particular behavioural performance.
>
> Mentoring: helping to shape an individual's beliefs and values in a positive way; often a longer term career relationship from someone who has "done it before."[5]

This group echoes the fundamental distinctions between coaching and mentoring prevalent today. Mentoring is imparting information, whereas coaching helps individuals discern their own personal goals and objectives.

Christian coaches Bob Logan and Sherilyn Carlton describe coaching in the same way.

> Sometimes we just need an outside set of eyes and ears to give us a sense of perspective.
>
> And coaching isn't about being an expert. Is there knowledge involved? Absolutely. But the most crucial knowledge focuses on areas like listening skills and asking good questions. Coaches don't need to have all the right answers so they can tell people what to do. It's not about listening to the coach—it's about helping others learn to listen to God for themselves.[6]

Their definition agrees with the basic tenets we've already observed. Coaching is about listening and asking good questions to help protégés determine the direction God is leading them.

Perhaps the best way to understand coaching and mentoring is by comparing them in the following chart.

Contrasting Mentoring and Coaching for Pastors and Christian Leaders

	Coaching	Mentoring
Duration	Short term	Long term
Relationship	Impersonal	Personal
Method	Asking directed questions to help protégé determine his or her own course of action	Giving direction from the mentor's past experiences
Age Difference	Does not matter	Normally the mentor is older with more experience
Focus	Self-discovery of solutions	Directed toward solutions that have been successful in the past in the life of the mentor

So, for the purposes of this volume, we will define *mentor* and *coach* in the following ways:

- A *mentor* is one who promotes the development of life and ministry skills for a protégé, primarily by imparting wisdom and skill from lessons learned from the mentor's own life and ministry experience.
- A *coach* is one who promotes the development of life and ministry skills for a protégé, primarily through asking probing questions about

a protégé's life, divine design, direction, and development so that the protégé grows primarily through self-discovery.

Some may question the legitimacy of these disciplines in the Christian walk. However, we find these methods used repeatedly in the Bible. Consider the following pairs of mentor/protégé teams found in Scripture: Moses and Joshua, Elijah and Elisha, Jesus and the disciples, Barnabas and Saul, Paul and Timothy, and Paul and Titus. Each of the mentors deeply influenced the protégés.

Here are two brief biblical examples, one of mentoring and the second of coaching. First, in 2 Timothy 2:2, Paul the mentor, instructs Timothy, the protégé, "And the things you have heard me say in the presence of many witnesses entrust to reliable people who will also be qualified to teach others." Paul charges Timothy to continue to use what he has given him to impact others. Pass on what you've learned—become a mentor!

Second, an incident in the life of Christ and Peter in Matthew 17:24–27 illustrates the principles of coaching.

> When they had come to Capernaum, those who received the temple tax came to Peter and said, "Does your Teacher not pay the temple tax?"
>
> He said, "Yes."
>
> And when he had come into the house, Jesus anticipated him, saying, "What do you think, Simon? From whom do the kings of the earth take customs or taxes, from their sons or from strangers?"
>
> Peter said to Him, "From strangers."
>
> Jesus said to him, "Then the sons are free. Nevertheless, lest we offend them, go to the sea, cast in a hook, and take the fish that comes up first. And when you have opened its mouth, you will find a piece of money; take that and give it to them for Me and you."

Jesus used a question and a statement to help Peter understand at least four essential truths.

- The Lord Jesus' position as the King even over the temple.
- Peter is a son of the King!
- Peter understood Christ's sovereign power, "cast in a hook!"
- Peter further learned a lesson about humility, that it is better to be defrauded than to cause an offense.

All of these lessons radiated from one question.

Defining Protégé

As we have seen in the above descriptions of mentoring and coaching, we would say that a protégé is a younger pastor who is taught and helped by an older pastor, a mentor, who has a lot of knowledge and experience. We will also use the term *protégé* when describing the relationship between a pastor and a coach, though age may not play as prominent a role.

We should also state that in most pastoral mentoring or coaching roles, both coaching and mentoring come into play. Wise coaches and mentors will use both approaches. This is the reason we often use the combination *mentor/coach*.

The Importance of Mentors and Coaches

THE IMPORTANCE OF MENTORS AND COACHES
Pastor Effectiveness
Mentor Effectiveness
Coach Effectiveness

Since our focus is on re-envisioning pastors, we need to ask how mentors and coaches are important to re-envisioning ministry. The answer to this question is threefold.

Pastor Effectiveness

A pastor's effectiveness varies greatly from pastor to pastor. All pastors are not created equal. The figure on page 192 shows the general breakdown of pastoral effectiveness in church turnaround and church leadership. Paul Borden originally presented this chart at a pastor cluster gathering. In Discovery 1 and Discovery 2 we found that one group of pastors, re-envisioning pastors, can enter into a plateaued or declining church and lead it through the process of turnaround. They know what to do. Their leadership capacity is great enough to lead the church in renewal. As we have seen, they number perhaps 6–15 percent of all pastors.

The second group, on the right in the figure, struggles tremendously in ministry. Most likely the divine design for these non–re-envisioning pastors does not fit pastoral ministry. This group would number perhaps 20 percent of all pastors.

The third and largest group of pastors, in the center of the diagram, consists of NREPs numbering about 65 to 74 percent of all pastors. These pastors have the capacity to grow in their leadership abilities. They may never become REPs but they can improve their level of leadership competency with help so that their church can begin to make a larger impact than is currently possible. For example, if a pastor of a church of 50 can lead his church to 75, a pastor of a church of 100 can lead his flock to grow to 150, and if a pastor of a church of 500 can grow in his competency, perhaps his church will grow to 600. All of these are wins and could become re-envisioning churches. The arrows at the bottom of the diagram indicate the ability of these pastors to grow in their leadership capacity.

The majority of pastors cannot lead well on their own. Most are managers, not leaders. They struggle to pull the leadership trigger. Andy Stanley speaks clearly to this issue.

> Pastors, preachers, and teachers who are not gifted in the area of leadership default to *management*. Best-case scenario, they take what's handed to them and nurture it, protect it, defend it, and in some cases, improve it. Worst-case scenario, they focus on pastoring, preaching and teaching, and delegate key leadership decisions to committees. They are reticent to move outside the lines they were hired into. It's neither intuitive nor comfortable for them to abandon the approach they inherited in order to lead out in a new direction. Consequently, they end up married to the model they were hired into.[7]

Re-envisioning pastoral ministry is about leadership, not management. Most pastors struggle to lead and need help. Coaches and mentors can help fill this leadership vacuum. They have the potential to make a huge difference, as we will see. With guidance from REPs who serve as mentors or coaches, their ability to move their churches to greater ministry effectiveness increases. Through this process, some pastors will undoubtedly become REPs.

Distribution of Re-envisioning and Non–Re-envisioning Pastors and Their Leadership Capacity[8]

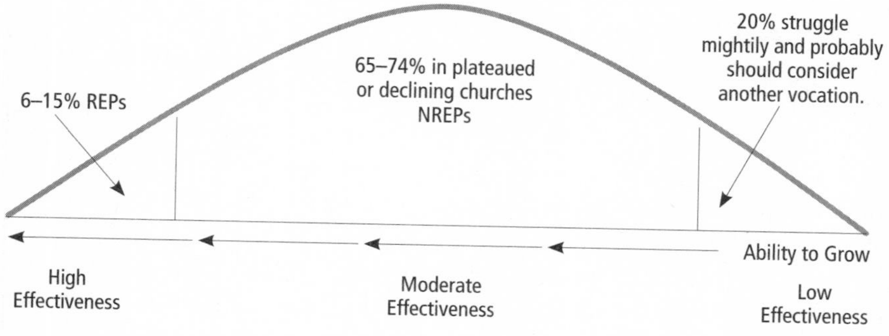

As a pastor, I (Gordon) have sought mentors and coaches from the very beginning of my ministry in a little church on the fringes of inner-city Dallas through four pastorates and one interim ministry. As my ministry expanded to include Fresh Start, I continued to seek wisdom when taking steps into the unknown. We will all face some monumental challenges that we never dreamed we would see. Jack Nivens, my pastor from Mesquite, Texas, came to my aid on numerous occasions. He walked me through some deadly minefields of "first church ministry." He helped me stay afloat while leading me forward in ministry effectiveness. Not only that, he is one reason I am still in ministry today. He proved to be that helpful!

After thirty-five years, I still find great value in contacting individuals to help clarify ministry issues that arise. As ministry responsibilities grow, so do challenges. I seek wisdom from others as I move into uncharted territory.

Mentor Effectiveness

In general pastors desire greater impact for the Savior. This was reflected in a number of interviews we conducted over the past several years. Mentoring can help provide that needed boost in ministry competency. Business research leaders Cynthia D. McCauley and Christina A. Douglas share the value of mentoring in the business world: "Research indicates that working with a mentor is associated with higher performance ratings, more recognition, greater compensation, more career opportunities, and more promotions."[9]

We see that business leaders are rediscovering biblical leadership practices, including mentoring. Mentoring works! We in the church ought to rediscover it too.

Coach Effectiveness

Just as mentoring produces increased effectiveness, coaching does the same. Andy Stanley, pastor of North Point Church in Atlanta, Georgia, one of the largest churches in America, speaks to the effectiveness of coaching: "You will never maximize your potential in any area without coaching. It is impossible. You may be good. You may even be better than everyone else. But without input you will never be as good as you could be. We all do better when somebody is watching and evaluating."[10]

Stanley adds:

> In the world of athletics, the coach does not withhold his opinion until asked. Neither does he sit back and watch his protégé make the same mistakes over and over without saying something. In the same way a good leadership coach will do

> everything in his power to ensure progress. Like an athletic coach, a leadership coach operates as if he has something on the line. . . . Good leadership coaches function as if they have something at stake in your performance.[11]

Coaching is vital to leadership development.

The Value of a Mentor/Coach

What is the value of a mentor/coach? We discovered the answer in our exploration of this topic with our pastors.

In Discovery 1, I (Gordon) asked two questions regarding mentoring: (1) In the first five years of your ministry did you have someone whom you regarded as a mentor/coach? (2) Do you currently have someone who mentors or coaches you in ministry? The questions were answered with a simple yes or no. The results were clear-cut. Mentoring made a huge difference in the lives of the turnaround pastors. Lack of mentoring made a huge difference in the non-turnaround pastors. The results are seen in the table below.

Coaches and Mentors from Discovery 1[12]

Questions	Turnaround Pastors	Non-Turnaround Pastors
Did you have a coach or mentor at the beginning of your ministry?	13 of 21 said yes—62%	4 of 7 said yes—57%
Do you currently have a coach or mentor?	13 of 21 said yes—62%	1 of 7 said yes—14%

The majority of turnaround pastors (62 percent) had coaches or mentors at the beginning of their ministry and 62 percent continue to have coaches and mentors today. In comparison, 57 percent, or four of seven, of the non-turnaround pastors had coaches at the beginning of their ministry. Currently only one non-turnaround pastor (14 percent) has a mentor. Two of the four who had mentors initially were previously leading growing, turnaround churches. As they moved into different churches, they no longer used a mentor, and their later ministries were not turnaround. Whether the loss of a mentor was the primary cause of this change is not completely clear. However, the result of this portion of the survey suggests a strong correlation between mentoring/coaching and effective turnaround ministry.

The question in Discovery 2 lacked the clarity of the two questions in Discovery 1. The question read, "Have you had in the past and do you now have a mentor or coach in your life?" On a four-point Likert Scale (with 1–true,

2–more true than false, 3–more false than true, and 4–false) to poll the pastors, the average response for a REP was 2.1 and for the NREP was 2.2. We believe the question was not definitive enough because we combined two questions from Discovery 1 into one question in Discovery 2. Nevertheless, the majority of pastors scored in the "more true than false" category.

In the interview processes for this book, I spoke with a pastor of one of the largest churches in our study. When I asked, "Do you have a mentor?" he responded, "I am always looking for a mentor who can help me move to the next level. I'm finding that pastors of churches larger than ours are not always helpful. They are too much into themselves!" So the key is not just finding someone who has done it bigger and better than you, it is finding someone who can help you in an area of need so that you can more easily take the next steps.

Another friend pastoring a large church for the first time has carefully sifted through a large roster of names to select a mentor who would help him move his church to the next level of ministry. Why? He was on a path he had never traversed before and recognized that he needed an experienced guide.

The Essential Characteristics of Mentors/Coaches and Protégés

THE ESSENTIAL CHARACTERISTICS OF MENTOR/COACHES AND PROTÉGÉS
Honesty
Vulnerability
Security in Christ
Trust
Commitment
Being Teachable and Coachable

Though not exhaustive, the characteristics we give here are essential for a growing, maturing mentor/coach and protégé relationship.

Honesty

Each party that is going to be involved in any of these of relationships must be honest with one another. Two individuals cannot build a relationship that will produce needed and desired change without honesty. You must be able to speak truth in love at every level of the relationship.

Vulnerability

To grow in one of these types of relationships, you must be vulnerable. Drop the smoke screens and show your true identity, both strengths and flaws, to grow and change in your ministry effectiveness.

Security in Christ

Over the years we have observed that pastors are some of the most insecure people we've ever met. Many pastors have been fired or live under the constant threat (sometimes perceived, sometimes real) of dismissal. Those feelings of insecurity will torpedo ministry effectiveness. If we're too worried about ruffling the wrong feathers, we cannot make the critical decisions that we need to make.

To counteract feelings of insecurity, we must understand that our identity is rooted in Christ. Neither our parents nor our congregation nor our church board nor our "success" or "failure" determine our approval. Jesus Christ does. We have been made whole and complete in him. Romans 14:8 speaks eloquently to our position: "If we live, we live for the Lord; and if we die, we die for the Lord. So, whether we live or die, we belong to the Lord." So we plunge ahead in ministry, serving by the grace of God for the glory of God. We serve first our Lord Jesus Christ and the church body second. Stated differently, what the Lord requires trumps what people demand.

Trust

Trust is a key element, a two-way street. The protégé must trust his or her teacher, and the teacher must trust the protégé. Honesty, vulnerability, and security play a large role in building trust. Trust will not be built overnight, but it can easily be destroyed by dishonesty and lack of vulnerability. Build trust and keep it!

Commitment

Relationships, such as the ones we will describe, take commitment on the part of the individuals involved. The relationship may last from a few months to many years. Individuals must maintain a high level of commitment for maximum impact. Appointments must be kept, assignments completed on time, and the use of time must be honored.

Being Teachable and Coachable

If the protégé is not teachable or coachable, then both parties are wasting time. Know-it-alls will never improve their skills through a mentor/coach.

The Expectations of a Mentor/Coach and a Protégé

Here are some key expectations for both mentor/coaches and protégés.

What You Should Expect from a Mentor/Coach

If you are a young pastor who is either turning around a church or wishing to, what should you expect from a seasoned veteran? Here are some expectations that should be fulfilled in your working with a mentor/coach. Don't be afraid to add your own.

A mentor/coach should:

- Define areas of your life and ministry that need work. You can expect your mentor/coach to help you in those areas of need.
- Help you, at a minimum, in the areas of learning, encouragement, accountability, and envisioning a new future for the church.
- Have the essential characteristics listed above.
- Be reliable.
- Help in completing and implementing a personal Leadership Development Plan.
- Be somewhat demanding. There is always pain associated with change. The old adage, no pain, no gain, is true in Christian ministry.
- Expect you to read and discuss books on leadership and ministry.

What a Mentor/Coach Should Expect from a Protégé

The mentor/coach should expect the following, at minimum, from his protégé:

- Reliability
- Inquisitiveness
- An overwhelming desire to grow
- Being coachable
- Possessing the essential characteristics
- An eager learner

Specialized Areas of Coaching and Mentoring

SPECIALIZED AREAS OF COACHING AND MENTORING
Defining an Internship
Defining an Apprenticeship
Examples of Internship and Apprenticeship Churches
Selecting a Church or Pastor for an Internship or Apprenticeship
Selecting an Intern or Apprentice

Specialized areas of coaching and mentoring consist of internships and apprenticeships. These tend to be available to pastors just entering full-time vocational ministry.

Defining an Internship

Internships allow for a time of ministry preparation that normally accompanies a course of study at a seminary or Bible college. It attempts to cross the yawning chasm that exists between the classroom and the real world of ministry. It offers a time to explore a person's divine design, direction, and development. Internships may focus on a particular area, such as youth ministry, or may concentrate on a more general area, such as pastoral ministry and all that entails.

The lengths of internships normally vary from three months to one year. Time commitments vary from a few hours each week to full-time ministry.

Defining an Apprenticeship

An apprenticeship affords the same opportunities as an internship. However, apprenticeships are normally of longer duration and intensity. This allows the student or young pastor to immerse himself in the wise tutelage of an experienced pastor. This is likewise a time for a young pastor to explore his divine design, direction, and development.

Time commitments for apprenticeships vary from a year to several years. Normally the longer apprenticeships include being on staff at a church. Implanting re-envisioning DNA into the life of a young apprentice ought to be a prime objective.

Examples of Internship and Apprenticeship Churches

A growing number of churches specialize in internships and/or apprenticeships. A large part of the ministry consists of imparting re-envisioning DNA to the intern or apprentice.

Bear Valley Church in Denver, Colorado, led the way in this arena in the mid-1980s. Frank Tillapaugh was skilled at imparting outwardly focused DNA into his leadership team. This church at one time had no less than fifty outreach ministries across the cities of the Denver Metro area, many of them led by apprentices and soon-to-be pastors. I (Gordon) know a number of pastors and leaders who were deeply impacted by that church. They caught the vision and continue to reproduce in much the same way. Some of the most effective pastors in our region originated at Bear Valley.

Northview Church in Abbotsford, British Columbia, is a large church (three thousand adults, five hundred children) that recognizes the great need to provide significant mentoring and training for young Christian leaders and pastors. In a recent interview Pastor Jeff Bucknam shared his passion with Gordon. "The church has dropped the ball in leadership development. I believe seminaries are doing it, but not in a complete way. I don't think they can. Most of the skills we do, we learn by doing those skills. Preaching is like that. Leadership is like that. If churches aren't committed to hands-on residencies, there will be few safe places for young men to learn how to pastor people. Instead, we will continue to have theologically astute but practically ignorant young men taking pastorates that neither they nor their church are prepared to handle. Seminaries can only do so much and, unfortunately, it's not enough given the gravity of our work. In every other field, lawyers article (that is, a lawyer's apprenticeship); doctors have to do a residency. I don't believe that lawyers and doctors do a more significant work than we do. I wish every church would take an intern and have a 'fire date.' Two years and you're gone. Then take another intern."[13]

As a second purpose, Jeff desires to bring more quality pastors into their Canadian context.

Currently Northview trains ten staff in mentorships. Eight of these are simply called interns. They are Bible college graduates who serve in the church for a one-year term. These are people who are exploring ministry possibilities. Two others are called teaching associates. These are seminary graduates who are being groomed for pastoral ministry. The teaching associates and the church both commit to a three-year term.

Northview recognizes the value of leadership training and the value of imparting the DNA of an effective church into young pastors. You will find their materials in appendix K.

Salem Evangelical Free Church in Fargo, North Dakota, is reworking their apprenticeship program. Pastor Glen Stevens has given us permission to include their program in this book. You will find a description of their *Joshua Project* in appendix K. This is a valuable tool for both young pastors and the churches that feel led to develop future leaders. You will also find Pastor Stevens's story in the mini-bio at the end of the chapter. Don't miss it!

Aspiring pastors would be wise to seek churches like Bear Valley, Northview, or Salem Evangelical Free Church for internships and apprenticeships. A person aspiring to be an apprentice or intern should check with seminaries and Bible colleges and denominational offices to locate potential churches and pastors who might facilitate this type of training. The number of these churches is growing but is still quite limited, given the needs we face in equipping young pastors for ministry.

Larger, healthy, growing churches ought to provide these venues for long-term leadership impact. A larger church can be 150 or more in worship attendance. The larger the church, the more potential interns or apprentices you can bring on board. For these ministries to occur, the field of influence of these churches must be larger than the local church. They must see themselves as fulfilling 2 Timothy 2:2.

Selecting a Church or Pastor for an Internship or Apprenticeship

A number of churches provide internships and a smaller number, apprenticeships. Some seminaries and Bible colleges require students to do an internship. If you are required to do so, do not treat it as simply another course requirement. Treat it as a valuable part of your ministry preparation. Research churches that fit your theological persuasion and your ministry development needs. Then apply. Make it a full year or longer of full-time internship, if possible.

Selecting an Intern or Apprentice

Please look back at the section on what to expect from a protégé, noting especially the essential characteristics. If you find someone who has these qualities, you should have a winner. Prayerfully seek those in whom you will invest yourself. Invest well. You and your protégé will be forever grateful.

Recruiting a Mentor/Coach or Protégé

In this section we give you some important information that will help you make wise choices when recruiting a mentor/coach or a protégé. Protégés can be either interns, apprentices, or pastors already in ministry.

Choosing a Mentor/Coach

If you are seeking a mentor/coach to help you in ministry, define your needs before you begin to look. What specific area of life or ministry are you seeking to improve? It may be personal evangelism, counseling, marriage and family issues (at home and with others), interpersonal relationship skills, and so on. At a minimum, follow the seven steps below. You may wish to add specific areas of expertise that you are seeking to add to your ministry skill set. For example, if you desire to become an executive pastor, find a competent executive pastor to mentor or coach you.

1. Determine the area(s) of need in your life.
2. Pray for direction before beginning the search.
3. Do a thorough investigation of those you are considering to make sure they are gifted and competent in the areas where you are seeking to grow.
4. Select a pastor who you feel can help you. He will probably be older with more experience than you and someone who has been successful in ministry. Remember, only 6–15 percent of pastors fall into this category.
5. Approach them to inquire about their willingness to help.
6. Remember to look for the essential characteristics discussed above.
7. Agree on the subject(s) you wish to cover, set a time frame and schedule, and begin to meet.

Choosing a Protégé

The process of choosing a protégé is similar to choosing a mentor/coach. First, you must decide if you have the time to invest in a protégé. There are dozens of young pastors who would love to have someone speak into their lives. Can you be one of them? As you think about the possibility, follow the steps below.

1. Determine your areas of strength.
2. Find a pastor or group of pastors in whom you might invest your life.
3. Pray for God's wisdom and direction in seeking a protégé or protégés.
4. Approach one or more pastors and offer your services.
5. Clearly spell out your expectations before you begin meeting. Let them know you have high expectations!
6. Agree on the subject(s) you wish to cover, set a time frame and schedule, and begin to meet.

Mentoring/coaching promises to make a huge impact in ministry. It is not a quick fix but it certainly will help the church in North America become more effective in reaching our generation for Christ. We must *invest now* if we hope to *see a return* in the future.

Why Become a Mentor or a Coach?

Why should you consider becoming a mentor or a coach? The answer to this question involves first a vision and then a challenge.

The Vision

Remember the vision of the apostle Paul that we referenced in chapter 3? His vision was to glorify God by reaching a growing number of unreached people groups with the gospel through (1) preaching the gospel, (2) planting churches, and (3) developing an ever expanding leadership base who would in turn (1) preach the gospel, (2) plant churches, and (3)develop an ever expanding leadership base! And so it continues.

That vision needs to be rekindled in North America. Pastors who have "it," the ability to re-envision a church, need to share "it."

Leadership coaches Robert Hargrove and Michel Renaud describe a major shift in business practice. They contend that now many business leaders make leadership development a primary focus of their work. They begin with what they call a New Paradigm in business leadership.

> New Paradigm #1. *CEO[s] and top executive[s] spend 25 to 50 percent of their time in leadership development*. The CEO is directly involved in leadership development in those companies that produce a graduation class of CEOs for other firms, as well as leadership bench strength. The most famous example is Jack Welch of General Electric, who said he spent 50 percent of his time on leadership development. He developed his successor, Jeff Immelt, Larry Bossidy of AlliedSignal, James McNerney of 3M, and Robert Nardelli of Home Depot. CEOs need to own leadership development, not automatically defer it to others. They must think of themselves as the top HR person in the company. They see leadership development and performance as totally integrated with performing, not a separate activity.[14]

Hargrove and Renaud also include the following remarkable quote from Jack Welch: "Developing leaders is more important than developing a strategy."[15] Welch recognized that if you train leaders to think and behave the right way, strategy will take care of itself.

If business leaders rediscovered the biblical principles of leadership development, perhaps we in the church should as well. Correcting the dearth of leadership in the church will take time. There are no quick fixes. Leadership development must occupy our thoughts and our actions if we hope to see the church revitalized in our generation! Coaching/mentoring, internships, and apprenticeships must play a major role in leadership development.

Concluding Challenges

Our present situation provides two challenges. First, young pastors long for people who can help them. Many have no one to whom they can turn. The pool of re-envisioning pastors is small, 6–15 percent of all pastors. Thus there are a limited number of qualified mentors who can help re-envision churches. Additional qualified leaders will be the key.

People who mentor or coach are investing in the big picture. They are thinking Church (with a capital "C," universal), not just church (little "c," their own personal little kingdom). Think beyond your own ministry zone and begin to think in terms of the greater harvest. Unlike Jack Welch, you probably cannot dedicate 50 percent of your time to leadership development, but think of the impact you can make by investing a day or two a month in other leaders. The results can be enormous.

Perhaps your church needs to develop a DNA Impartation Station where young pastors-to-be can catch a vision for re-envisioning ministry. Make room in your budget for an intern a year (or more if you are a larger church). Build into the lives of these aspiring pastors a passion and the wherewithal to lead a church from decline to growth. This must be caught. It is not taught.

If you are an older, fruitful pastor who has done well in ministry, why not share the wealth? Become the leader of a pastor cluster, bring on an intern or apprentice, or select a promising young pastor and pour your life into him. Increase your impact. Become a mentor or coach for the glory of God!

Invest, invest, and invest.

Mini-Bio of a Re-Envisioning Leader

Glen Stevens is just a regular guy who grew up in a Christian home in Minot, North Dakota—no superstar, no extraordinary person, just a normal, down-to-earth individual whom God is using in spectacular ways. He is an encouragement to other "ordinary" people who would like to pastor in extraordinary ways.

How did this ordinary guy become such an effective pastor? He helped start Crossroads Evangelical Free Church in Albert Lea, Minnesota, and it grew from 125 to 725 in 13 years. That's tremendous, steady growth. Now he has returned to the place where his ministry began, Salem Evangelical Free Church in Fargo, North Dakota. In 3 years the church has grown from 511 to 800. How is all this possible for a guy who is so down-to-earth?

It began with an apprenticeship at age twenty-eight. After completing his coursework toward an M.Div., he called Salem to see if he could become an intern. At that time the pastor at Salem, Dr. Greg Scharf, helped develop the Trinity Pastoral Apprenticeship Program with Trinity Evangelical Divinity School. Rather than landing an internship, Glen secured a two-year apprenticeship. In his words, "The apprenticeship was a practical component to go along with the academic side of preparation for ministry. I received five years' experience in two years." Pastor Greg taught Glen how to be a pastor in the church setting.

After thirteen years in Minnesota, Glen returned to his pastoral roots to take the reins at Salem. Glen not only pastors, but he has become a coach for other pastors. He also developed a new apprentice ministry for Salem and continues to pass on to others the gift so freely bestowed on him.

Glen's apprenticeship helped him answer basic ministry questions, such as:

- Where do I begin?
- What makes a pastor effective?
- What are the next steps I need to be taking?
- How do I relate to my church board?
- What should I do to handle difficult people?
- How do I balance the pressures of ministry and my family?
- What should my schedule look like?

Pastor Scharf laid a great foundation on which to build an extraordinary ministry!

Questions for Reflection, Discussion, and Application

1. For younger pastors: As an aspiring preacher, which of the four models of leadership development appeals to you—mentoring, coaching, internship, or apprenticeship, or a combination?

2. Which category in the bell curve figure in this chapter best fits you? Your position on the curve will dictate the direction you must choose.
   a. If you are a REP, consider how to expand your impact with other pastors in need.
   b. If you are a NREP in the middle section, consider identifying a coach or a mentor and enter a relationship with that individual.
   c. If you are a NREP in the right-hand section, you should seriously examine your divine design and direction. If you continue in vocational ministry, by all means secure a mentor or a coach. On the other hand, perhaps the Lord has wired you for something entirely different. Discover that and pursue it with passion.
3. If you are a REP, is your church outwardly focused enough to begin investing in interns and/or apprenticeships? If the answer is yes, then pursue that avenue. If the answer is no, what steps do you need to take to get to yes?
4. How do your essential characteristics stack up? Where are your strengths and your weaknesses?
5. When we described Glen Stevens's ministry in the mini-bio, we said that God uses ordinary people in extraordinary ways. Do you agree with this statement? If so, what might God do through you?

13

Preparation, Process, and Practice

The primary focus of this investigation, unlike most books on the topic, is *who*. Who re-envisions churches? Our exploration of re-envisioning pastors has provided the church with important answers to this question based on temperament studies and demonstrable, behavioral characteristics unique to re-envisioning pastors. However, we must address the *how*. Both REPs and especially NREPs need a re-envisioning process that will help them lead their churches in a turnaround. Many REPS know how to do this intuitively. In our exploration we have come across some (CSs and SCs) that did not share the characteristics of REPs but who re-envisioned churches because they knew how to do so. Therefore, it is imperative that we cover the preparation, process, and practice of re-envisioning a church.

Introduction: Process versus Model

The Model Mentality

A typical response for many struggling pastors who are leading plateaued and dying churches is to attend a megachurch conference sponsored by a church that is led by an envisioning or re-envisioning pastor. These struggling, often discouraged pastors

RE-ENVISIONING A CHURCH
Stage 1: The *preparation* for re-envisioning a church
Stage 2: The *process* for re-envisioning a church
Stage 3: The *practice* of re-envisioning a church

are searching for a model they can mimic and hope that its application will turn their churches around. The thinking is that if we just do what these successful churches are doing, we will experience the same results.

This seldom works, because mimicking a model doesn't produce churches that are authentic to who they are (their identity), when they are (their times), and where they are (their geography). You can't reproduce a North Point in Little Hope, Texas!

The Pursuit of a Process

Instead of aping or mimicking some successful super church, a struggling church needs to pursue a process that results in a model that's not only authentic but unique to the church and its culture. This process consists of three stages for church development: the preparation, process, and practice stages.

Stage 1: The Preparation for Re-Envisioning the Church

STAGE 1: THE PREPARATION FOR RE-ENVISIONING THE CHURCH
Step 1: Gain Support
Step 2: Draft a Strategic Leadership Team (SLT)
Step 3: Communicate Constantly
Step 4: Embrace a Theology of Change
Step 5: Conduct a Church Analysis
Step 6: Recruit a Coach or Mentor
Step 7: Lay a Spiritual Foundation

Before we attempt to lead our churches through the revitalization process, we must prepare them for what is to come. If we jump right into it, without preparing our people, chances are excellent that such an effort will fail. Thus preparation must precede process. The following seven steps outline this necessary preparation.

Step 1: Gain Support

First, you must gain the support of the empowered leadership of the church. We are not using the term *empowered* here in a negative sense. Every church will have a locus of power. In many churches it is the pastor; in others it is the board, a patriarch or matriarch, or even a prominent family. Regardless of who it is, if they are not supportive of the process, it will not happen. This step, then, serves as an indicator of whether to move forward with the re-envisioning process. If the power person or people are not ready, then the Holy Spirit who prepares people for the process is telling you to wait until they are ready. Otherwise you could waste a lot of time and money on a failed process.

Step 2: Draft a Strategic Leadership Team (SLT)

You will need a team of leaders to lead by proxy your church through the process. We refer to them as the strategic leadership team (SLT), because they are the key servant leaders in your church. They know the church best and will likely have the favor and support of the congregation. When congregants know that their leaders are on the team, they recognize that other leaders besides the pastor are a part of the process. This encourages them to be supportive of the team and its work.

Step 3: Communicate Constantly

A vital factor in preparing a church for a turnaround is trust. We have a truism in the Malphurs Group: "You can't lead people if they don't trust you." And one vital way to engender people's trust is to communicate with them. As much as is feasible, keep them abreast of the SLT's work. Use every means possible to connect with the congregation. This would include announcements, bulletin inserts, and progress reports posted on the church's website, Facebook page, as well as Twitter.

Step 4: Embrace a Theology of Change

Often people are willing to embrace change when they understand that, according to the Bible, it is okay to change. Thus you need to develop and regularly communicate a theology of change that consists of *function, form*, and *freedom* (the three *F*s).

1. *Function* refers to what the church does, such as worship, evangelism, fellowship, service, and so on. These were the functions of the first-century church and are still true for the church today. They do not change.
2. The functions of the church are manifest in its *forms*. For example, the church's worship (a function) may be classical, traditional, or contemporary (forms of worship). The form, not the function, may change and probably must change if the church is to stay relevant to its culture.
3. The church has a lot of *freedom* in terms of the forms it uses to accomplish its functions. This does not sit well with legalistic churches.

Step 5: Conduct a Church Analysis

Just as people have four vital signs (pulse, respiration, blood pressure, and temperature), so does the church. If you want to know how you are doing physically, then you regularly check your vital signs. And if you want to know how your ministry is doing spiritually, you check its vital signs. One vital sign to check is congregational worship attendance. Is the worship attendance growing, plateaued, or declining? Check congregational giving or stewardship. Is the giving growing, plateaued, or declining? A third vital sign to check is the church's strengths. Ask, where are we strong and what do we do well? The fourth sign is the church's weaknesses. Ask, where are we weak? What are we not doing so well and how might this be vital to the life of our church?

Step 6: Recruit a Coach or Mentor

When I (Gordon) explored the characteristics of revitalizing pastors, I discovered that most had a mentor or coach. Often these were older, wiser pastors, who were willing to come alongside the pastor and coach or mentor him. Coaches function primarily to ask pastors the kinds of questions about themselves and their ministries that they need to be asking but are not. Mentors function to help pastors think through some aspect of the church's life and its ministries. Both also serve as needed accountability partners for pastors who may not be accountable to anyone, though this is desperately needed.

Step 7: Lay a Spiritual Foundation

It is imperative that we keep in mind that the preparation and process are spiritual in nature. It is possible that a pastor could lead his church through the re-envisioning process through the power of the flesh and not the Spirit. Churches are spiritual organisms, and such an approach would spell disaster. Consequently, we must prepare our churches spiritually for the process. Spiritual preparation includes such practices as the confession of sin, righting wrongs, addressing gossip, seeking and offering forgiveness, dealing with anger, addressing grievances, and other similar practices.

STAGE 2: THE PROCESS FOR RE-ENVISIONING A CHURCH
Step 1: Develop the Church's Biblical Mission
Step 2: Discover the Church's Core Values
Step 3: Develop the Church's Vision
Step 4: Design the Church's Strategy

Stage 2: The Process for Re-Envisioning a Church

At this point, the church should be well prepared to address the re-envisioning process. We have intentionally and strategically built this process around certain vital biblical texts that address in some way Christ's church. This process involves four steps.

Step 1: Develop the Church's Biblical Mission

Every church must have a mission. The mission provides the church with its direction and function. The direction spells out where the church is going, and the function addresses what it is supposed to accomplish. The Savior has already given the church its mission back in the first century. The mission is to make disciples, according to Matthew 28:19; Mark 16:15; and Luke 24:45–49. The problem is determining what this means. We don't use the term *disciple* much today outside the church. We believe that making disciples includes both evangelism in particular (see Mark 16:15; Luke 24:45–49) and edification in general (Matt. 28:20; 10:34–39).

I (Aubrey) ask the churches that we work with in the Malphurs Group to develop a short, memorable, and biblical mission statement that the congregation will find easy to remember. We ask that it be short enough to fit on a business card. One church came up with: "To know Christ and make him known." Another's mission was: "To present Christ as Savior and to pursue him as Lord."

I can't emphasize enough the importance of a church's mission statement. Recently I had two retired military officers in one of my courses at Dallas Seminary. One day they made an amazing statement about the importance of the mission. They said that the military would never send troops into a battle without a clear understanding of its mission. We need to think the same in our churches.

Early in the twenty-first century, there's a growing movement for church's to focus specifically on reaching people in their neighborhoods. And to do so means that the church needs to consider the tangible as well as emotional needs of the people around it. The emphasis is less on being invitational—inviting people to your church—and more on being incarnational—living the life of Christ among our neighbors outside the church. This is referred to as the missional church movement. While this is a relatively new emphasis among Anglo and Asian churches, it has long been practiced by African American churches, specifically in their communities.

JERUSALEM CHURCH'S CORE VALUES
Worship
Fellowship
Biblical instruction
Evangelism
Service

Step 2: Discover the Church's Core Values

A church's core values are its constant, passionate, and biblical core beliefs that both guide and empower its ministries. What does this mean? The church's values will be constant—they will not change much; they desperately cling to life. The church's values are what its people care deeply and feel strongly about. That is passion. And the values must be biblical.

An example of the Jerusalem church values are found in Acts 2:41–47. They were evangelism (vv. 41, 47), fellowship (vv. 42, 44–46), worship (vv. 42–43, 46–47), biblical instruction (v. 42), and service (v. 45). We're convinced that spiritually healthy churches will hold to and live these as actual, not aspirational, values.

The core values both empower and drive the church. They dictate what a church will and will not do. For example, if a church does not value evangelism, they will do little evangelism. The same holds for the other ministries of the church. We in The Malphurs Group help churches discover their core values because, by definition, they dictate what churches will and will not do. We use a values discovery process called storyboarding. If you would like to know more about this process, you will find a description of it on pages 42–44 in *Advanced Strategic Planning*.[1]

Step 3: Develop the Church's Vision

The vision, as well as the mission, is important to the church, because it too addresses the church's ministry direction. You will recall from chapter 10 that a vision is a clear, exciting picture of God's future for your church as it can and must be. Since we've already written the chapter on vision, we'll make a few comments and then move on to the strategy.

While both mission and vision address the future of the church, the mission addresses where the church is going for planning purposes, while the vision is what makes people want to go there. If this is not happening, then the church needs to assess its current vision and consider developing a more relevant vision.

Step 4: Design the Church's Strategy

The ministry's mission and vision address in their own ways where the church is going. It is the strategy, however, that clarifies how it will get there. A good strategy will consist of five core concepts: reaching the community, making disciples, building a team, analyzing the setting, and raising the finances.

DESIGNING A CHURCH STRATEGY
Reach the community
Make disciples
Build a team
Analyze the setting
Raise the finances

Reach the Community

Community is the people you will reach. In the business world it is commonly referred to as your customers. The church's community is the people who live in its geographical sphere of spiritual influence. It spells out where and with whom the church's ministries will take place geographically. Luke clarifies this for the Jerusalem church in Acts 1:8 where Jesus states the church is to be a witness in Jerusalem, Judea and Samaria, and to the ends of the earth. The important community question for the church is, What or where is your Jerusalem?

There are two answers. First, you must decide where the geographical boundaries lie for your church's community. Much depends on whether you are located in the inner city, suburbia, or a rural community. Generally speaking, it will be somewhere between one to three miles, represented by concentric circles with the church's facility in the center.

Next, you need to investigate who lives within your Jerusalem. The key to this is demographics that will provide you with all kinds of information about your Jerusalem, and much of this information is free. When Rick Warren did this exercise, he named the typical person in Saddleback's community Saddleback Sam. If you want to know who is Saddleback's customer, it's Saddleback Sam.

When working through this exercise with churches, I (Aubrey) like to ask them a most thought-provoking question, Why would your community want to attend your church? With all that Saturday nights and Sunday mornings have to offer—sports, movies, outdoor activities, and so forth, why would they be attracted to your church?

Make Disciples

As we know, the church's mission is to make disciples, which involves both evangelism (winning people to Christ) and edification (helping them mature in Christ). I (Aubrey) like to ask churches this question: Do you have a clear, simple, memorable pathway for making disciples through your church that most people understand and know where they are along that pathway? The normal response is either a blank stare or a shaking of heads from side to side.

To help churches think through this, I use what I refer to as the discipleship or maturity matrix. I create it first by drawing a horizontal line across the top of a four-by-eight-foot white board. On the line I write what I believe are a congregant's characteristics of maturity: worship, fellowship, biblical instruction, evangelism, and service or ministry. (Note that these are also the church's values.) My view is that a mature disciple will manifest these characteristics much of the time.

Next, I draw a vertical line down the left side of the white board. Then I list the church's primary ministries along that vertical line. There will likely be only a few of these—usually somewhere between two to as many as six or seven, as is the case with Willow Creek Community Church in Chicago. The primary ministries are those that primarily help people realize the characteristics of maturity in their lives and experience them daily. They also make up a church's unique ministry model that is to focus on evangelism and edification. Some examples are a church's worship service, Sunday school, and small groups.

The ideal is that each primary ministry helps people to embrace one of the several characteristics of a mature believer. The people who attend and those who lead a primary ministry should know why they are doing what they are doing or the purpose of the primary ministry. For example, the purpose of small groups ministries is fellowship.

Build a Team

BUILD A TEAM
Mobilize the congregation
Develop the staff
Train the board

Most churches will have two or three teams they will need to build.

1. The *congregation* makes up the team that is to do the ministry, according to Ephesians 4:11–13. The job of the church is to mobilize them so that they follow through and actually do the ministry, not the pastor.
2. The *church's staff* may be as few as 1 or 2 people in a small church to 150 to 200 in a megachurch. Our view is that the primary role of the church's staff, in addition to operating in their areas of expertise, is to develop leaders who are attracted to and minister in those areas and beyond.
3. A *church's governing board*, such as an elder board, needs to know why they exist and how they are to function and receive training to fulfill their role. The church must decide if they are merely advisory or if they have some power. And if the latter, how does their power compare to that of the pastor? I (Aubrey) answer these and other important board questions in my book *Leading Leaders*.[2]

Analyze the Setting

ANALYZE THE SETTING
Locate strategically
Address shifting ethnicities
Invite a "mystery attender"

Your setting is where your ministry takes place. It consists of a facility and the location of that facility. Re-envisioning churches attempt to locate strategically in their geographic communities. They ask, Where can we have the greatest impact in and on our community? The missional church movement has de-emphasized the need for a facility and location, focusing instead on being out in their community and meeting in facilities such as a retirement center, school, movie theater, park, restaurant, and so forth. Since some church facilities are in bad shape, we suspect that they would benefit by selling these facilities and using the income for other purposes such as planting churches in their Jerusalem.

Some churches are concerned about shifting ethnicities. The people who have moved into the community are not like the people in the church who have moved out of the community. They are of a different color, speak a different language, and may live at a lower level of income. The obvious approach would be to attempt to reach these new people. However, the church will need to make some serious changes in what it does and how it does it. For example, it might need to change the worship music and the instruments. It might need to bring on a pastor or staff persons who are of the same ethnicity and speak the same language as the community.

The Malphurs Group encourages such churches to do what is known in some circles as the "mystery shopper." Ours is known as the "mystery attender." The church invites someone who does not know the church to visit on a Saturday evening or Sunday morning. They would observe the culture and watch what takes place and then report back to the church staff. How are they treated? Do people welcome them or ignore them? Are the facilities clean and properly maintained? When a newcomer has a negative response in these areas, it sends the message that the people of the church don't seem to care anymore, and the church is on its last legs. After their first visit, they will probably never return.

Raise the Finances

RAISE THE FINANCES
Determine who is responsible for the finances
Manage the finances
Determine ways to increase giving

Re-envisioning churches are often short on finances. Their pastors may be confused as to who should raise funds, how much, and how. Certainly most church cultures look to the pastor to raise and manage their finances, and there may be some biblical evidence that supports this (1 Tim. 3:4; 5:17). The problem is that most pastors either do not know how or do not want to take on this job. They tend to be chaplains who spend their time teaching and preaching the Bible or visiting congregants in their homes and in the hospital. What pastors must realize is that raising capital is part of leadership and it is in their job description, whether they like it or not. It is important that they not neglect it and learn how to do it. We will cover this shortly.

How much must they raise? The answer addresses a key tool in the pastor's arsenal—the budget. And critical to the budget is the proper allocation of funds. The problem is that too many church budgets are written in accounteze. Some accountant helped them set up their budget, not realizing that church finances are different from business finances. We recommend that all churches allocate a certain percentage of their funds to four items: 10 percent to missions and evangelism, 50 percent to personnel, 20 percent to ministries, and 20 percent to facilities. Also keep in mind that if you adjust these allocations (we suggest that you do not), you will have to account for the funds some other place in the budget. I (Aubrey) have worked with several churches who pride themselves on giving to missions. One such church allocated around 23 percent for missions. The only problem is that this large amount meant that funding in other areas had to be less. In this case it affected personnel, who were underpaid.

How can the re-envisioning pastor raise funds? The following are some ways.

- *Cast the church's vision.* As we learned in the chapter on vision, people will give to a strong, compelling vision.
- *Set aside one month annually to preach and teach stewardship.* Have any Sunday school classes and small groups follow up by providing more information and challenging people to give. Use the small groups to hold people accountable.
- *Make it easy to give.* Provide online services or whatever it takes, depending on the age and culture of the church, for people to give regularly. Some churches still provide special envelopes.
- *Hold a new members and/or a newcomers class.* People tend to be more interested in giving when considering and/or joining the church. Let them know the church's expectations. The church would also be wise to provide some type of financial classes or counseling for those who struggle financially due to debt and easy credit.
- *Have an occasional capital campaign* to raise funds for missions or for revamping or updating the facilities or both.
- *Cultivate the church's giving champions*—those with the gift of giving. The pastor can meet with these champions and let them know the church's needs in addition to ministering to and counseling them personally.
- *Challenge the congregation to increase their giving* 1–2 percent more than last year. This is not a lot of money for most congregants, but will add up over time for the church.
- *Finally, an area that many churches have not thought about is the ministry of deferred giving.* This involves wills, living trusts, charitable trusts,

life insurance, real estate, endowments, and so forth. The advantage of such giving is that it benefits the church long after the giver has gone to be with Christ, enjoying his presence and fellowship in heaven.

Stage 3: The Practice of Re-Envisioning a Church

The practice of re-envisioning the church involves evaluation and implementation.

Evaluation

In Revelation 2–3 there is good precedent for some type of church evaluation. Every church will experience evaluation. For example, how often has a couple been driving home from a service or a visit at a church and discussed the pastor's sermon? Did you like it? Why or why not? Common questions for people's kids are, Did you like the children's program? What did you learn? Do you want to go back? This is informal evaluation and it takes place every week in some form.

My (Aubrey's) suggestion is that, since evaluation takes place anyway, why don't we make it formal and do it once a year? We suggest at the very least that the church consider evaluating the senior pastor and any staff. The senior pastor and the staff must have a job or ministry description that serves as a basis for such a formal evaluation. That way there is no question as to what they are being evaluated for. Many prefer a 360-degree evaluation format where the person being evaluated is evaluated by his or her supervisor, peers, and those who work for them. They also evaluate themselves. We have found the self-evaluation to be most effective.

Implementation

We want to stress the importance of implementing or executing your process. Without implementation, nothing happens. Without implementation, much money and time has been wasted.

We suggest that you recruit the leaders of your implementation process from the strategic leadership team and let them draft others to work with them. Each team will take responsibility to implement parts of the strategy such as community outreach, disciple making, and so forth. While we have placed this at the end of this chapter and the planning process, that does not mean that we wait until the end to launch implementation. We recommend that you begin execution early in the process. Then, as you cover each piece of the strategy, the team has the necessary information to act. And by the time you get to the end of the process, the teams are up and running.

Questions for Reflection, Discussion, and Application

1. The authors believe that the pastor or person who attempts to lead a church through the re-envisioning process is as important as the process itself. They argue that *who* comes before *how*. Do you agree with them? Why or why not?
2. The authors also believe that how you re-envision the church is important since some NREPs have led their churches through a turnaround because they knew how to do it. Do you agree or disagree? Why or why not?
3. The authors believe that you must prepare a church for the re-envisioning process before you launch the process. Does this make sense? Why or why not?
4. Do a church ministry analysis on your church that includes checking the church's four vital signs. Are your attendance and giving growing, plateaued, or in decline? Why? What are some of your strengths as a church? What are your greatest strengths? What are some of your weaknesses? What are your greatest weaknesses?
5. Does your church have a mission statement? Why or why not? If so, what is it? Does it align with the Great Commission? Why or why not? Is it short and memorable? Do your people know what it is should a visitor ask?
6. Have you identified your core values as a church? What are they? Are any outward focused? How do your core values align with the five that the authors noted in Acts 2:41–47? What values, if any, are missing?
7. Does your church have a vision statement? Why or why not? If so, what is it? Does the congregation know what it is and does the vision excite them? Why or why not?
8. Does your ministry have in place a plan for reaching your community? Why or why not? Where is your community or Jerusalem? Who is included in your Jerusalem? What are some ways you can reach out to your community?
9. Do you have a clear, simple, memorable pathway for making disciples that most in your church understand and know where they are along that pathway? If so, what is it? If not, why not and what will you do about this?

10. Do your people believe that it is the pastor's or the people's job to do the ministry? What does Scripture teach? Do you have in place a process for mobilizing your congregation for ministry? Why or why not?
11. Does your church have any paid ministry staff? If not, why not? If yes, who are they and what do they do? Within their expertise, are they involved in developing leaders for the church?
12. Is your church facility located strategically to reach your community for Christ? If yes, explain how you are strategically located. If not, why not and what can you do about it?
13. In your church who leads in the area of its finances? Why? Is your budget easy to decipher or do you have a serious case of accountanteze? If the latter, what will you do about it? Who, if anyone, is responsible for raising funds for your church's ministry? How do they raise funds? How might they better raise funds?
14. Do you have a plan in place to implement your re-envisioning process? Why or why not? Do you have a formal evaluation process? Why or why not? If so, who gets evaluated and how?

14

Re-Envisioning Seminaries, Denominations, and Networks

With the decline of the church across America has come a decline in most major denominations, judicatories, networks, associations, and so forth. However, we're convinced that this does not and should not have to be. Rather than throw in the towel on them, I would prefer to throw down the gauntlet to them—to challenge them to re-envision themselves and what they do. Like so many churches, somewhere along the way, they have lost their vision—assuming they had a vision in the first place. I am convinced that it can be a new day for these parachurch organizations.

I would also say the same to our seminaries and Bible colleges. Times have been tough for them as well. Over the past thirty years, many of our smaller Bible colleges have not survived, leaving us with the bigger schools such as Moody and a few others. Some of our seminaries have struggled, as many—even the larger ones—have seen a decline in enrollment and donor giving. As with the denominations, I believe it can be a new day for seminaries and some Bible colleges as well. This involves re-envisioning.

Re-Envisioning Seminaries

Identity

Seminaries are parachurch ministries that have come alongside churches to help them accomplish what they likely would not do by themselves. For example, they can provide in-depth Bible teaching that would be difficult but not impossible to find in a local church. They also cultivate scholars who can pour their lives into apologetics and other important disciplines that address defending the faith. Another advantage is they can accomplish much of this in a shorter period of time than the local church. The typical seminary program lasts two to three years, whereas the church might need five or more years to accomplish the same thing.

Strengths

What are seminaries doing well? Most seminaries do an excellent job of teaching the Bible. For example, Dallas Seminary, unlike most others, has a department of English Bible. The goal of this department is to introduce students and future pastors to the entire Bible by surveying all of its books. Seminaries are also good at teaching theology and church history, which often go together. Many offer language study, which you rarely see in a church. They teach Hebrew and Greek and guide the use of these languages to exegete and apply the Old and New Testaments. Another more practical area is homiletics or preaching. And a good homiletics curriculum will guide students not only in how to preach but in how to preach exegetical and topical sermons and narrative portions of the Bible as well as the Epistles.

Weaknesses

We must also ask, What are they not doing well that is vital to the church? What are the weaknesses? Perhaps the most important answer that affects the church is the development of leaders. Seminary-trained pastor Andy Stanley writes:

> I attended a highly respected seminary for four years. You know how many leadership classes my school required me to take? I bet you do. None. Not a one. And my degree was the degree designed for those who felt called to lead a local church. Worse than the fact that leadership wasn't taught was the implicit message: Leadership isn't important. If you know the Bible, you know all you need to know to lead a local church. But knowing the Bible does not a leader make.[1]

So what kind of pastors do seminaries produce? They tend to develop scholar pastors who function as chaplains primarily in small churches.

Suggestions

SUGGESTIONS FOR SEMINARIES
Help students discover God's direction for their lives
Guide students in crafting a leadership development plan (LDP)
Partner with churches that can provide internships and residencies
Require students to enlist a mentor or coach

Discover God's Direction

Having taught in a seminary for over thirty years, I (Aubrey) have several suggestions for seminaries. One is to help students determine their ministry directions. Another term for this is *God's will for their vocational direction*. My experience is that it is rare to find a student who knows this and can take courses that develop and equip them to serve in their ministries. This could be addressed in the very first semester of the first year, by helping students discover their divine design. As you recall from an earlier chapter, design dictates direction. This would take place both in the seminary and the local church where students can test their wiring in the cauldron of real-life ministry.

Require a Leadership Development Plan

Seminaries need to require students to develop a leadership development plan (LDP) and guide them in doing it. This assumes that they have a good sense of what God plans to do with them in ministry. Such a plan would help students know what courses they should take and the importance of the local church in ministry preparation.

Partner with Churches

Seminaries should work closely with churches that can provide the kind of experience that will prepare students for church-related ministries. This would include internships and residencies, much like those offered in a teaching hospital. They can provide students with opportunities to confirm their divine design and ministry direction. They could give them a broad range of ministry experiences they would never get in a seminary. Interns would have opportunities to look over the pastor's or staff's shoulders as they do ministry.

Enlist a Mentor or Coach

Students need an advisor or, better, a coach or mentor. This could be someone on the faculty of the seminary or a pastor or staff person in their church. I am not aware of anyone who does not believe in or support the use of coaches and mentors for training in ministry.

Re-Envisioning Denominations, Judicatories, and Networks

Identity

Like seminaries and other schools, denominations and judicatories are parachurch organizations. They too have come alongside churches to help them accomplish what they and seminaries cannot do by themselves.

Strengths

A major strength of denominations is their size, which enables them to accomplish what individual churches could never accomplish on their own. This includes such things as providing chaplains for the armed services, offering lower rates for various kinds of insurance (medical, automobile, house, and so on), and retirement plans. Some are able to support missionaries so that the missionaries themselves do not have to raise support. A denomination can also weigh in on some national issues, such as abortion, homosexuality, and other similar concerns. Being a part of a bigger organization brings with it a sense of belonging to something bigger than oneself. Finally, those within a denomination will come to know others in the area with whom they can enjoy fellowship and camaraderie.

Weaknesses

Denominations also have their weaknesses. They can become so large that they lose contact with the individual pastor. They may expect loyalty to the denomination that may not be realistic. They may have too much power over the individual churches that make up the organization. And many have lost their way or reason for being and are losing their following.

Suggestions

Questions that these organizations should be asking are, What can we do to grow and develop pastors that the seminary cannot or is not accomplishing? What are the gaps in seminary training and other pastoral training that a network or judicatory can address?

Leadership Development

I have already pointed out the important area of leadership in general and leader development in particular. Denominations must address the training of REPs and NREPs for turnaround ministry. This could take place in the context of boot camps, seminars, and leader development clusters.

SUGGESTIONS FOR DENOMINATIONS AND NETWORKS
Provide leadership development opportunities
Provide mentors and coaches
Offer vocational counseling
Assist churches with their pastoral search process
Encourage pastoral research
Outsource some ministry services

Mentors and Coaches

Denominations should provide mentors and coaches for established church pastors, as they have for those involved in church planting. These people could be of immense help in advising REPs and NREPs. The denominations should pursue REPs and invite them to become mentors and coaches for churches in the denomination.

Vocational Counseling

Denominations should provide counsel for struggling pastors. As addressed earlier in this book, struggling churches are often led by struggling pastors who are questioning themselves and their ability to lead a church. Many are beginning to doubt whether they should be in ministry at all and are considering dropping out and even pursuing another profession. In addition to vocational doubts some are facing problems in their marriages that are impacting their leadership. Counsel for these problems is vital and can be provided by the church's denomination.

The Pastoral Search Process

Churches would benefit from help with their pastoral search process. My (Aubrey's) experience is that most churches are not good at finding senior pastors and staff, and this only complicates the pastoral leadership problem. Churches may not realize that they need lots of help in this area. I was consulting with a church several years ago, and during the breaks, various people would come to me and complain about their pastor. I would ask, "Why did you hire him in the first place?" They obviously did not know what they were doing. The denomination could advise churches to look for a REP to assist them in the search process.

Encourage Research

Due to doctor of ministry programs, dissertations, and theses, there is lots of good information available on various topics that relate to pastoral ministry.

I (Aubrey) have one doctor of ministry student who has done an excellent job of investigating what local churches, large and small, are doing, if anything, to develop leaders. I have a master of theology student who researched and wrote an outstanding thesis on vision that has impacted my thinking on whether vision statements should be short or long.

I'm not aware of any of this kind of research that is being done at a denominational or judicatory level, and our leaders desperately need it. Because of my position at a seminary, I am aware of some of the research that is being done, but most denominations and networks are not involved in research. I believe that the solution to this lack of knowledge is for them to sponsor research in the various aspects of pastoral leadership that will greatly assist pastors in their ministries. One example is the use of temperament tools, such as the Personal Profile (DISC) and the Myers-Briggs Type Indicator (MBTI). These tools can be used to discover if there are specific characteristics that make up the profile of an executive pastor, a youth pastor, a worship pastor, and others. The denomination could offer their pastors (especially those with the doctor of ministry degree who are familiar with research) a stipend and the opportunity to present their research in seminars at its annual and other meetings.

Outsourcing Services

Not just anybody can provide the kinds of training pastors need, and it is doubtful that denominations have such a person on their staff. To provide this level of training, then, top people or experts in their fields must be brought in to train pastors. For example, who is known for strategic planning, vision development and casting, community outreach, disciple making, and so forth? Bring these people into your meetings and have them conduct workshops that walk pastors and staff through their areas of expertise. For example, I regularly conduct workshops on how to craft a leadership development process that affects leaders at every level of the church. The goal is for each person to walk away from the workshop with such a plan in hand, ready to be implemented.

Mini-Bio: A Glimmer of Hope

David DeWitt, a likeable, faithful, middle-aged pastor, is currently serving his third church. This church resulted from the merger of two unhealthy congregations about eighteen years ago. Then the church suffered a split over a doctrinal issue a year and a half after David's arrival.

His leadership profile and Pastoral Leadership Assessment would mark him as a non–re-envisioning pastor. His church statistics support this. He attended a boot camp led by Gary McIntosh and me (Gordon), in September 2012. We gave essential tools for turnaround to the leaders assembled. We also organized two pastor clusters to help follow up with the participants.

David was an eager learner. He took lots of notes, asked many questions, and readily engaged in the discussions generated during camp and after hours.

When he returned home, he told us, "I told the church everything we talked about at the boot camp. The church responded, 'Let's do it together!'" The church continues to work through changes a year later, including a name change, adding a Celebrate Recovery ministry, planning a second service, and restructuring the church board. David stated, "I had thought about many of the things you covered, but the boot camp helped crystallize my thinking." (In many cases, pastors search for "permission" to do what God has already ordained them to do. Though permission does not need to be granted, the effect of doing so releases pastors for fruitfulness they never dreamed possible!)

This is perhaps a good way to sum up a book on re-envisioning pastoral leadership. As we have seen, the majority of pastors struggle to lead their churches to positive growth, health, and vitality. But given the right tools with coaching and mentoring, many of these pastors will become more useful instruments in the Master's hand. And as we have noted, two elements are necessary for church revitalization: a capable pastor and a willing congregation. Both of these are developing at United Wesleyan Church, soon to be CrossPoint Wesleyan Church, in Mount Orab, Ohio—the church David pastors.

May the tribe of capable pastors and willing congregations grow exponentially for the glory of our great God and Savior, Jesus Christ!

Questions for Reflection, Discussion, and Application

1. What are your thoughts about seminary preparation? Have you attended a seminary or Bible college? Do you agree with the authors' assessment of seminary preparation? Why or why not? Would you add any strengths of seminaries they may have missed? If so, what? Would you add any weaknesses that they did not list? If so, what?
2. What are your thoughts about the authors' suggestions for seminaries? What do you agree and disagree with? What would you add to the list of suggestions?

3. What do you think about the authors' critique of denominations and networks? Do you agree with the strengths given? Why or why not? Are there any you would add to the list? If so, what? Do you agree with their list of weaknesses? Why or why not? What have they missed?
4. Do you believe that the authors' suggestions for denominations are right? Why or why not? What would you add to their list?

Appendix A

Temperament Indicator 1

Instructions

Read the four terms listed across each line. Then rank each characteristic for how well it describes you in a ministry or work-related situation.

Number 4 is most like you, and number 1 is least like you. Each word should have a number 1, 2, 3, or 4 (see sample below). When you are finished, total the number in each column and write that number in the space provided below that column.

_4_ Direct	_1_ Popular	_2_ Loyal	_3_ Analytical

___ Decisive	___ Outgoing	___ Dependable	___ Logical
___ Controlling	___ Expressive	___ Steady	___ Thorough
___ Competent	___ Influential	___ Responsible	___ Skeptical
___ Blunt	___ Enthusiastic	___ Sensible	___ Compliant
___ Competitive	___ Persuasive	___ Cooperative	___ Serious
___ Callous	___ Impulsive	___ Submissive	___ Accurate
___ Volatile	___ Manipulative	___ Conforming	___ Picky
___ Persistent	___ Personable	___ Harmonious	___ Creative
___ Productive	___ Animated	___ Restrained	___ Fearful
___ Self-reliant	___ Articulate	___ Predictable	___ Diplomatic
___ *Total*	___ *Total*	___ *Total*	___ *Total*
(Doer)	*(Influencer)*	*(Steady)*	*(Thinker)*

Appendix B

Type Indicator 2

Instructions

1. As you take this indicator, please keep in mind that there are no correct or incorrect answers.
2. Read each statement and circle the item (a or b) that best represents your preference in a ministry or work-related environment.
3. Do not spend a lot of time thinking over your answers. Go with your first impulse.

Questions

1. When around other people, I am
   a. expressive
   b. quiet
2. I tend to
   a. dislike new problems
   b. like new problems
3. I make decisions based on my
   a. logic
   b. values
4. I prefer to work in a
   a. structured environment
   b. nonstructured environment
5. I feel more energetic after being
   a. around people
   b. away from people
6. I work best with
   a. facts
   b. ideas
7. People say I am
   a. impersonal
   b. a people-pleaser
8. My friends at work say I am very
   a. organized
   b. flexible

9. I get more work accomplished when I am
   a. with people
   b. by myself
10. I like to think about
    a. what is
    b. what could be
11. I admire
    a. strength
    b. compassion
12. I make decisions
    a. quickly
    b. slowly
13. I prefer
    a. variety and action
    b. focus and quiet
14. I like
    a. established ways to do things
    b. new ways to do things
15. I tend to be rather
    a. unemotional
    b. emotional
16. Most often I dislike
    a. carelessness with details
    b. complicated procedures
17. In my relationships I find that over time it is easy to
    a. keep up with people
    b. lose track of people
18. I enjoy skills that
    a. I have already learned and used
    b. are newly learned but unused
19. Sometimes I make decisions that
    a. hurt other people's feelings
    b. are too influenced by other people
20. When my circumstances change, I prefer to
    a. follow a good plan
    b. adapt to each new situation
21. In conversations I communicate
    a. freely and openly
    b. quietly and cautiously
22. In my work I tend to
    a. take time to be precise
    b. dislike taking time to be precise
23. I relate well to
    a. people like me
    b. most people
24. When working on a project, I do not
    a. like interruptions
    b. mind interruptions
25. Sometimes I find that I
    a. act first and ask questions later
    b. ask questions first and act later
26. I would describe my work style as
    a. steady with realistic expectations
    b. periodic with bursts of enthusiasm
27. At work I need
    a. fair treatment
    b. occasional praise
28. In a new job I prefer to know
    a. only what it takes to get it done
    b. all about it
29. In any job I am most interested in
    a. getting it done and the results
    b. the idea behind the job
30. I have found that I am
    a. patient with routine details
    b. impatient with routine details

31. When working with other people, I find it
    a. easy to correct them
    b. difficult to correct them
32. Once I have made a decision, I consider the case
    a. closed
    b. still open
33. I prefer
    a. lots of acquaintances
    b. a few good friends
34. I am more likely to trust my
    a. experiences
    b. inspirations
35. I consistently decide matters based on
    a. the facts in my head
    b. the feelings in my heart
36. I prefer to work
    a. in an established business
    b. as an entrepreneur

Instructions for Scoring

1. Place a check in the a or b box below to indicate how you answered each question.
2. Add the checks down each column and record the total for each column at the bottom.
3. The highest score for each pair indicates your temperament preference.
4. For each pair subtract the lower from the higher score to discover the difference in your preferences. A higher number indicates a clear choice or preference but does not indicate the measure of development. For example, a higher score for extroversion means that you prefer it over introversion. It does not mean that you are a strong extrovert.

	a	b		a	b		a	b		a	b
1	___	___	2	___	___	3	___	___	4	___	___
5	___	___	6	___	___	7	___	___	8	___	___
9	___	___	10	___	___	11	___	___	12	___	___
13	___	___	14	___	___	15	___	___	16	___	___
17	___	___	18	___	___	19	___	___	20	___	___
21	___	___	22	___	___	23	___	___	24	___	___
25	___	___	26	___	___	27	___	___	28	___	___
29	___	___	30	___	___	31	___	___	32	___	___
33	___	___	34	___	___	35	___	___	36	___	___
Total	___	___	Total	___	___	Total	___	___	Total	___	___
	E	I		S	N		T	F		J	P
	Extrovert	Introvert		Sensing	Intuition		Thinking	Feeling		Judgment	Perception

Appendix C

Leadership Style Survey

Gordon developed a twenty-three-question survey to probe pastoral leadership styles. These comments reflect the average responses given by pastors in the Leadership Style Response questions in Discovery 1. The answers are based on a five-point Likert Scale with the following values:

5: SA—Strongly Agree
4: A—Agree
3: U—Uncertain
2: D—Disagree
1: SD—Strongly Disagree

With this assessment tool, effective pastors tend to have higher scores: the higher the score, the more effective the ministry.

The responses are divided into four groups. In each case, the responses refer to the turnaround pastors (TAPs) in comparison to the non-turnaround pastors (NTAPs).

- Large Difference: a difference of 25 percent or more (Each full point in this scoring system represents a difference of 25 percent)
- Moderate Difference: a difference of at least 0.5–0.9, 12.5–22.5 percent
- Little Difference: less than 0.2–0.4 or 5.0–10.0 percent difference
- No Difference: 0.0–0.1 or 0.0–2.5 percent difference

Leadership Style Responses

Statements	TAPs	NTAPs
Large Difference in Responses (25% or more)		
More outgoing	4.3	3.3
More innovative than traditional	3.8	2.4
Works better with a team of people	4.0	2.7
Moderate Difference in Responses (12.5–22.5%)		
More self-motivated	4.5	3.9
More energetic	4.2	3.6
Better at delegation	4.0	3.3
Better at developing new leadership	4.3	3.4
More focused and determined	4.5	3.7
Better at developing strong relationships	4.5	4.0
More directive type leader	3.3	2.8
Better communicator	4.7	4.0
Better at handling conflict and resolving problems	4.4	3.9
Little Difference in Responses (5.0–10.0%)		
Better at empowering and encouraging others in ministry	4.4	4.0
Tends to be pushy when working toward a goal	2.9	2.6
Able to lead and have people follow	4.2	3.9
Controlling	2.3	2.1
No Difference in Responses (0.0–2.5%)		
More caring and loving	4.2	4.1
Goal or results driven	4.0	3.9
Impatient with people who disagree with me	2.6	2.6
Centrality of Scripture in all things	5.0	4.9
Reaching people for Christ is top priority	3.6	3.6
Making the gospel relevant	4.4	4.4
Preaching more challenging than comforting	3.8	3.7

Observations

- TAPs outscored the NTAPs on 20 of 23 questions.
- Turnaround pastors are significantly more outgoing than their non-turnaround counterparts. This is extremely important for a church to grow by reaching new people.

- Turnaround pastors are not afraid to break the mold and try new things; non-turnaround pastors are more reserved. This fits well with NTAPs being High S and High C in the DISC profile. Pastors wired this way like stability and sameness.
- Turnaround pastors appear to be better team players. Teamwork is essential in a growing church. Teamwork, delegation, and empowering leadership are essential, as no single person or small group can carry the load required for turnaround.
- TAPs are self-motivated. They do not require someone to look over their shoulder and urge them forward.
- Turnaround ministry requires a tremendous amount of energy. Turnaround pastors are more energetic.
- New leadership opens new doors and avenues for ministry. Developing new leaders and delegating responsibilities work well with growing churches.
- Turnaround leaders are very focused in what they do. They are driven by a sharply defined vision to accomplish what cannot be accomplished by a shotgun approach to ministry.
- Both groups have strong relational capabilities. Turnaround leaders have the edge in this category. It is difficult for any church to grow without a relational pastor. Relational pastors tend to produce relational people who produce relational churches.
- TAPs tend to be direct, rather than passive, leaders. They are "take charge" leaders.
- Good communication is necessary for life. It is no less true in the church. The turnaround pastors have a significant lead in this category.
- Change produces conflict and problems. In order to be a TAP, one must have skills in conflict management and problem solving.
- TAPs also will push to accomplish their agenda. However, their responses would indicate that they gently nudge others rather than steamrolling them.
- Both sets of pastors scored very low on the issue of being controlling. One might think that turnaround pastors would be seen as more forceful, but even the lay leaders gave low scores to both turnaround and non-turnaround pastors on this question. Both sets of pastors were patient when dealing with those who disagree with them. These responses point to servant-leadership as a core value of all the pastors in Discovery 1.
- The foundation for good ministry, theology, and methodology is the Word of God. All of the pastors hold the Scriptures in high regard, as they should. This is a prerequisite to sound pastoral ministry at any level.

Appendix D

The Expanded Temperament Indicator 1

We have designed the following material to help you confirm your true temperament and further understand it. You may be predominantly one profile but more likely are a combination of two. Read through the strengths and weaknesses of each profile and determine which is most like you.

1. The Dominance Profile (D)

Strengths

Action oriented	Determined	Persistent
Adventurous	Direct	Pioneering
Bold	Doer	Problem-solver
Brave	Driver	Productive
Competent	Efficient	Resourceful
Competitive	Enterprising	Results oriented
Confident	Fast paced	Risk taker
Courageous	Firm	Self-starter
Daring	Goal oriented	Takes charge
Decisive	Immediate results	Vigorous

Weaknesses

Aggressive	Avoids relationships	Busy
Argumentative	Blunt	Callous
Assertive	Bossy	Cocky

Controlling
Demanding
Dominant
Forceful
Impatient
Impulsive
Independent
Inflexible
Insensitive
Insistent
Opinionated
Outspoken
Overbearing
Overlooks facts
Pushy
Restless
Self-reliant
Strong willed
Stubborn
Tactless
Unyielding
Volatile
Workaholic

2. The Influential Profile (I)

Strengths

Animated
Appealing
Articulate
Attractive
Captivating
Change oriented
Charming
Cheerful
Confidant
Convincing
Dramatic
Emotional
Encouraging
Energetic
Enthusiastic
Expressive
Extroverted
Fast paced
Friendly
Fun loving
Good mixer
Group oriented
High-spirited
Influential
Inspiring
Jovial
Joyful
Lighthearted
Magnetic
Motivating
Optimistic
Outgoing
Personable
Persuasive
Playful
Poised
Popular
Promoter
Risk taker
Sociable
Spirited
Spontaneous
Stimulating
Talkative

Weaknesses

Attacks
Egotistical
Exaggerates
Flippant
Ignores details/facts
Illogical
Impatient
Impulsive
Jumps to conclusions
Lacks follow-through
Loud
Manipulative
Misses details
Noisy
Obnoxious
Overbearing
Overestimates
Oversells
Phony
Poor concentration on tasks
Poor use of time
Scattered
Shallow
Showy/showoff
Unfocused
Unpredictable
Talks too much

3. The Steadiness Profile (S)

Strengths

Accommodating
Adaptable
Agreeable
Amiable
Calm
Compassionate
Considerate
Cooperative
Dependable
Even-tempered
Friendly
Generous
Good listener
Good-natured
Harmonious
Helpful
Inspiring
Kindhearted
Lenient
Likeable
Moderate
Modest
Neighborly
Nondemanding
Obedient
Obliging
Patient
Peacemaker
Relational
Reliable
Responsible
Restrained
Satisfied
Sensible
Sincere
Steady
Submissive
Supportive
Sympathetic
Tolerant
Willing

Weaknesses

Avoids confrontation
Can be taken advantage of
Cautious
Codependent
Conforming
Contented
Conventional
Dependent
Dislikes change
Doesn't initiate
Easygoing
Gives in
Indecisive
Loyal
Misses opportunities
Nonconfrontational
Predictable
Retiring
Slow

4. The Conscientious Profile (C)

Strengths

Accurate
Agreeable
Analytical
Careful
Conscientious
Consistent
Correct
Creative
Detailed
Diplomatic
Discerning
Disciplined
Factual
Humble
Inquisitive
Insightful
Logical
Observant
Orderly
Perceptive
Persistent
Practical
Precise
Quality

Respectful
Responsible
Scheduled
Soft-spoken
Systematic
Tactful
Thorough
Thoughtful

Weaknesses

Avoids controversy
Bogged down in details
Boring
Cautious
Change resistant
Compliant
Conventional
Critical
Fearful
Fussy
Idealistic
Indecisive
Introspective
Introverted
Needs reassurance
Perfectionistic
Pessimistic
Picky
Private
Refined
Reserved
Rigid
Sensitive to criticism
Serious
Skeptical
Slow to make decisions
Stuffy

Appendix E

The Expanded Type Indicator 2

We have designed the following material using Myers-Briggs terminology to help you confirm your true temperament and further understand it. Read through the material and determine which is most like you, an extrovert or an introvert, sensing or intuition, thinking or feeling, and judgment or perception.

1. Question: Where do you prefer to focus your attention that energizes you?

Extroversion	Introversion
Seeks verbal interaction	Seeks quiet
Likes to be with others	Likes to be alone
Interacts with many	Interacts with few
Energy increases over time	Energy diminishes over time
Acts first, thinks later	Thinks first, acts later
Initiates conversation	Waits for others to initiate conversations
People stimulate and energize them	People drain their energy reserves

Extroversion	Introversion
Explores the world to understand it	Seeks to understand world to explore it
Prefers many friends with brief contact	Prefers fewer friends with more contact
Speaks easily with strangers	Has little to say to strangers
Focuses on the outer world of people	Focuses on inner world of ideas
Easy to approach	Not as easy to approach
Prefers breadth	Prefers depth
Extensive	Intensive
Interaction	Concentration

2. Question: How do you acquire information?

Sensing	Intuitive
Gains information through the five senses	Gains information through a sixth sense
Sensible person	Imaginative person
What is	What could be
Does things the accepted way	Does things their own way
Focuses on facts	Focuses on possibilities
Life as it is	Life as it could be
Visionaries may annoy them	Visionaries fascinate them

Sensing	Intuitive
Common sense person	Questions common sense
Practical	Fanciful
Prefers details	Prefers the big picture
Literal	Figurative
Uses current skills	Develops new skills
Experience	Hunches
Realistic	Speculative
Perspiration	Inspiration
Utility	Fantasy

3. How do you make decisions?

Thinking	Feeling
Decisions based on principles	Decisions based on values
Convincing	Touching
Uses logic (head)	Uses values or needs (heart)
Makes decisions objectively	Makes decisions subjectively
Uses analysis	Uses person-centered values
Objective	Subjective
Logical judgments	Values judgments
Cool head	Warm heart
Facts-oriented	People-oriented

Thinking	Feeling
Seeks objective truth	Seeks harmony
Justice-based	Grace-based
Impersonal data	Personal values
Analytical	Sympathetic
Consistent thought	Harmonious relationships
Firm	Gentle
Too objective	Too passionate
Head rules	Heart directs
Organized	Adaptable
Principles	Values

4. How do you relate to the outer world?

Judging	Perceiving
Wants matters settled	Leaves matters open
Chooses carefully	Chooses impulsively
Planned	Flexible, open-ended
Organized	Spontaneous

Judging	Perceiving
Punctual	Leisurely
Serious	Easygoing
Quick decision maker	Slow decision maker
Controls the world	Responds to the world

Judging	Perceiving
Makes decisions	Leaves options open
Completes tasks	Explores tasks
Scheduled	Unscheduled
Routine	Whimsical

Judging	Perceiving
Sets deadlines	Whenever
Work comes first	Work can wait
A sense of urgency	Plenty of time
Settled	Pending

Appendix F

Sampling of Church Growth Statistics from Discovery 2

This appendix contains statistical information gathered from 146 pastors and the 285 churches they served. The chart includes pastoral tenure, statistics on the growth or decline in church attendance for each church served, percentage of growth, and the average annual growth rate (AAGR) arranged in order from the least to the greatest. Because of the enormous size of the database, we will present only a sampling of the statistics of this discovery project.

A word of clarification is in order to explain the table itself. The table consists of seven columns. These columns provide essential information about each of the churches. Each row contains information for one church.

- Column 1 gives the pastor's number as assigned in our survey results. We simply catalogued the pastor's information in the order we received it.
- Column 2 provides two important pieces of information. The first number tells us the order of this particular church served by this pastor. The second number tells us how many churches this pastor has served. Thus 2/4 designates that this is the second church served by this pastor out of four churches served.
- Column 3 informs us as to the length of tenure at this church. This figure along with the attendance figures are used to calculate the AAGR.
- Columns 4 and 5 list the attendance at the beginning of the ministry and at the end of the ministry respectively. These numbers are used to

calculate the percentage of growth. In addition, the calculation of total growth or decline results from subtracting the "attendance at the end" from "the attendance at the beginning."

- Column 6 displays the percentage of growth.
- Column 7 shows the results of the tabulation of the Average Annual Growth Rate (AAGR) for each church. All of the figures contained in this chart are arranged from the least AAGR to the greatest.
- Re-envisioning pastors are depicted by normal font while non–re-envisioning pastors are shown in **bold**.

The following statements explain the methods and procedures used to determine the pastors who qualified as re-envisioning pastors and those who are considered non–re-envisioning pastors.

We faced two major challenges as we wrestled with the data. First, we had to determine how we would evaluate pastors to label them as either a re-envisioning or a non–re-envisioning pastor. In a sampling this large, we discovered that many pastors had a mixed bag of results; a number of them have led both turnaround and non-turnaround congregations. Second, the status of a few pastors changed as they moved to their final church. In several cases when we discovered an apparent change in status, we decided that a tenure of one year or less at their final church was not enough to justify changing their status from REP to NREP or from NREP to REP. So we established the following criteria in the evaluation process.

- A pastor's status as either a REP or an NREP was determined by the last church served with the following exception.
- In the case of a pastor who was serving at his last appointment for one year or less, his status was determined by the ministry that immediately preceded the last appointment. Pastor #115 (the second line in the chart) is an illustration of this. The AAGR at his first church was 5.8 percent for eleven years while he was –20.0 percent in his second appointment where he has served only one year.

These determinations explain why some pastors who have an Average Annual Growth Rate (AAGR) of 2.4 percent or less in a given church are still considered REPs and why some who directed churches to grow at a rate greater than 2.5 percent are still considered NREPs. Pastor 101 is a good example of this phenomenon. He struggled for seven years in his first church (AAGR of –3.8%) while doing much better in the second church (AAGR +4.3%).

Sample of Churches with an AAGR from –29.3% to –2.6% (30 total churches)

Pastor #	Church Order	Years at Church	Attendance at Start	Attendance at End	Percent of Growth	AAGR
125	1/1	5	85	15	–82%	–29.3%
115	2/2	1	125	100	–20%	–20.0%
105	1/3	1.5	75	55	–27%	–18.7%
143	1/1	7	104	50	–52%	–9.9%
85	3/3	5	115	75	–35%	–8.2%
105	2/3	4	60	46	–23%	–6.4%
26	1/1	19	50	20	–60%	–4.7%
124	1/1	2.5	2800	2500	–11%	–4.4%
101	1/2	7	50	38	–24%	–3.8%
77	3/3	10.5	125	90	–28%	–3.1%

Sample of Churches with an AAGR from –2.5% to +2.5% (42 total churches)

Pastor #	Church Order	Years at Church	Attendance at Start	Attendance at End	Percent of Growth	AAGR
67	3/3	10	45	35	–22%	–2.5%
22	4/4	16	45	32	–29%	–2.1%
105	3/3	8	110	98	–11%	–1.4%
117	1/1	22	20	15	–25%	–1.3%
84	2/3	15	60	60	0%	0.0%
20	2/2	26	100	150	50%	1.6%
134	1/1	38	300	550	83%	1.6%
103	3/4	7	3000	3500	17%	2.2%
3	2/2	15	75	105	40%	2.3%
147	1/3	10	130	165	27%	2.4%

Sample of Churches with an AAGR from 2.5% to 10% (81 total churches)

Pastor #	Church Order	Years at Church	Attendance at Start	Attendance at End	Percent of Growth	AAGR
61	2/2	20	52	87	67%	2.6%
33	3/3	8	1300	1600	23%	2.6%
120	1/1	37	130	375	188%	2.9%
17	2/2	10.5	65	90	38%	3.1%
139	1/3	13	45	70	56%	3.5%
45	2/2	13	125	200	60%	3.7%
77	2/3	9	25	35	40%	3.8%
101	2/2	4	389	460	18%	4.3%
137	2/2	3	65	75	15%	4.9%

Pastor #	Church Order	Years at Church	Attendance at Start	Attendance at End	Percent of Growth	AAGR
103	2/4	22	950	3000	216%	5.4%
104	2/3	5	73	95	30%	5.4%
139	2/3	15	80	185	131%	5.7%
37	2/3	15	950	2200	132%	5.8%
115	1/2	11	70	130	86%	5.8%
66	1/2	10	18	32	78%	5.9%
11	4/7	8	100	162	62%	6.2%
122	2/2	17	27	80	196%	6.6%
112	2/2	18	130	450	246%	7.1%
121	2/3	12	250	575	130%	7.2%
128	3/3	19	20	75	275%	7.2%
11	1/7	4	15	20	33%	7.5%
11	2/7	4	75	100	33%	7.5%
11	3/7	4	175	237	35%	7.9%
1	3/3	16	175	600	243%	8.0%
37	3/3	4	2200	3100	41%	9.0%
109	2/2	14	325	1152	254%	9.5%

Sample of Churches with an AAGR from 10.1% to 512% (132 total churches)

Pastor #	Church Order	Years at Church	Attendance at Start	Attendance at End	Percent of Growth	AAGR
11	7/7	1.2	200	225	13%	10.3%
82	2/3	21	35	300	757%	10.8%
130	1/1	29	25	550	2100%	11.2%
2	1/1	20	140	1200	757%	11.3%
8	1/1	26	70	1250	1686%	11.7%
5	1/4	8	45	110	144%	11.8%
50	1/1	2.5	300	400	33%	12.2%
118	3/3	6	125	250	100%	12.2%
121	1/3	18	80	650	713%	12.3%
126	1/1	22	30	500	1567%	13.6%
20	1/2	10	25	90	260%	13.7%
10	2/2	10	18	65	261%	13.7%
38	1/1	25	150	4000	2567%	14.0%
11	5/7	14	75	600	700%	16.0%
102	2/2	3	511	800	57%	16.1%
39	1/1	20	220	4400	1900%	16.2%

Pastor #	Church Order	Years at Church	Attendance at Start	Attendance at End	Percent of Growth	AAGR
11	6/7	5	80	175	119%	16.9%
28	1/1	24	126	5500	4265%	17.0%
15	1/2	8	15	75	400%	22.3%
43	2/2	11	80	900	1025%	24.6%
12	1/1	4	90	325	261%	37.9%
135	3/3	2	75	163	117%	47.4%
60	2/3	1	150	230	53%	53.3%
52	1/1	7	13	300	2208%	56.6%
131	3/3	1	25	80	220%	220.0%
63	1/1	0.5	30	60	100%	300.0%
78	3/3	0.33	55	100	82%	512.0%

Notes on the chart:

1. There were 72 churches that fell below the 2.5% AAGR, 213 that scored above.
2. Note the AAGR for pastors # 2, 8, 28, 38, 39, 82, 126, and 130. Each of the churches has AAGRs between 10.8% and 17.0%. In each case the pastor has been at the church a minimum of 20 years. These pastors were able to lead the churches in long, sustained growth!
3. One pastor (#11) served 7 churches and all 7 turned around. All 7 are included in appendix F.
4. Consider also pastors who have served 20 years or more who are NREPs. Their AAGRs range from -1.3% to 1.6%. Once again, many factors enter into the growth and lack of growth in a church. This demonstrates that long tenure is not a guarantee of growth.
5. Generally, the best way of comparing growth is through the compilation of the AAGR. The one problem with the AAGR is in short-tenure situations. The AAGR is accentuated when the divisor is small and especially if it is less than one year. This is why we use caution in evaluating churches of first-time pastors who have served less than two and a half years. Pastor #78 is an example of an inflated AAGR (the last line). He had served his latest church for only 4 months and the resulting AAGR is 512%. This is why we have also included total growth, percentage of growth, and the Average Annual Growth Rate. An examination of all three calculations gives a full-orbed view of the growth or decline of a church.
6. This abbreviated chart includes pastors from all geographical sections of the United States, as well as Canadian pastors.

Appendix G

Pastoral Leadership Audit Scores

We developed a twenty-five-question survey to probe pastoral leadership tendencies. These comments reflect the average responses given by pastors in the Pastoral Leadership Audit in Discovery 2. The answers are based on a four-point Likert Scale with the following values:

1: True
2: More true than false
3: More false than true
4: False

With this assessment tool, effective pastors tend to have smaller scores: the smaller the score, the more effective the ministry.

The responses are divided into four segments listed immediately below. In each case, the responses refer to the re-envisioning pastors (REPs) in comparison to the non–re-envisioning pastors (NREPs).

- Large Difference: a difference of at least 0.8 or 26.7 percent or more (Each full point in this scoring system represents a difference of 33.3 percent)
- Moderate Difference: a difference of at least 0.4–0.7, 13.3–23.3 percent
- Little Difference: less than 0.2–0.3 or 6.7–10.0 percent difference
- No Difference: 0.0–0.1, 0.0–3.3 percent difference

The responses in the table below are grouped into three categories: re-envisioning pastors (REPs), REPs in churches with an average worship attendance of 500 or more, and the non–re-envisioning pastors (NREPs). These are to be compared with one another.

Note that on every question but one, REPs scored higher than their NREP counterparts. The statement "I prefer to work with a team" shows identical results between REPs and NREPs.

Pastoral Leadership Audit

Statements	REPs	REPs in 500+ churches	NREPs
Large Difference in Responses (26.7% or more)			
Better leader than manager or administrator	1.5	1.3	2.1
Inspiring preachers and communicators	1.3	1.1	2.0
Inspiring, visionary leaders	1.7	1.4	2.3
Better at leading churches in turnaround	1.4	1.3	2.6
Moderate Difference in Responses (13.3–23.3%)			
Has a clear compelling vision for next 5–10 years	1.5	1.3	1.9
Has above average people skills	1.4	1.3	1.8
More energetic	1.6	1.4	2.0
Better at delegation	2.0	1.8	2.2
Exerts more influence than NREPs	1.2	1.1	1.6
Better at resolving conflict	1.8	1.7	2.3
Better at solving problems	1.6	1.5	2.0
A more directive than passive leader	1.7	1.5	1.9
Better at developing new leadership	2.1	2.0	2.5
Passionately communicates vision	1.5	1.2	1.9
A self-starter	1.4	1.1	1.6
More effective at leading multiple generations through change	1.6	1.5	2.2
Little Difference in Responses (6.7–10%)			
More innovative than traditional	1.8	2.0	2.0
One who thinks "young" regardless of age	1.6	1.6	1.8
Reasonably quick to embrace change	1.6	1.5	1.8
Better at empowering people to use their giftedness in ministry	1.6	1.5	1.8
Worse at maintaining strong personal relationship	1.6	1.6	1.4
Better at using coaches or mentors	2.1	2.0	2.2
More willing to pay the price when leading change	1.4	1.3	1.6
An extrovert	1.8	1.8	2.0
No Difference in Responses (0.0–3.3%)			
I prefer to work with a team	1.8	1.7	1.8

Notes of Importance

The Canadian responses in both the DISC and the Pastoral Leadership Assessment were significantly different from the American responses. There was little distinction between the REPs and NREPs among Canadian pastors. This indicates that the Canadian pastors and churches are more relaxed and it also indicates that the Canadian churches demand less from their pastors than their American counterparts.

Pastors of larger churches have lower PLA scores. Thus, if an individual wants to improve pastoral skills, working on the traits in the PLA is a great place to begin. Include these characteristics in your Leadership Development Plan.

Comments on the Statements

The following are observations from the Pastoral Leadership Audit. The notes represent the differences between the REPs of larger churches (500+) and NREPs. Keep in mind, no REP displays all these characteristics but will display a majority of them.

- In two leadership statements, the abilities of the REPs greatly surpass those of the NREPs (better leader than manager and inspiring, visionary leader).
- Preaching and communication play an enormous role in transforming a church. REPs are significantly more adept in this area.
- Three statements concerning vision (inspiring, visionary leader; compelling vision; and passionately communicating vision) demonstrate a large difference in the envisioning skills in REPs when compared to NREPs. Positive change requires a visionary leader.
- REPs re-envision churches! This question asked whether or not a pastor had led a church in turnaround. The responses showed the greatest difference between the two groups of pastors in the twenty-five areas we probed.
- Good people skills aid greatly in producing turnaround.
- A great deal of energy is required to re-envision a church. REPs have a distinct edge on energy.
- Delegation is essential for an expanding ministry. Re-envisioning pastors are better at this.
- REPs are more influential than their NREP colleagues.
- Change creates conflict and problems. Consequently, conflict resolution and problem solving are essentials in church renewal. The evidence points to the superiority of REPs in these two areas.

- Churches require directive leadership. Re-envisioning pastors deliver.
- In order for new church growth to occur, the leadership base must expand. Those who produce new growth develop new leaders.
- Self-motivation is key to pastoral effectiveness and REPs are self-starters. No one needs to direct them as their motor is always running!
- Pastors must be able to minister to all generations, especially the younger ones, for effective turnaround to take place. REPs prove to be more able in this arena of ministry. That is why one must "think young" to bridge the gap between generations.
- Flexibility and innovation mark those who lead churches in transformation. Rigidity and reliance on old practices inhibit change that is needed for turnaround to occur.
- We anticipated that REPs would be more innovative than traditional, better at empowering leadership, and those who use coaches or mentors in ministry. In each case, the REPs exceeded the NREPs. However, the degree of difference was less than anticipated. These are still important areas of need for re-envisioning ministry.
- There was little separation in the responses of the groups of pastors in terms of working with teams. Both groups scored extremely well in this area.
- One area of great surprise involved the area of maintaining strong personal relationships. This is the only area where NREPs exceeded the REPs. Perhaps this is because the re-envisioning pastors are more focused on the task than on the people. This is similar to the apostle Paul, who chose not to take John Mark on the second missionary journey. The mission held greater importance to him than the missionary. Barnabas was just the opposite. It should be noted that both REPs and NREPs scored well here.

Appendix H

Vision Style Audit

Instructions

Circle the letter (A or B) that best describes your preference in a ministry situation. Be sure to go with your first impression.

1. I like courses that focus on
   A. fact
   B. theory
2. I prefer the company of
   A. realistic people
   B. imaginative people
3. People view me as
   A. a practical person
   B. an ingenious person
4. I like best people who
   A. prefer the "tried and true"
   B. come up with new ideas
5. People say that I am
   A. conventional
   B. unconventional
6. I like to pursue matters
   A. in the accepted way
   B. in my own unique way
7. I prefer
   A. the facts
   B. ideas
8. I'm comfortable with
   A. certainty.
   B. theory
9. I like best
   A. building things
   B. inventing things
10. I am convinced that
    A. seeing is believing
    B. believing is seeing
11. That which appeals most to me is
    A. the concrete
    B. the abstract
12. I'm most comfortable with
    A. the known
    B. the unknown

13. I prefer to be known as
    A. a realist
    B. a visionary
14. I like to think more about
    A. what is
    B. what could be
15. I'm more likely to trust
    A. my experience
    B. my intuition
16. I'm known as someone with
    A. common sense
    B. vision
17. I think it's more important to
    A. adjust to the facts
    B. see the possibilities
18. I prefer to
    A. support established methods
    B. address unsolved problems
19. I'm more interested in
    A. what is actual
    B. what is possible
20. I see best
    A. what's right in front of me
    B. what can only be imagined

Scoring

Total the number of As that you circled and then the number of Bs. Which is the greater number?

Interpretation

If you circled more As than Bs, you're the type of leader who catches a vision by visiting another ministry and seeing it for yourself. You are a "vision catcher." Your focus is more on the present than the future.

Your vision style: **Vision Catcher**

If you circled more Bs than As, you're the type of leader who creates a vision in your head (you see it in your mind). You are a "vision creator." You focus primarily on the future.

Your vision style: **Vision Creator**

Questions

Does your ministry call for a Vision Catcher or a Vision Creator? Does it really matter?

Appendix I

Character Assessment for Leadership

Over the years, leaders have discovered that godly character is critical to effective ministry for Christ. However, no one is perfect, and all of us have our weaknesses and flaws as well as strengths. This character assessment is to help you determine your character strengths and weaknesses so that you can know where you are strong and where you need to develop and grow. The characteristics are found in 1 Timothy 3:1–7 and Titus 1:6–9.

Instructions

Circle the number that best represents how you would rate yourself in each area.

1. I am "**above reproach**." I have a good reputation among people in general. I have done nothing that someone could use as an accusation against me.

   Weak 1 2 3 4 5 Strong

2. I am the "**husband of one wife**." If married, I not only have one wife but I am not physically or mentally promiscuous for I am focused only on her.

   Weak 1 2 3 4 5 Strong

3. I am "**temperate**." I am a well-balanced person. I do not overdo in my use of alcohol, etc. I am not excessive or given to extremes in beliefs, etc.

   Weak 1 2 3 4 5 Strong

4. I am "**sensible.**" I show good judgment in life and have a proper perspective regarding myself and my abilities (humble).
   Weak 1 2 3 4 5 Strong

5. I am "**respectable.**" I conduct my life in an honorable way, and people have and show respect for me.
   Weak 1 2 3 4 5 Strong

6. I am "**hospitable.**" I use my residence as a place to serve and minister to Christians and non-Christians alike.
   Weak 1 2 3 4 5 Strong

7. I am "**able to teach.**" When I teach the Bible, I show an aptitude for handling the Scriptures with reasonable skill.
   Weak 1 2 3 4 5 Strong

8. I am "**not given to drunkenness.**" If I drink alcoholic beverages or indulge in other acceptable but potentially addictive practices, I do so in moderation.
   Weak 1 2 3 4 5 Strong

9. I am "**not violent.**" I am under control. I do not lose control to the point that I physically or verbally strike or cause damage to other people or their property.
   Weak 1 2 3 4 5 Strong

10. I am "**gentle.**" I am a kind, meek (not weak), forbearing person who does not insist on his rights nor resort to violence.
    Weak 1 2 3 4 5 Strong

11. I am "**not quarrelsome.**" I am an uncontentious peacemaker who avoids hostile situations with people.
    Weak 1 2 3 4 5 Strong

12. I am "**not a lover of money.**" I am not in ministry for financial gain. I seek first his righteousness, knowing that God will supply my needs.
    Weak 1 2 3 4 5 Strong

13. I "**manage my family well.**" If I am married and have a family, my children are believers who obey me with respect. People do not think they are wild or disobedient.
    Weak 1 2 3 4 5 Strong

14. I am "**not a recent convert.**" I am not a new Christian who finds myself constantly struggling with pride and conceit.
    Weak 1 2 3 4 5 Strong

15. I have "**a good reputation with outsiders.**" Though lost people may not agree with my religious convictions, they still respect me as a person.
    Weak 1 2 3 4 5 Strong

16. I am "**not overbearing.**" I am not self-willed, stubborn, or arrogant.
    Weak 1 2 3 4 5 Strong

17. I am "**not quick-tempered.**" I am not inclined toward anger (an angry person) and I do not lose my temper quickly and easily.
    Weak 1 2 3 4 5 Strong

18. I am "**not pursuing dishonest gain.**" I am not fond of or involved in any wrongful practices that result in fraudulent gain.
    Weak 1 2 3 4 5 Strong

19. I "**love what is good.**" I love the things that honor God.
    Weak 1 2 3 4 5 Strong

20. I am "**upright.**" I live in accordance with the laws of God and man.
    Weak 1 2 3 4 5 Strong

21. I am "**holy.**" I am a devout person, whose life is generally pleasing to God.
    Weak 1 2 3 4 5 Strong

22. I "**hold firmly to the faith.**" I understand, hold to, and attempt to conserve God's truth. I also encourage others while refuting those who oppose the truth.
    Weak 1 2 3 4 5 Strong

When you have completed this character assessment, note those characteristics that you gave the lowest rating (2 or below). The lowest of these are to become the character goals or challenges that you focus on and develop.

Appendix J

Sixteen Make-or-Break Questions

The following sixteen make-or-break questions will help you as a church discern how you are really doing.

1. Do you have your finger on the church's pulse so that you can regularly read your critical vital signs?
2. Do you have a contagious, memorable mission that serves as a compass to navigate your church through whitewater change? Does it roll off your tongue with clarity and conviction?
3. Do you habitually consult your mission statement when making any and all decisions that affect the future direction of your church?
4. Have you carefully identified your actual core values so that you understand why you are successful in some areas and struggle in others, such as evangelism?
5. Has your church's impact in your community been such that if you were to suddenly disappear, it would leave a serious hole in your community?
6. Do your people view themselves as merely the church's members or Christ's missionaries?
7. Do you have a clear, simple pathway for making disciples that most in your church understand and know where they are on that path?
8. Does your staff team enthusiastically align with your core values, mission, and vision?
9. Do you have an intentional process for increasing and empowering lay volunteers to lead and do the church's ministries?

10. Do you have a staffing blueprint that provides crystal clarity about the next ministry to launch and who will lead it?
11. Do your facilities contribute functionally to the realization of your vision in the community?
12. Do you have a biblical strategy in place for raising finances that has resulted in an increase in giving over the last few years in spite of the recession?
13. Does your church's vision cast a clear, compelling picture of your future? In the last thirty days have you overheard a church member articulate or discuss your vision?
14. Do you have an intentional process for developing key leaders at every level in your church? Can you outline it on a napkin over a cup of coffee?
15. Have you crafted a personal, individualized leader development plan for your own growth as a leader in your church?
16. Has your pastor or anyone on staff identified and enlisted a coach to help him or her grow and stay fresh as a leader?

How is your church doing in response to these make-or-break questions? Need some help?

Appendix K

Examples of Successful Internship and Apprenticeship Ministries

In this appendix you will find information from two proactive, visionary churches—Northview Community Church in Abbotsford, British Columbia, and Salem Evangelical Free Church in Fargo, North Dakota. Both churches recognize that primary responsibility for leadership training falls to the local church, not to seminaries and Bible colleges. It is also significant that both are training leaders to serve in churches other than their own. We are grateful to Pastor Jeff Bucknam and Pastor Glen Stevens respectively for freely sharing their vision and these practical tools to help you as you consider what your response might be to the Christian leadership challenges facing the church in North America. If you would like further information concerning their ministries, please check out the church websites: www.northview.org and www.salemefc.org.

The information is given first for Northview Community Church in two parts: Teaching Associate's position designed for seminary graduates who intend to pursue pastoral ministry and Internship for Bible College graduates who desire exposure to a number of different ministry options. The last portion of this appendix contains information on the Joshua Project of Salem Evangelical Free Church.

Teaching Associate at Northview Community Church

About Northview Community Church

Northview Community Church is located in Abbotsford, British Columbia, Canada. Weekly attendance is approximately 3,500 over 6 services. Established in 1980, Northview has approximately 1,300 members and belongs to the Canadian Conference of Mennonite Brethren Churches.

Abbotsford, British Columbia

Abbotsford is a unique urban setting, framed by the coast and Cascade mountain ranges and massive land areas dedicated to farming. Abbotsford lies in the heart of the Fraser Valley, 68 kilometres (42 miles) east of Vancouver and 190 kilometres (118 miles) north of Seattle, Washington.

Abbotsford's economy is fueled primarily by the agriculture, manufacturing, and aerospace industries. Surrounded by plenty of fertile grounds, Abbotsford is the largest farm gate in the province, producing close to half a billion dollars annually.

Abbotsford is home to many outdoor activities. Cyclists find excellent territory on both flat, country roads and forest trails on Sumas and McKee mountains. Hiking trails are prolific in Abbotsford, nearby Chilliwack, and throughout the Lower Mainland of British Columbia. Several ski resorts are within an easy hour or two drive.

Young families and working professionals continue to relocate to Abbotsford, drawn by affordable real estate. One of the fastest growing economies in Canada, Abbotsford has grown to become the fifth largest city in British Columbia.

Abbotsford has a growing Sikh population that accounts for more than 60 percent of Abbotsford's total immigration in the last 10 years. Very few people of East Indian descent attend Northview, which poses enormous potential for community outreach.

Quick Facts

- Population of 139,000 (estimated 2011), approximately 45 minutes from Vancouver, BC.
- Population of the Metro Vancouver area is approximately 2.3 million.
- 27% of Abbotsford residents were born outside Canada.
- 39 languages are spoken in Abbotsford.
- Abbotsford is also diverse in terms of age; almost 1/3 of residents are children.
- 13.7% of Abbotsford residents speak Punjabi.

Growth and Outreach at Northview

Church Growth

People joining Northview attribute their attendance to the following:

- People are attracted to the clarity of preaching, characterized by an unwavering adherence to the truth of Scripture, even if it's not popular. This seems to be a cross-generational value among new members.
- Many families state they started attending Northview because of their children. Their kids simply weren't interested in programs at the church they were attending; they are excited about KidsTown (weekend service children's ministry), Middle School or High School groups and are growing in their knowledge of the Bible and their faith in Jesus.
- Young adults are attracted to the pastorate model (medium-sized groups) of discipleship and connecting in community.
- People see Northview as a serving church and are attracted because they have opportunities to get involved.

Reaching the Community

Abbotsford has been labeled part of the "Bible Belt" of British Columbia. While there are many churches in Abbotsford (more than 90), the political and moral conservatism of the city's culture can be generally attributed to the city's largest religious groups: Christians and Sikhs.

Both Christianity and Sikhism are conservative in nature and profess family values; moreover, a large majority of Abbotsford's Christian population is of Mennonite heritage, which has a number of similarities to the Sikh community. Both Sikhs and Mennonites are conservative within their traditional ethnic origins. They are both characterized by a high view of religion and tradition. Both groups experienced persecution in their native land and chose to separate themselves from mainstream society. Younger generations of both groups are less concerned with ethnic roots and traditions, have more postsecondary education than their parents, and are more integrated into the culture at large.

Pluralism is a value and ideal that permeates Canadian society. This pluralistic outlook in combination with Abbotsford's moral conservatism means that the culture, and younger generations in particular, lean toward a worldview that is characterized by therapeutic moralistic deism.

Geographically, there is a growing disconnect in the community between West and East Abbotsford in terms of ethnicity. West Abbotsford is largely populated by people of East Indian descent, while East Abbotsford is dominated by people of European Caucasian descent.

In the last few years, Northview has undergone a major paradigm shift from an attractional ministry that focused on bringing people to the church for programs, to missional ministry that focuses on equipping people for expressing and explaining the Gospel in their everyday life. One of the results of this paradigm shift is a slow growth in the ethnic diversity of Northview's attendance, though this is not yet to the extent that is proportionate to Abbotsford's ethnic populations.

Abbotsford has a growing university (University of the Fraser Valley), which is largely a commuter school. The student population is approximately 15,000 students.

Our Mission

Leading people to passionately follow Jesus.

Our Vision

Loving God, one another, and the world.

Our Core Values

Loving God

- We value dependence on God expressed through prayer.
  (Acts 17:24–25; Phil. 4:6; 1 John 5:14)
- We value living in obedience to the authority of Scripture.
  (2 Tim. 3:16–17; James 1:22; Luke 6:46–49)
- We value yielding to the Holy Spirit.
  (1 Cor. 12–14; Rom. 12:4–8; Gal. 5:22–23)
- We value acts of worship in response to who God is and what He has done.
  (Luke 7:36–47; Rom. 12:1–2; Eph. 5:18; Pss. 95:1–2; 96:1–3; Rom. 12:1)

Loving Others

- We value equipping people for transformation and ministry.
  (Luke 10:1–12; Eph. 4:11–16)

- We value healthy family life.

  (Gen. 1:26–27; 2:21–25; Matt. 19:1–12; 1 Cor. 7:1–16; Eph. 5:18–6:4; Col. 3:18–4:1)
- We value authentic community.

  (Eph. 4:25–32; Mark 3:31–35; Rom. 12:9–16; John 17:20–21; 1 John 3:16–18)
- We value being a church that reflects the ethnicity and inter-generational makeup of our local community.

  (Rev. 7:9–17; Eph. 2:14–22; Acts 10:34–35; Gal. 3:28)

Loving the World

- We value doing justice and mercy as an outgrowth of the Gospel both locally and globally.

  (Micah 6:8; Isa. 1:17; 58:6–7; Amos 5:14–15; Luke 4:16–21; Matt. 25:31–46; James 2:14–17)
- We value speaking the Gospel in culturally relevant ways in our community and around the world.

  (Rom. 10:14–15; Matt. 28:18–20; Acts 16:25–34; 1 Cor. 15:1–8)
- We value reflecting the reign of Christ in every area of life and society.

  (Genesis 2; Phil. 4:8)

Our Governance

Council of Elders

Northview is led by the Council of Elders, which is comprised of volunteers, who are discerned and affirmed by Northview members. The Council of Elders meets monthly. Elders serve an indefinite term, subject to reaffirmation every six years. Elders serve as chair or member of one of the board committees.

Senior Leadership Team

Northview staff are led by the Senior Leadership Team, comprised of the Lead Pastor, Executive Pastor, Pastor of Outreach, Pastor of Prayer and Discipleship, and the Pastor of Worship. Northview values the biblical directives for church leadership set forth in 1 Timothy 3 and Titus 1. For this reason, the Senior Leadership Team makes decisions as a plurality in mutual submission to one another. All five members of the Senior Leadership Team sit on the Council of Elders as non-voting members.

About the Residency

The Teaching Associate is a 3-year residency designed to raise up pastoral leaders who have a passion for the local church. This position will focus primarily on developing teaching and preaching skills by experiencing multifaceted local-church ministry.

The Teaching Associate will have opportunity to teach in every ministry within Northview Community Church. These include, but are not limited to, preaching or teaching to children, middle school and high school youth, young adults, seniors, and adult education classes. The incumbent will develop materials for pastorates (mid-sized community groups) and life groups (small community groups). The Teaching Associate will preach at Northview's weekend services and related venues as appropriate. Over the three-year term, the Teaching Associate's area of teaching will progressively be focused and refined to a specific area of passion and expertise.

The Teaching Associate reports to the Pastor of Prayer and Discipleship. He will receive extensive mentorship from the Lead Pastor and Pastor of Prayer and Discipleship.

Intended Purpose

The intended purpose of the Teaching Associate residency is to provide a graduate student with an intensive immersion in church ministry. This role provides the future pastor with a multitude of ministry experiences that will equip him to function at different levels of leadership.

Intended Outcome

The intended outcome of the position is to lead to a full-time role as lead/associate teaching pastor in an established church setting, or a supported role in a church plant setting.

Specific Responsibilities

1. Teaching

Opportunity will be provided to teach in a variety of ministry settings:

- Teaching weekly theology classes on a rotational basis following the curriculum developed by the teaching pastors.
- Teaching as part of the Adult Christian Discipleship Classes.

- Speaking periodically at various ministry events, such as Seasons (Senior Ministry), SOLA (Young Adults Ministry), Elevate (High School Ministry), and Vertical Edge (Middle School Ministry).
- Teaching at church-wide leadership meetings and various other leadership training events held within different church ministries.
- Preaching during the weekend services (1–4 times per year).

2. Resource Development

Assisting various ministry leaders with the development of curriculum for their specific department:

- As a member of the teaching team, contribute to the development of the sermon series.
- Assist the Pastor of Prayer and Discipleship with developing curriculum for discipleship classes.
- Oversee the development of weekly devotional guides corresponding to the sermon series.
- Assist the Pastor of Community with creating a small group leadership development program.

3. Administrative Duties

Involvement in the leadership of the church:

- Attend Council of Elder and committee meetings as requested.
- Attend pastoral, staff, and Senior Leadership Team meetings as required.
- Any other duties that may be required from time to time.

Qualifications

1. Must be in agreement with the theological doctrines of Northview.
2. Master's Degree from an accredited seminary.
3. Gifted communicator with a call to full-time teaching ministry.
4. Preference will be given to Canadian citizens or permanent residents. Must be eligible to be employed in Canada.
5. Has a reputation of living a lifestyle that honours and uplifts the name of Christ.

The person called to this ministry must be in agreement with Northview's confession of faith, mission, vision, and core values, and must have a passion for the ministry of the church. The incumbent must also have the qualifications of an Elder, as outlined in 1 Timothy 3 and Titus 1.

The incumbent must make Northview Community Church their home church.

Selection Process

What Should Interested Graduates Submit?

1. Résumé
2. Preaching video/audio (whichever is convenient)
3. Philosophy of Ministry
4. Theological Questionnaire (see appendix). Allow yourself 1–1.5 hours.

Application Deadline: April 5, 2012

Candidates selected for interview will be contacted in April to arrange interviews for later in the Spring. Final selection should be completed by June. Start date is August 15, 2012.

Please submit the above documents to Ashley Wall, Administrative Assistant for Prayer & Discipleship, at ashley@northview.org. Large audio and video files can be submitted via www.yousendit.com or similar file transfer sites.

Additional Information

Additional information, including Northview's statement of faith, list of current staff and elders, and program details, are available on our website: www.northview.org

Appendix

Northview Community Church, Pastoral Search, Theological Interview Questions

Note: It is anticipated that your response to each question will be 2–3 paragraphs.

1. Have you read NCC's confession of faith? Are there any concerns or hesitations with it?
2. Explain your understanding of the gospel.

3. What are your views regarding how Divine Sovereignty and human responsibility coexist? Would you call yourself a Calvinist or an Arminian or something else? Why?
4. What are your views regarding the gifts of the Spirit? Do you believe the gifts of tongues, prophecy, and healing are for today? If yes, how should they function in the local church today?
5. What are your views regarding the role of women in ministry leadership? Why do you hold the viewpoint you do on this matter?
6. What are your views on eschatology? Do you consider yourself amillennial, premillennial, or something else? Please explain why you hold the view you do.
7. Who are some of your favorite Christian authors and speakers? Please explain what you appreciate about each one.
8. What are your views on baptism? Do you baptize infants or only adults?
9. What are your views on war and nonviolent resistance?
10. What are your spiritual gifts and how have they been affirmed in your life?
11. In your opinion, what are the most pressing issues or challenges facing North American Christians in the beginning of the 21st century?
12. What are the most dangerous false teachings in the contemporary evangelical church in your opinion?
13. What is your view of hell? Duration of it. Nature of it. Does anyone go there? If so, who?
14. Regarding other world religions, would you consider yourself an exclusivist, inclusivist, or pluralist?
15. What is your view of Scripture? Do you believe the Bible contains errors? What is your process for interpreting the Bible?

Internship Program at Northview

Internships: Equipping People for Transformation and Ministry

At Northview, we believe in helping to train people for ministry. Interns participate in a structured program that exposes young leaders to practical church ministry in almost every area of the church and theological training.

The goal is to provide a place to gain experience, be exposed to a variety of ministries in the church, mentor under one of our pastors, develop a solid theological base, and develop the gifts that God has given. Internships are 10–12 months long and are paid positions of 40 hours a week.

Who Can Apply?

The ideal candidate for our program is a Bible College graduate who is looking for some practical experience in a church. They should be longing to grow deeper in their faith, willing to be stretched personally, seeking to develop their ministry/leadership gifts, wanting a deeper understanding of church ministry, and desiring to be equipped for future ministry.

We believe that our program is ideal for a grad that is looking to flesh out the education they have received in a real-life church experience before going into full-time ministry or pursuing further education. It may also be ideal for people who are questioning their call to work in full-time ministry. Be involved for a year and see how God leads in and through that experience!

We are, however, open to people that have not yet finished their degree or are looking at pursuing ministry in the future. We desire to be flexible yet committed to what we believe God has called us to.

A Typical Week

- prayer meetings
- a 2-hour theological class
- a 1-hour class with one of our pastors to talk about their ministry and Q&A
- visits to other ministries of the church
- one-on-one mentoring time with the pastor under whose ministry the intern is working
- significant involvement in a specific ministry area
- time for self-evaluation

In addition to this, there will be special events/opportunities to be a part of. Examples include working in our Alpha program, attending various seminars and conferences, mission trips, etc.

Intern Positions

College
High School
Middle School
Church Community
Children's Ministry
Worship and Arts
Missions
Women's Ministry

Internships run for 10 months from late August through the end of June.

Internship Program, Salem Evangelical Free Church, Fargo, North Dakota, the Joshua Project

Salem Evangelical Free Church has a rich history of training next-generation leaders for ministry in the local church. The "Joshua Project" seeks to provide greater definition for the future leadership development of young ministry-minded individuals as Salem continues to mentor and deploy young laborers for the harvest. Three types of opportunities are defined: "Pastoral Apprentice" for those pursuing a seminary degree to serve as a vocational pastor, "Ministry Internship" for those considering vocational ministry in a local church or the mission field, and "Academic Internship" for those receiving academic credit or on-the-job experience in a church setting towards a non-seminary degree.

Pastoral Apprenticeship

Much can be learned in a classroom in preparation for a pastoral career. Much can also be learned in on-the-job experience. But the ideal learning environment is found when the student is taking classes and working in the local church at the same time. One's ministry efforts and colleagues enrich and strengthen the learning happening in the classroom. Through this process, what's learned in the classroom can be immediately applied and evaluated in the context of church ministry, all under the supervision of a seasoned Senior Pastor and pastoral team. The Salem Apprenticeship provides this optimal learning environment for future pastors. This is a gift to the Church at large, because the individuals coming out of Apprenticeship will bring all their experience in church ministry with them into their first pastoral role. They will be uniquely equipped to handle the various challenges of pastoral ministry in the 21st century.

Ministry Internship

As young men and women look at the possibility of a career in ministry, one of the best ways to discover what such a calling would be like is through an intensive ministry internship under the supervision of one of Salem's pastors. The internship gives them hands-on experience and exposure to ministry in the local church, which can assist them in their own career decision-making process. It also serves the local church because the Intern will actively be engaged in ministry at Salem, providing help for the ministry in which their internship is based.

Academic Internship

NDSU, MSUM, and Concordia are significant centers of higher education in Salem's Metro. Occasionally a student seeking a degree in a role that Salem uses for ministry support may want to do an academic internship for school credit. Usually this student wants to explore what a career in their field (for example, accounting) might be like in a church or ministry setting. This creates a potential win-win for both student and Salem.

General Provisions

- Approval and Compensation: Positions, funding, and compensation are approved by the Elder Board based on a position description developed with and submitted by the supervising Ministry Staff member (pastor or operations manager). For Pastoral Apprentices, the supervisor is the Senior Pastor. For academic interns, the position description needs appropriate approval from the school, the position is typically unpaid, and external fund-raising is not allowed.
- Time frames:

  Apprentice: Up to six years (for example, distance education) depending on seminary degree progress.

  Intern: Up to one year. Beyond one year, the intern will either need to be hired to a non-term position or apply for the Apprenticeship Program and enroll in a seminary distance learning program. Apprentices and interns may apply for open Salem positions.
- Hours and compensation: Apprenticeships will typically be full-time positions with full-time employee benefits but with no housing allowance. Paid intern positions can be up to 30 hours per week with limited benefits defined in the Personnel Policy Manual based on approved work hours. Overtime should be avoided and in all cases requires approval by the intern's supervisor and the Operations Manager. To comply with Federal Labor laws, the position description and practice should clearly distinguish between paid activity and volunteer ministry.
- Funding: Funding sources for positions may include the Salem general fund, self-funding (e.g. employment outside of Salem or savings), reserves in the Joshua Fund (specific account for supporting interns), and support-raising from friends and family outside of Salem via the Joshua Fund.
- General: Apprentice and intern positions are subject to the Personnel Policy Manual. All positions/employment are at-will.

Notes

Introduction

1. Ron Sellers, "Pastors Think Pastors Should Stay Put," *Facts & Trends* 51, no. 5 (September/October 2005), 4–5.

2. http://toddbreiner.wordpress.com/2010/12/20/where-oh-where-has-my-youth-pastor-gone/.

3. http://www.thomrainer.com/2009/06/8–traits-of-effective-church-leaders.php.

Chapter 1 The State of Pastoral Leadership in America

1. Win Arn, *The Pastor's Manual for Effective Ministry* (Monrovia, CA: Church Growth, 1988), 41, 43.

2. David T. Olson, *The American Church in Crisis: Groundbreaking Research Based on a National Database of over 200,000 Churches* (Grand Rapids: Zondervan, 2008), 179.

3. Ibid., 180.

4. Thom S. Rainer, *Breakout Churches: Discover How to Make the Leap* (Grand Rapids: Zondervan, 2005), 45.

5. Ibid., 245.

6. These figures were given during a presentation to the Great Commission Research Network, November 10–11, 2011, Biola University, La Mirada, CA.

7. "The State of the American Church," http://www.theamericanchurch.org/ (accessed July 26, 2013).

8. Olson, *The American Church in Crisis,* 35.

9. David Kinnaman, *You Lost Me: Why Young Christians are Leaving the Church . . . and Rethinking Faith* (Grand Rapids: Baker, 2011), 22.

10. Barry A. Kosmin and Ariela Keysar, "American Religious Identification Survey (ARIS 2008): Summary Report" (Hartford, CT: Trinity College, March 2009), 5.

11. Ibid.

12. Ibid.

13. Ibid.

14. ReligionLink, "Pagans Go Mainstream: Wiccans and Druids and Goddesses—Oh, My," October 20, 2009, http://www.religionlink.com/.

15. Olson, *The American Church in Crisis,* 176.

16. Ibid.

17. There is debate as to the identity of the seven angels. The debate focuses on the meaning of the term *aggelos.* The question is whether the *aggelos* are angels or messengers, that is, the pastors. The view chosen greatly impacts the meaning of the passage. The term *aggelos* is defined in the following two ways. One is human messengers: an envoy, one who is sent by men or by God. The other is supernatural powers, such angels as messengers of God (Walter Bauer, F. Wilbur Gingrich, William F. Arndt, and Frederick W. Danker, *A Greek-English Lexicon of the New Testament and Other Early Christian Literature,* 2nd ed. [Chicago: University of Chicago Press], s.v. *aggelos*).

New Testament scholar Mark Wilson (Mark Wilson, "Revelation," *Zondervan Illustrated Bible Backgrounds Commentary* [Grand Rapids: Zondervan, 2002], 4:259) believes the "angels" to be supernatural beings. Pastor-scholar W. A. Criswell and John Walvoord, noted prophetic scholar, believe these angels to be the human messengers to the church, the pastor-teachers. Walvoord's comments are instructive.

> The Greek word *aggelos*, which has been transliterated in the English word *angel*, is frequently used in the Bible of angels, and this seems to be its principal use as noted by Arndt and Gingrich. However, it is often used also of men in Greek literature as a whole, and in several instances this word referred to human messengers in the Bible (Matt. 11:10; Mark 1:2; Luke 7:24, 27; 9:52). It is properly understood here as referring to human messengers to these seven churches. These messengers were probably the pastors of these churches or prophets through whom the message was to be delivered to the congregation. (John F. Walvoord, *The Revelation of Jesus Christ: A Commentary* [Chicago: Moody Press, 1966], 53.)

We are in agreement with Criswell and Walvoord. In this view, the communication chain is as follows: the message made its way from God to Christ, from Christ to a supernatural being (an angel), from the angel to John, and from John to the messengers, the pastor-teachers, the spokesmen of the seven churches. It is significant that the messengers were the ones being evaluated by the Lord. That ought to cause every pastor to stop and weigh the seriousness of the work committed into their hands.

18. Bob Humphrey, "Fresh Start Ministries" (Rockport, IL: Fresh Start Ministries Strategic Church Consulting, n.d.), 3–4.

19. Bill Hybels, *Courageous Leadership* (Grand Rapids: Zondervan, 2002), 23.

20. Ibid., 27.

Chapter 3 The Biblical Basis for Re-Envisioning Ministry

1. Phone interview with Robert Humphrey by Gordon Penfold, June 25, 2009.

2. Lorin Woolfe, *The Bible on Leadership: From Moses to Matthew—Management Lessons for Contemporary Leaders* (New York: American Management Association, 2002), 37–38.

3. Charles Caldwell Ryrie, *Revelation* (Chicago: Moody Press, 1968), 21.

4. Ibid., 20–32.The citations are not verbatim, but Ryrie's succinct style has influenced this chart significantly.

5. Revelation 2:7, 11, 17, 29; 3:6, 13, 22 (NASB).

6. Peter Wiwcharuck, *Building Effective Leadership* (Alberta, Canada: International Christian Leadership Development Foundation, 1987), 23.

7. Phone interview with Pastor Dary Northrup, Timberline Church, Fort Collins, Colorado, by Gordon Penfold, October 26, 2010.

8. Nikki (last name not given), email correspondence, August 5, 2013.

9. Larry Baker with Becky Lyles, *It's a God Thing*! (Enumclaw, WA: WinePress, 2000), 31–32.

10. Ibid., 32.

Chapter 4 Design, Direction, and Development

1. Bill George, *True North* (San Francisco: Jossey-Bass, 2007), 8.

2. The Spiritual Formation department at Dallas Theological Seminary has developed and used these four *H*s in helping seminarians discover their divine designs and ministry directions.

3. Aubrey Malphurs, *Building Leaders* (Grand Rapids: Baker, 2004).

Chapter 5 The Leader's Behavior

1. David Keirsey, *Please Understand Me* II (Del Mar, CA: Prometheus Nemesis, 1998).

2. Sylvan J. Kaplan and Barbara E. W. Kaplan, *The Kaplan Report: A Study of the Validity of the Personal Profile System* (Chevy Chase, MD: Performax Systems, 1983).

3. Isabel Briggs Myers and Mary H. McCaulley, *Manual: A Guide to the Development and Use of the Myers-Briggs Type Indicator* (Palo Alto, CA.: Consulting Psychologists Press, 1985), chap. 11.

4. Roland Kenneth Harrison, *Introduction to the Old Testament* (Grand Rapids: Eerdmans, 1969), 1004.

5. Ibid., 1007–8.

6. Ibid., 1006.

7. Ibid., 1007.

8. Derek Kidner, *Proverbs: An Introduction and Commentary* (Downers Grove, IL: InterVarsity, 1964), 17.

9. David Ward, "Theologically Justifying Personality Type Training" (a student paper presented at Dallas Theological Seminary, Dallas, Texas, 1992), 3.

10. This chart reflects the statistics in Aubrey Malphurs, *Planting Growing Churches for the 21st Century*, 3rd ed. (Grand Rapids: Baker, 2004), 103.

Chapter 6 Our Initial Exploration

1. Gary L. McIntosh (class lecture, "Growing and Multiplying Churches in North America," Talbot School of Theology, La Mirada, CA, January 2009). McIntosh's source

is C. Peter Wagner, "Principles and Procedures of Church Growth," February 5–16, 1979, in the section "Reporting Church Growth," p. 5. Wagner's statistics were undoubtedly based on a live birth rate of 25 births per 1,000, which was the birth rate in the late 1950s. The birth rate in 2010–11 is 13.68 births per 1,000 or 1.4 percent (www.iknfolplease.com/pa/A0005067.html, accessed April 14, 2013). The AAGR for the United States population from 1990 to 2010 is 1.1 percent. For our purposes, a turnaround church will average 2.5 percent AAGR, which means it keeps its biological growth and keeps up with the population growth in the United States. It is also of note that in our research, there is a natural break between TAP and NTAP (non-turnaround pastor) at the 2.5 percent AAGR mark.

Total growth, percentage of growth, and average annual growth rate are different ways of examining growth or decline. Numerical growth is important but doesn't tell the whole story. AAGR is a way to measure growth in the same way financiers measure compound interest over time. So when you think of AAGR, think of compound interest. In the chart below, notice the differences in evaluating growth based on each of the three methods. In each case the numerical growth was 100.

Years of Ministry	Beginning Attendance	Ending Attendance	Numerical Growth	Percentage of Growth	AAGR
1	100	200	100	100%	100%
5	100	200	100	100%	14.9%
10	100	200	100	100%	7.2%
20	100	200	100	100%	3.5%

Notice that the best way of evaluating the growth is through the compilation of the AAGR. The one problem with the AAGR is in short-tenure situations. The AAGR is accentuated when the divisor is small and especially when it is less than one year. This is why we do not use churches of first-time pastors who have served less than two and a half years. One pastor in our study is an example of an inflated AAGR. He served his latest church for only four months and the resulting AAGR is 512 percent. For this reason we have included total growth, percentage of growth, and the average annual growth rate.

2. Olson, *The American Church in Crisis*, 25. Olson notes the following reasons for using worship attendance to measure the spiritual climate of a church. Olson writes, "A growing number of religious researchers believe that weekend church attendance is the most helpful indicator of America's spiritual climate. Attendance gives a more accurate picture of a person's religious commitment than membership. As the philosopher Ludwig Wittgenstein said, 'If you want to know whether a man is religious, don't ask him, observe him.' Attendance is a real-time indicator, a weekly appraisal of commitment. Membership reflects a commitment to a church made in the past but may not be reflective of current actions. The value of membership also differs by generation. The builder generation (born 1920–45) loved to join organizations. The boomer cohort (born 1946–64) resists institutional commitment. Looking at attendance rather than membership diminishes the effect of this generational difference."

3. I anticipated that most TAPs would exhibit strengths in evangelism and leadership. In this pool of pastors, 62 percent of TAPs and 43 percent of NTAPs had the gift of leadership. I assumed that a much higher percentage of TAPs would exhibit the gift of leadership and

a much lower percentage of NTAPs would demonstrate the gift of leadership. I also felt that the preponderance of TAPs would have the gift of evangelism. Only 29 percent of the TAPs and 14 percent of the NTAPs listed evangelism in their top four gifts. I was shocked. Teaching was in the top four gifts of twenty-six of twenty-eight pastors who completed the Modified Heights Spiritual Gifts Inventory.

4. George Barna, *Turnaround Churches* (Ventura, CA: Regal Books, 1993), 67.

5. Gordon E. Penfold, "Defining Characteristics of Turnaround Pastors among Evangelical Churches in the Rocky Mountain States" (D.Min. diss., Biola University, 2011), 161–63.

6. Ibid., 68.

7. Gary L. McIntosh, *Taking Your Church to the Next Level: What Got You Here Won't Get You There* (Grand Rapids: Baker, 2009), 90–95.

8. Paul D. Borden, *Direct Hit: Aiming Real Leaders at the Mission Field* (Nashville: Abingdon, 2006), 98.

9. This figure was given in response to Gordon's inquiry as to the number of TAPs in Wayne Wager's Central New York District of the Wesleyan Church.

10. In response to Aubrey's question as to the number of turnaround pastors in his association, David Bowman, the executive director of the Tarrant Baptist Association in Fort Worth, Texas, shared this figure at the Great Commission Research Network meeting on the campus of Biola University in 2011.

11. Gordon E. Penfold, "Turnaround Pastors: Characteristics of Those Who Lead Churches from Life-Support to New Life" (a paper presented to the Great Commission Research Network, November 10–11, 2011, Biola University, La Mirada, CA), 23.

12. Bob Dean, the executive director of the Dallas Baptist Association gave Aubrey this figure when he inquired as to the percentage of churches in the DBA that were led by turnaround pastors.

13. After a trip to the Northern Plains District of the Evangelical Free Church of America, district superintendent Daryl Thompson gave these very sound figures as to the number of turnaround pastors in his district. Gordon agrees with his figures after examining the church growth statistics for the district.

Chapter 7 Our Follow-up Exploration

1. Patrick Lencioni, *The Advantage* (San Francisco: Jossey-Bass, 2012), xvii.

2. Though this is not an intensely statistical study, we gathered a great amount of statistical information. Gordon's analytical background as a researcher and engineer certainly played a large role in amassing and interpreting the data gathered.

3. A second pastor (NREP) had served only 9 months. We did not use their results in calculating the AAGR, because they had not served the mandated 2.5 years. However, we did use the short-tenured pastors who had served less than 2.5 years in computing the average ministry experience and tenure.

4. Barna, *Turnaround Churches*, 67.

5. Ibid., 68.

Chapter 8 Four Critical Questions

1. Andy Stanley, *Deep and Wide: Creating Churches Unchurched People Love to Attend* (Grand Rapids: Zondervan, 2012), 300.

Chapter 10 How to Create and Cast a Compelling Vision

1. Haddon Robinson in Aubrey Malphurs, *Developing a Vision for Ministry in the 21st Century* (Grand Rapids: Baker, 1999), 10.

2. "Study: McDonald's Logo More Recognizable than Christian Cross," *Dallas-Fort Worth Heritage*, October 1995, 6.

Chapter 11 Creating a Culture for Change

1. Lyle E. Schaller, "A Passion for the Mission," *Net Fax*, a service of Leadership Network, no. 84 (November 1997): 1.

2. Jeff Chu, "Teachings from the Summit: Highlights from the 2010 Conference," *Fast Company* (December 2010–January 2011), 131.

3. Aubrey Malphurs, *Advanced Strategic Planning*, 2nd ed. (Grand Rapids: Baker, 2005).

Chapter 12 Recruiting a Mentor or Coach

1. Howard G. Hendricks and William Hendricks, *As Iron Sharpens Iron: Building Character in a Mentoring Relationship* (Chicago: Moody, 1995), 17–18.

2. Ibid., 158.

3. Don Hahn, "Similarities and Differences in Coaching and Mentoring," http://www.champtrainer.com/documents/Similarities%20and%20Differences%20in%20Coaching%20and%20Mentoring.pdf.

4. http://www.management-mentors.com/resources/coaching-mentoring-differences/.

5. http://www.brefigroup.co.uk/coaching/coaching_and_mentoring.html.

6. Bob Logan and Sherilyn Carlton, *Coaching 101: Discover the Power of Coaching* (St. Charles, IL: ChurchSmart Resources, 2003), 19.

7. Stanley, *Deep and Wide*, 295.

8. Paul Borden, chart presented at Rocky Mountain Church Network Cluster Meeting (First Baptist Church, Rocky Ford, CO, September 2011). Used with permission.

9. Cynthia D. McCauley and Christina A. Douglas, "Developmental Relationship," in Cynthia D. McCauley and Ellen Van Veslor, eds., *Handbook of Leadership Development*, 2nd ed. (San Francisco: Jossey-Bass, 2003), 92.

10. Andy Stanley, *The Next Generation Leader* (Sisters, OR: Multnomah, 2003), 104.

11. Ibid., 109.

12. Gordon E. Penfold, "Defining Characteristics of Turnaround Pastors among Evangelical Churches in the Rocky Mountain States" (D.Min. diss., Biola University, 2011), 158.

13. Skype interview and email correspondence with Jeff Bucknam by Gordon Penfold, August 15, 2013.

14. Robert Hargrove and Michel Renaud, *Your Coach (in a Book): Mastering the Trickiest Leadership, Business, and Career Challenges You Will Ever Face* (San Francisco: Jossey-Bass, 2004), xv.

15. Ibid., xii.

Chapter 13 Preparation, Process, and Practice

1. Aubrey Malphurs, *Advanced Strategic Planning*, 3rd ed. (Grand Rapids: Baker, 2013), 42–44.

2. Aubrey Malphurs, *Leading Leaders* (Grand Rapids: Baker, 2005).

Chapter 14 Re-Envisioning Seminaries, Denominations, and Networks

1. Stanley, *Deep and Wide*, 294–95.

Aubrey Malphurs, Ph.D.

- Aubrey is the founder of the Malphurs Group (www.malphursgroup.com).
- He also teaches in the Pastoral Ministries and Leadership Departments at Dallas Seminary.
- His email: amalphurs@dts.edu; aubrey@malphursgroup.com.
- His cell phone: 469-585-2102.

Gordon Penfold, D.Min.

- Gordon is pastor of First Baptist Church, Holyoke, CO.
- He is also the director of Fresh Start Ministries, www.startingfresh.net.
- His email: gordonpnfld@gmail.com.
- His cell phone: 970-631-6740.

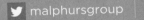